KINGDOM OF FOOTBALL

KRISTIAN COATES ULRICHSEN

Kingdom of Football

Saudi Arabia and the Remaking of World Soccer

HURST & COMPANY, LONDON

First published in the United Kingdom in 2025 by
C. Hurst & Co. (Publishers) Ltd.,
New Wing, Somerset House, Strand, London, WC2R 1LA
© Kristian Coates Ulrichsen, 2025
All rights reserved.

The right of Kristian Coates Ulrichsen to be identified as the author of this publication is asserted by him in accordance with the Copyright, Designs and Patents Act, 1988.

A Cataloguing-in-Publication data record for this book is available from the British Library.

ISBN: 9781911723660

This book is printed using paper from registered sustainable and managed sources.

www.hurstpublishers.com

EU GPSR Authorised Representative

Easy Access System Europe Oü, 16879218

Address: Mustamäe tee 50, 10621, Tallinn, Estonia

Contact Details: gpsr.requests@easproject.com, +358 40 500 3575

Printed and bound in Great Britain by Bell and Bain Ltd, Glasgow

CONTENTS

Acknowledgments	vii
List of Abbreviations	ix
Introduction	1
1. A Brief History of Football in Saudi Arabia	9
2. Mohammed bin Salman, a Prince in a Hurry	31
3. Vision 2030 and the Public Investment Fund	51
4. Rebranding Saudi Arabia as a Destination	67
5. The 2023 Breakthrough	87
6. The Sportswashing Debate	105
7. Will Vision Become Reality?	121
8. The Road to 2034	141
Notes	163
Bibliography	207
Index	225

ACKNOWLEDGMENTS

As a lifelong football fan and a longtime analyst of the Gulf, *Kingdom of Football* brings together two of my personal and professional interests. I hope that the passion I feel for both is reflected in the writing. Thanks are due to Michael Dwyer for suggesting that I head down this particularly enjoyable rabbit-hole, and to the entire team at Hurst Publishers for their support and assistance. I am grateful also to my family and friends, as well as to my colleagues at Rice University's Baker Institute for Public Policy, for enduring months of Gulf-related football focus.

LIST OF ABBREVIATIONS

AFC	Asian Football Confederation
ARAMCO	Arabian American Oil Company
CEDA	Council of Economic and Development Affairs
CEO	Chief Executive Officer
CONCACAF	Confederation of North, Central America and Caribbean Association Football
CPSA	Council of Political and Security Affairs
CSL	Chinese Super League
GDP	Gross Domestic Product
FIFA	International Federation of Association Football
FII	Foreign Investment Initiative
KAEC	King Abdullah Economic City
KSA	Kingdom of Saudi Arabia
MLS	Major League Soccer
NASL	North American Soccer League
PACE	Player Acquisition Center of Excellence
PIF	Public Investment Fund
RHQ	Regional Headquarters Program
SABIC	Saudi Basic Industries Corporation
SAMA	Saudi Arabian Monetary Agency
SAMI	Saudi Arabian Military Industries
SME	Sports Mega-Event
SPL	Saudi Pro League

LIST OF ABBREVIATIONS

SRI	Stanford Research Institute
UAE	United Arab Emirates
UEFA	Union of European Football Associations
WWE	World Wrestling Entertainment

INTRODUCTION

"After using their petrodollars to buy conglomerates, hotels and famous paintings, Arab moneymen now have turned to the world of sport and launched an ambitious, free-spending campaign to buy some of the world's top soccer talent from Brazil."[1] Such began the opening paragraph of a breathless report in the *Washington Post*, seeking to explain to an American readership the significance of Brazil's captain signing a contract to play in Saudi Arabia. It was 1978 and the star in question, Roberto Rivelino, who played alongside Pele in Brazil's 1970 World Cup winning side, had just signed for Al-Hilal, a team based in Riyadh in a league that was only two years old. The days that followed saw feverish speculation that others would follow as the Saudis "have let it be known that they do not intend to settle for just one Brazilian star." Rumours abounded that an offer of $5 million, which would have shattered the record transfer fee for the time, was on the table for Zico, to be split between the player and his club, Flamengo.[2]

Fast forward to 2022, and another captain at a recently-concluded World Cup was on his way to Riyadh to sign for city rivals Al-Nassr. Cristiano Ronaldo had endured a difficult tournament in Qatar which had seen him dropped for the knockout games and his contract terminated by Manchester United. At his unveiling, which began with Ronaldo mistakenly telling the watching world that "for me it's not the end of my career to come to South Africa," the Portuguese superstar added that "I want to give a different vision of this country and football. This is why I took this opportunity. I am coming here to win, play, enjoy, and be part of the success of the country and the culture of the country."[3] The fact that Ronaldo was seated in front of a "Visit Saudi" backdrop emblazoned with the phrase "Saudi, Welcome to Arabia" only reinforced the notion that his latest career move was about more than football alone.

Saudi pride was piqued in 1978, as Iran became the first country in the Middle East to qualify for the World Cup, and again in 2022, when the tournament was staged in the Arab world for the first time, in Qatar next door. In addition, the United Arab Emirates, another state on the Arabian Peninsula, led the way in the 2000s in using football sponsorship to strengthen brand awareness of Dubai and Abu Dhabi, with Emirates and Etihad gaining global recognition as a result of their links with leading European clubs.[4] In each case, Saudi Arabia was upstaged by a geopolitical rival (Iran) or by far smaller neighboring states (Qatar and the UAE). For a country so dominant in terms of geographical size, population, and conventional power metrics, Saudi Arabia risked being left behind by fast-moving regional peers, whether in terms of economic development, sporting prowess, or soft power accumulation.[5]

Written from the perspective of a lifelong football fan and longtime analyst of the Gulf States, this book examines Saudi Arabia's rise to footballing prominence against the backdrop of the dizzying array of developments associated with Mohammed bin Salman—a process of change one Saudi commenter likened in 2019 to "riding in the back seat of a speeding car. We can't see where we are going. We just pray the driver knows so we avoid crashing."[6] Since he burst onto the scene in 2015, the millennial Crown Prince has transformed the Saudi political and economic landscape in ways that amount to a remaking of the country he intends to rule as King for many decades. If he lives as long as his father, King Salman, Mohammed bin Salman will be on the throne in the 2070s, barring unforeseen circumstances, and already, as Crown Prince, he has concentrated decision-making authority to an unprecedented extent. Any story of Saudi Arabia in the 2020s is also one of Mohammed bin Salman, the two are so intertwined, and by the time the FIFA men's World Cup opens in Saudi Arabia in 2034, Mohammed bin Salman will almost certainly be King, barring exceptional longevity on his father's part.

INTRODUCTION

Simultaneously, and seemingly from nowhere, the Kingdom has emerged as a hub for sport in general, and football in particular, as owner, sponsor, host, and participant. The FIFA "vote" by acclamation to allocate the 2034 World Cup to Saudi Arabia was remarkable for how inevitable such a decision appeared in 2024, when a few years earlier it would have seemed unthinkable. Barely a week goes by without a sports personality, or even an entire sport, being linked to Saudi Arabia in some way, amid heated debates about "sportswashing," a label only coined in the early 2010s which has entered the vocabulary of 2020s football.[7] The fact that Mohammed bin Salman's ascendancy to political power was marred by egregious missteps in domestic and regional policymaking added an air of controversy to subsequent tie-ups with Saudi state entities after the murder of Jamal Khashoggi inside the Saudi Consulate in Istanbul in October 2018 in an operation of appalling barbarity that U.S. intelligence agencies assessed to have been conducted with the approval of the Crown Prince.[8]

There is a relative dearth of literature in English on football in the Gulf aside from the focus on Qatar and the 2022 World Cup, which generated many books, edited volumes, and journal articles as well as acres of newsprint and social media commentary of varying quality.[9] Journalists such as Ahmed Al Omran, James Dorsey, James Montague, and John Duerden have followed football in Saudi Arabia and the broader region for years, but they are exceptions who stand out. Among publishers, Routledge has developed a significant catalog of textbooks, handbooks, and monographs that have centered the study of sport in all its political, economic, social, and cultural aspects, as well as its marketing and business models.[10] A 2023 volume, *The Geopolitical Economy of Sport*, was notable for its inclusion of a section on the Gulf, with two of the co-editors (Simon Chadwick and Paul Widdop) writing a critical analysis of the debate on sportswashing, which, they argued, was "marked by the inflammatory language of binary ideologists intent on asserting their own position rather than understanding a complex phenomenon (...) examining the ways in which countries have deployed sport for political purposes is not an attempt to sidestep serious issues nor to excuse one country or another for the misdemeanors in which they have engaged. Instead, it is about establishing a breadth of knowledge and depth of understanding, which the present diatribe fails to do."[11]

The chapters which follow put the development of football in Saudi Arabia into political and economic as well as historical and comparative context. The current era is not the first attempt to transform Saudi football, as shown by the Rivelino signing more than forty years ago. In 1976, Jimmy Hill, the managing director of Coventry City and charismatic television pundit, was appointed technical director to the Saudi Arabian Football Federation with a remit to modernize the domestic game. A plethora of English managers duly came and went, with one complaining that "What you wanted was a 10-year plan but they had money so they thought success was going to come right away," and Hill acknowledged that the impatient Saudi press were quick to declare, "the British have completely failed to improve our football team's standard."[12] A generation later, Saudi Arabia not only qualified for its first World Cup, in the USA in 1994, but also became the first Arab side to qualify from the group stage, after a Maradona-esque goal from Saad Al Owairan secured a memorable 1–0 victory over Belgium. Performances later regressed to the point where Saudi Arabia did not win another game at the World Cup until 2018, with an 8–0 thrashing by Germany in 2002 and a 5–0 defeat to Russia, in front of a watching Mohammed bin Salman in 2018, two low points.[13]

The eight chapters in this book examine the different aspects of the Saudi investment into football, domestically and internationally, since 2016, the year Vision 2030 was launched. *Kingdom of Football* is therefore a book both about football and about the broader political and economic context of decision-making in the Saudi Arabia taking shape under Mohammed bin Salman. It is not devoted to sportswashing, although the term is scrutinized, because of the need to link the moves into football to political and policy priorities both domestically and internationally. Football (and sport in general) has become intertwined with, and integral to, key elements of Vision 2030. These include the highly ambitious (and possibly unachievable) targets of attracting hundreds of millions of visits and tens of millions of new residents to Saudi Arabia's "giga-projects" (such as Neom) when they are completed as well as more practical policy objectives of creating new job opportunities and boosting social cohesion and public health.

INTRODUCTION

It is the somewhat uneasy symbiosis between the realistic and the fantastic aspects of what the Saudi authorities are trying to do which renders Vision 2030 such a high-stakes gamble on securing the Kingdom's future.

Chapter One provides an overview of the development of the domestic football scene in Saudi Arabia. Although a national Saudi league was only launched in 1976, the oldest Saudi club, Al-Ittihad, was established in Jeddah as early as 1927. Most of the major clubs in the Kingdom predate by several decades the Saudi league system, reflecting how the early growth of football occurred in fits and starts but also in ways broadly recognizable to the game's development in many other settings around the world. Much the same pattern is evident in the periodic attempts to engage external consultants to kickstart development, and in the on-off attempts to privatize the teams and move away from the model of state funding and support. This opening chapter takes the reader to 2020, a period which includes the transition of power in Saudi Arabia in 2015 (when Salman became King, aged 79), its aftermath as Mohammed bin Salman accumulated decision-making authority, and the disruption of the Covid-19 pandemic.

In Chapter Two, the focus shifts to Mohammed bin Salman and his plans to transform Saudi Arabia. Aged twenty-nine when he was appointed Minister of Defense and Deputy Crown Prince in 2015, there is every indication that Mohammed bin Salman views himself as the twenty-first century equivalent of his grandfather, Abdulaziz bin Abdulrahman Al Saud, the founder of the modern Kingdom of Saudi Arabia. Just as 'Ibn Saud' ruled for more than fifty years (1902–1953) and established the parameters of the Saudi state that six of his sons, from Saud to Salman, have continued to rule ever since, so Mohammed bin Salman sees it as his mission to overhaul and restructure core aspects of the Kingdom's political economy. While Saudi Arabia has often been labeled an "absolute monarchy" by critics and analysts alike, the practical reality for most of the post-1953 era in Saudi Arabia was that authority was spread among many senior princes and power was not untrammeled.[14] Since the early 2010s, unofficial guardrails and informal checks and balances in the ruling system have nevertheless fallen away, for a variety of reasons.

Chapter Three examines the two drivers of Saudi policymaking that frame and guide the investment into football (and so much else). These are Vision 2030, the policy roadmap to diversify the Saudi economy and lessen the Kingdom's reliance on oil, and the Public Investment Fund, for much of its existence a low-profile locally-focused entity which has, since 2015, been transformed into a global powerhouse.[15] It is the PIF which has been at the forefront of Vision 2030 initiatives and Saudi forays into sport (such as LIV Golf and esports) and football (such as Newcastle United and the majority acquisition of four Saudi clubs). Mohammed bin Salman launched Vision 2030 in April 2016 at a time of significant economic and fiscal pressure caused by collapsing oil prices and a ballooning budget deficit, leading the then Deputy Crown Prince to declare that "2015 was the year of the quick fix. 2016 is the year of the more organized quick fix, and 2017 is the year the vision will begin."[16] 2023 marked the midpoint of the Vision 2030 timeline, and it is critical to Mohammed bin Salman's credibility that its targets be met and its objectives realized.

In Chapter Four, the analysis moves onto the use of sport as a tool for rebranding, in Saudi Arabia's case highlighting the changes taking place and promoting the Kingdom as a destination. Governments and political regimes have long recognized the value of using sport for political purposes, and the authorities in Saudi Arabia are no exception, save for the sheer resources they can deploy. The investment into football internationally, and the attraction of stars to Saudi Arabia either as players or as brand ambassadors, represents an attempt to harness the global appeal of football to spread the message that the Kingdom is changing (at least superficially) to an international audience of potential investors, visitors, and residents needed to populate the giga-projects as they become operational over the next decade.

Chapter Five examines 2023 as the year everything changed for Saudi football. The year began with Ronaldo's arrival in a country giddy from the victory over Argentina at the World Cup, and continued with the transformation of the Saudi Pro League into one of the most talked-about leagues in the world. Not all the arrivals worked out, as Jordan Henderson quickly returned to Europe and Neymar suffered a season-ending injury soon after he joined Al-Hilal, and

INTRODUCTION

attendances at many of the games which did not involve the big Saudi clubs remained stubbornly small, and comparable to the third tier in England. While rumors of foreign players being unhappy with their new surroundings circulated, most of those who arrived in 2023 remained for a second year, and many performed well at the Euro 2024 finals in Germany, but questions remained about the depth and durability of the league's transformation in the longer term.

The buzzword in much of the Western media coverage of Saudi moves into football is "sportswashing," a neologism that did not exist when a member of Abu Dhabi's ruling family acquired Manchester City in 2008 and Qatar won the right to host the 2022 FIFA World Cup in 2010—developments that dramatically raised the profile of the Arabian Peninsula as an emerging hotspot in the "new" geopolitics of football. The term became ubiquitous in Britain, Scandinavia, and much of Northern Europe in 2022 and in the U.S. in 2023, in the latter case as a result of the Saudi backing for LIV Golf in its struggle with the PGA Tour. Chapter Six explores how the term "sportswashing" came about and assesses its relevance for analyzing the Saudi moves into sport, which are part of a broader strategy rather than an end-goal in itself. That said, the chapter ends by examining the purchase of Newcastle United by a consortium led by the Public Investment Fund in 2021, and arguing that this is the closest approximation to sportswashing in practice.

Chapter Seven assesses the prospects for the Saudi transformation project, in its footballing and broader sense, and examines the likelihood that vision may become reality (and what sort of reality). Lessons from other footballing startups, such as the North American Soccer League (NASL) and Major League Soccer (MLS) in the United States, the J-League in Japan, and the Chinese Super League, provide useful historical and comparative insight into the challenges ahead. These include the difficulties of building organically, achieving sustainable growth, and attracting and replacing star talent, as the difficulties in the post-Pele period in the U.S. showed. Those leagues which have taken a longer-term approach, such as MLS and the J-League, have generally succeeded better than those which sought instant success, such as NASL and the Chinese Super League, although even these leagues faced periods of significant uncertainty that at times put their survival at risk. No two cases (or countries) are ever the same, and the chapter explores how the Saudi approach might evolve, especially in light of the apparent scaling back of some of the giga-projects and the challenges of aligning rhetoric and reality in implementing and delivering results.

The book ends by looking ahead to 2034, the year the FIFA men's World Cup is set to be hosted in Saudi Arabia. The decade ahead will see Mohammed bin Salman crowned King and the deadline for Vision 2030 reached, although it remains to be seen how many of the giga-projects come to fruition and at what scale. The trajectory of the 2029 Asian Winter Games, to be held in an as-yet unbuilt mountain resort at Trojena, a part of the gigantic Neom development, will be a bellwether of the viability of plans which look impressive as glitzy presentations when they come up against delivery deadlines and external timetables. By contrast, there may be less risk associated with the World Cup preparations, given the decade-long timeframe, the staging points along the way, such as the AFC Asian Cup in 2027, and the comparatively less fantastical requirements of building new football stadiums rather than developing a ski and winter sports facility in an area with little snow. Instead, it is the many non-football targets which the Saudi investment in football is intrinsically linked to which are likely to be harder to achieve, whether in time for 2030 or by 2034, particularly if the challenges of financing such projects to completion begin to mount.

1

A BRIEF HISTORY OF FOOTBALL IN SAUDI ARABIA

For many people in the United Kingdom and in Europe, the first inkling of a football world in the Arabian Peninsula came in 1977. That July, Don Revie, the celebrated former manager of Leeds United, sensationally left the England job to take over the national team of the United Arab Emirates, a federation of seven emirates created just six years earlier. In the British media frenzy which followed, Revie was dubbed "Don Readies" and accused of selling out his country for Arab oil money, despite the fact that many in the media had been calling for his head after a run of poor performances.[1] For good measure, the English Football Association launched disciplinary proceedings against Revie and banned him from football for ten years in a move that was later ruled unlawful in the High Court. By then, the damage to Revie's reputation was done, and he never managed in England again, although he is more fondly recalled in the UAE, which reached its first (and, so far, only) World Cup in 1990, a decade after his tenure ended.[2]

This chapter weaves the development of football in Saudi Arabia into the political, economic, and social context of a country that was itself in the process of state formation after its unification by Ibn Saud into the modern Kingdom of Saudi Arabia in 1932. An opening section details the origins and early development of football from the 1920s to the formation of the first national league in 1975. A second section examines a series of challenges and breakthroughs between the 1970s and the 1990s, a period which saw Saudi clubs, as well as the national team, establish themselves on the international stage, and welcome the first high-profile foreign players and coaches. Section three documents the rise of regional competition in the 2000s as the United Arab Emirates and Qatar became active and highly visible participants in football on and off the pitch, as owners, sponsors, and hosts. The early 2000s were a time of relative inertia in Saudi football, which is documented in the fourth section, and the chapter ends by looking at the domestic football landscape on the cusp of great change by 2020.

Origins and early development

The 1970s were a decade of rapid change in the six Gulf States which, together with Yemen, make up the Arabian Peninsula. Oil prices quadrupled in the aftermath of the Yom Kippur War in October 1973 and Arab oil embargo, and the flow of revenues into state treasuries increased exponentially. Saudi government revenue in 1975 was forty times higher than in 1965, with the figure rising from $655 million to $26.7 billion.[3] The budget allocated to Saudi Arabia's second five-year plan, which began in 1975, was nine times that of the first five-year plan, launched in 1970.[4] Tales abounded of white elephant projects of varying degrees of feasibility, such as a plan to use tugboats to tow an iceberg from Antarctica to the Red Sea where the melting ice would meet demand for fresh water in the Kingdom.[5] A Saudi prince and French polar explorer organized an International Symposium on Icebergs in Paris in June 1977, which decided that "the ideal iceberg would be rectangular to help prevent tipping, weigh about 100 million tons, be about a mile long, 900 yards wide, and 750 yards high, and be nudged along at about one mile per hour."[6] However, a trial in October ended in failure as a test iceberg (from Alaska) melted in five days.[7]

It was in this same decade that football in Saudi Arabia began to take its modern form based on a national league which replaced the hitherto-regionalized system in 1976. The first clubs had been formed in the 1920s and 1930s and were concentrated in Jeddah, the center

A BRIEF HISTORY OF FOOTBALL IN SAUDI ARABIA

of the comparatively more developed Hijaz region, with Al-Ittihad starting out in 1927 and Al-Ahli ten years later. Unlike in other parts of the region, such as Iran and the smaller Gulf States, the origins of the earliest clubs in Saudi Arabia were more organic, rather than linked to foreign oil workers or colonial projects, although football was also popularized by Muslim pilgrims from the Malay Peninsula and Indonesia.[8] In this respect, they had more in common with the formation of sports clubs in urban centers across the Middle East, such as in Baghdad, Cairo, Damascus, and Istanbul, by local metropolitan elites in the post-Ottoman era. This was illustrated by the fact that the first clubs in the Kingdom emerged in the Hijaz, a part of this "space," rather than in the Eastern Province (where oil was discovered in 1938) or in the central Najd region around Riyadh.[9] Indeed, Al-Ittihad had its roots in the Hijazi Sports Club, a multi-sport entity founded by urban elites in the city.[10]

The matches that took place were between teams in the same area. These gradually became organized into three regional frameworks: east, central, and west, although the early popularity of football both as a pastime and as a spectator sport periodically unnerved the authorities. Football was banned in Jeddah (but not Mecca) in 1934 as a British official observed that "It is not the football itself which has fallen under suspicion, but the fact that it brings young men together in clubs."[11] After Saudi oil exports began in earnest after the Second World War, the pioneering clubs in the Hijaz in the west were augmented by clubs in the Eastern Province, with Al-Ettifaq emerging in 1945 from a combining of local teams in Dammam, the epicenter of the nascent oil sector. Riyadh, by comparison, was more austere and less developed, and while its first team, Al-Shabab, appeared in 1947, it was only in the mid-1950s that Al-Nassr and Al-Hilal followed suit.[12]

1956 saw the creation of the Saudi Arabian Football Federation, led by Prince Abdullah al-Faisal, the eldest son of the Crown Prince and Prime Minister, Prince Faisal, who subsequently became King in 1964 and ruled until his assassination by a nephew (whose own much younger half-brother would later be active in football with Al-Hilal and Sheffield United) eleven years later. Prince Abdullah had a lifelong attachment to Al-Ahli, one of the "big four" that would much later be one of the clubs acquired by the Public Investment Fund in 2023, and is remembered today as one of the most important figures in the modern development of football in Saudi Arabia. His nephew, Prince Abdulaziz bin Turki al-Faisal, who was appointed the Kingdom's first dedicated Minister of Sport in 2020, has been prominent in the successful Saudi bid to host the 2034 men's World Cup, and appears set to play a key role in the decade-long preparation for the tournament.

Development of football and its supporting infrastructure followed broader patterns of state-making in the modern Kingdom of Saudi Arabia. The city of Jeddah, and the Hijaz region on the Red Sea coast, was a cosmopolitan space with relatively advanced political and economic structures prior to its subjugation by the forces of Ibn Saud in 1924 and its incorporation into the emerging Saudi state.[13] In the east, oil was discovered in 1938 and exports began in May 1939, although further exploration and extraction had to wait until after the Second World War.[14] The political economy of development was thus focused on the western and eastern coastlines of Saudi Arabia, in the urban centers of the Hijaz and the Eastern Province, respectively, with their long histories of transnational intellectual and cultural exchanges.[15] It was not until Saudi government ministries were moved from Jeddah in the 1970s (with foreign diplomatic compounds following in the 1980s) that Riyadh established its dominant position in state structures.[16]

Saudi Arabia joined FIFA in 1956, the year the Saudi football federation was created, and nine years before the Kingdom joined the International Olympic Committee. Egypt had been the first Arab state to join FIFA, in 1923, with Lebanon and Syria following in 1936 and 1937, and Iraq in 1950.[17] Across the waterway of the Gulf, Iran formed a football association in 1946 and joined FIFA in 1948, but the Iranian sporting landscape was dominated by the popularity of wrestling in the period up to the revolution in 1978.[18] The smaller sheikhdoms joined FIFA in the aftermath of their emergence as sovereign states in 1961 (Kuwait) and 1971 (Bahrain, Qatar, and the UAE), while Oman, preoccupied with internal issues for much of the 1970s, was the last Gulf State to join FIFA, in 1980.[19] However, it took until the 1978 World Cup for the Saudi national team to enter the qualifiers for the first time, where they defeated Syria on their qualifying debut but lost home and away to Iran, the eventual Asian and Oceanian representative in Argentina.

A domestic knockout competition, the King's Cup, took place for the first time in 1957 and was won by Al-Wehda from Mecca. Al-Ittihad and Al-Hilal dominated the tournament in the two decades prior to the emergence of the national league in 1976, the year that Al-Nassr defended the trophy they had won for the first time the year before. 1970 saw the formation of the Arabian Gulf Cup, a regionwide competition for national teams, dominated in its early years by Kuwait, the regional leader in football (as in so many other walks of life at the time). Saudi Arabia hosted the second Gulf Cup, in 1972, but did not win the tournament until 1994, the year of their World Cup heroics in the USA. In 1990, the Saudis withdrew from that year's cup, which took place in Kuwait six months before the Iraqi invasion, in protest at an emblem they considered a reminder of Kuwait's defeat of Ibn Saud's forces at the Battle of Jahra back in 1920.[20]

Eight teams entered the inaugural Saudi Premier League in 1975 (which was rebranded into its current name, the Saudi Professional League in 2008), but the first season was cut short by the assassination of King Faisal in March and the cancellation of the remaining games. Four of the teams hailed from Riyadh, reflecting the capital's growing centrality in the Kingdom, two from Jeddah, and one apiece from Mecca and from Khobar in the Eastern Province. A second and third tier (known as the First and Second Divisions) were established in 1976, creating a three-step pyramid linked by promotion and relegation. Al-Hilal won the first national championship, in 1976–77, and in 1977–78 the league expanded to ten teams with the addition of Al-Ettifaq and Al-Tai, and the signing of foreign players was permitted for the first time. Clubs received core funding from the state (with the ministry responsible evolving over time from the General Presidency of Youth Welfare in 1974 to the General Sports Authority in 2016 and finally to the Ministry of Sport in 2020) and supplemented it with sponsor and broadcast revenues, along with donations from fans, including sizable sums in some cases from princely and other wealthy supporters.[21]

KINGDOM OF FOOTBALL

Challenges and breakthroughs

The Jimmy Hill era began in 1976 with an approach from a Saudi prince to the former professional who had gained widespread recognition in British football in 1961 from his successful campaign to force the Football League to abolish the maximum wage, first introduced in 1903, that footballers could then earn.[22] After retiring, Hill began a long association with Coventry City, as manager and later managing director, and also moved into broadcasting with the BBC. Hill formed a company, World Sports Academy, and hired a team of twenty, including David Icke, himself a former youth-team player at Coventry and, as Hill tactfully noted, "later proclaimed Son of God." However, Icke found it difficult to adapt to living in Riyadh and quickly returned to the U.K., as did Hill's first choice as national team manager, Bill McGarry, the decidedly old school Wolves manager who replaced the Hungarian legend Ferenc Puskas.[23] Another of the retired pros brought in by Hill "found it hard to adapt to the extreme cultural differences" and caused further offence by refusing to learn his players' names and referring to them by their shirt numbers.[24]

Other aspirational plans to bring in top-notch English managers, with Brian Clough, Bob Paisley, and Bobby Robson all floated as possibilities, also went nowhere, and Hill later commented that "the thought was that an inspirational coach, manager or messiah might help them to move up the football ladder in double-quick time."[25] Hill thus alluded to the search for instant success, and the sense of failure was magnified by press reports of the budget of tens of millions of pounds he had been allocated by the authorities. David Woodfield, the former Wolves defender who was another of the coaches brought over, stated later that "What you wanted was a 10-year plan but they had money so they thought success was going to come right away."[26] Perhaps unsurprisingly, the English interlude was met with sustained hostility from the Saudi media, and the advisory contract was not renewed in 1979, after the Saudis only finished third in the Gulf Cup in Baghdad (in which Revie's UAE job also ended in ignominy following 7–0 and 5–0 defeats to Kuwait and Iraq). That said, Hill oversaw the development of a youth system at under 21, under 18, and under 16 levels, which was followed within

A BRIEF HISTORY OF FOOTBALL IN SAUDI ARABIA

a few years by the first major breakthroughs at club and national team levels as Saudi Arabia began to make its mark on Asian football and the global game in the mid-1980s.

Rivelino was the first foreign superstar to play in Saudi Arabia, as noted in the opening to this book. His three-year spell at Al-Hilal was a success, on and off the pitch, as the club pipped Al-Nassr for the title in his first season and added a King's Cup the following year with a win against Al-Shabab in 1980. Media reports claimed that Rivelino had been offered a salary that was seven times higher than his existing one in Brazil, in an echo of the contracts offered to Ronaldo, Neymar, Jordan Henderson, and others in 2023. In addition to being flown from Rio to Riyadh on Concorde, Rivelino was reportedly lodged in a "spare palace" belonging to Al-Hilal's chairman, a nephew of King Khalid.[27] Here, too, was another echo of 2023, when another Brazilian superstar, Neymar, was flown to Riyadh to sign for the same team, Al-Hilal, in a jet arranged by another royal nephew, in this case Prince Alwaleed bin Talal, nephew of King Salman.[28] Looking back fondly to his time in Saudi Arabia four decades earlier, Rivelino told *Arab News* in 2020 that "It was almost amateur football at the time" and recalled that there was only one stadium in Riyadh but three teams, so "we trained from 6 to 7 pm, the next team from 7 to 8 and then the third from 8 to 9."[29]

Saudi Arabia in the 1980s and 1990s faced a challenging set of political, social, and economic headwinds which had an impact on all aspects of policy. The Saudi leadership was shaken to the core by the seizure of the Grand Mosque in Mecca by Sunni religious extremists in November 1979 and by sustained protests by Shia communities in the Eastern Province at almost exactly the same time.[30] Although the two events were unconnected, they occurred in the immediate aftermath of the geopolitical shockwaves generated by the Islamic revolution in Iran. The Al Saud responded to these developments by becoming more conservative, expanding and enforcing a religious turn in domestic policymaking and supporting pan-Islamic causes abroad, such as in Afghanistan in the 1980s and Bosnia in the 1990s.[31] This took place against the backdrop of a sustained slump in oil prices that began in 1981, bottomed out in 1986, and lasted until the end of the 1990s.[32] The downturn hit public finances hard, as income from oil plunged 90 percent between 1981 and 1986 and state revenues decreased by nearly 80 percent in the same period.[33]

Despite these pressures, Saudi football made a number of breakthroughs in the final two decades of the century, especially on the regional and international stage. The national team won the AFC Asian Cup for the first time in 1984, defeating China 2–0 in the final in Singapore. This was the first of five successive finals in the tournament, as the Saudis defended their crown in 1988, won for a third time in 1996, and finished runners-up to Japan in 1992 and 2000. The five consecutive Asian Cup finals remain unmatched, and the Kingdom's back-to-back triumphs in the 1980s was not emulated until Qatar followed their inaugural title in 2019 with a win on home soil in 2024. At club level, Al-Hilal became the first Saudi side to reach the final of the Asian Club Championship (today the AFC Champions League), in 1986, and the first to win the competition, in 1991, when they beat Iranian rivals Esteghlal in the final in Qatar. Other Saudi clubs, such as Al-Nassr, Al-Qadsiah, and Al-Shabab, also enjoyed continental success in the 1990s, and Al-Nassr represented Asia in the inaugural FIFA World Club Championship in 2000, where they played three games in the group stage and lost to Real Madrid and Corinthians but beat Raja Casablanca 4–3.[34]

On the global stage, June 1989 saw the Saudi under-16 team crowned world champions as they came back from 2–0 down to defeat Scotland on penalties in the final of the U-16 World Cup in front of a packed crowd of 51,000 at Hampden Park in Glasgow. Earlier in the tournament, the Saudis had also retrieved a two-goal deficit against a Portuguese side featuring a young Luis Figo who scored the opening goal. However, the triumph was marred by allegations, both at the time and subsequently, that the Saudi side fielded over-age players. The apparent discrepancies were noticed by the popular *Saint & Greavsie* television show with Ian St. John remarking that many of the Saudi players looked over 16 and were much stronger than their Scottish counterparts, especially as the game went on.[35] Twenty years on, the sense of Scottish injustice was still palpable, as the by-now retired secretary of the Scottish Football Association claimed that "it was so obvious—the Saudi keeper looked like Peter Shilton," referring to England's 40-year-old goalkeeper at the time,

A BRIEF HISTORY OF FOOTBALL IN SAUDI ARABIA

and alleged that one of the Saudi players was "married with three children and was a captain in the Royal Guard—all that and he was playing in the Under-16 World Cup."[36]

The highpoint for Saudi football in the 1990s was undoubtedly their maiden appearance at the World Cup finals in 1994. The Saudis entered the tournament in some disarray after going through four managers in a year, including one who resigned after being told by a prince to make a substitution during a qualifying game, before alighting on Jorge Solari, reportedly after King Fahd spoke with the President of Argentina, Carlos Menem.[37] Their captain, Majid Abdullah, the all-time top scorer for Al-Nassr and the national team, hailed from a Sudanese background in Jeddah and was known variously as the "Arabian jewel" and the "Desert Pele."[38] After losing narrowly to the Netherlands in their opening game, in which they led at half-time, the Saudis defeated Morocco 2–1 and then beat Belgium 1–0 with a goal from Saeed Al Owairan after a run from his own half that was strikingly similar to Diego Maradona's famous second goal in the "Hand of God" quarterfinal between Argentina and England in 1986.[39] Having become the first Middle East nation, and only the second from the broader region, after Morocco, to qualify for the knockout stage, the Saudis' run ended with a 3–1 defeat by Sweden in the round of 16. However, the national team did not win another World Cup game for another 24 years, a period which saw heavy defeats to France in 1998, Germany in 2002, Ukraine in 2006, and Russia in 2018, and a failure to qualify in 2010 and 2014.[40]

The 1990s additionally saw Saudi Arabia play a critical role in the creation of what became the FIFA Confederations Cup, a tournament for continental champions that was held every two years until 2003 and every four years between 2005 and 2017 as a warm-up event for the host of the following year's men's World Cup. The tournament began as the King Fahd Cup and was played for the first time in Riyadh in October 1992 as a four-nation affair with Argentina and Saudi Arabia defeating the Ivory Coast and the United States in the semifinals before the Argentines beat the hosts 3–1 in the final in front of a capacity 75,000 crowd. In January 1995, an expanded King Fahd Cup brought together Saudi Arabia, Denmark, Japan, Argentina, Mexico, and Nigeria in two groups of three, before a final in which the Danes beat the Argentinians 2–0. Two years later, Riyadh hosted the event for the third time but under the rebranding of the FIFA Confederations Cup rather than the King Fahd Cup. The 1997 edition featured two groups of four with World Champions Brazil joining the continental champions (with the Czech Republic standing in for Germany as the tournament clashed with the Bundesliga's winter break), before a knockout stage which culminated in Brazil thrashing Australia 6–0 with hat-tricks from both Ronaldo and Romario. From 1999, the tournament was played outside Saudi Arabia and did not return to Riyadh as the event became tied to the hosting cycle of the men's World Cup.[41]

Rise of the UAE and Qatar

On a regional level, the 2000s saw the rise of the UAE and Qatar, as much off the pitch as on it, with the advent of state-linked investments in the global football ecosystem. This, again, was consistent with wider political and economic trends as the two much smaller neighbors of Saudi Arabia assumed far more visible and proactive roles in regional and international affairs. The UAE had much earlier, between 1986 and 1989, organized the Dubai Champions Cup as a contest between the champions of England and Scotland, at a time when English clubs were serving an indefinite ban from UEFA competitions as a result of the Heysel tragedy at the European Cup final between Juventus and Liverpool in 1985.[42] All three editions went to penalties, with Liverpool and Celtic trading victories over each other either side of Rangers overcoming Everton despite having six goals disallowed by the referee. The final game took place in April 1989, a week before the Hillsborough stadium disaster, and the event did not recur, as UEFA readmitted teams from England into its competitions in 1990, with Liverpool serving an additional one-year ban until 1991.[43]

Qatari and Emirati involvement in football accelerated rapidly after the turn of the century as the two countries became regional powerhouses in a changing Middle East and began to create a truly international imprint. The early 2000s saw the rebranded Qatar Stars League attract a succession of aging international stars to the country in a manner that prefigured by two decades the moves to the Saudi

A BRIEF HISTORY OF FOOTBALL IN SAUDI ARABIA

Pro League in 2023. Pep Guardiola, Gabriel Batistuta, Fernando Hierro, and Stefan Effenberg were among the big names who ended their playing careers in Qatar, as did Xavi a decade later.[44] At home, the Qatari authorities invested heavily in the Aspire Academy for Sport Excellence, with Pele and Maradona making a rare joint appearance at its grand opening in 2005.[45] The Aspire Academy assisted in the development of a generation of footballers, some drawn from regional states, which formed the nucleus of the Qatar side which won the AFC Under-19 Championship in 2014 and the full AFC Asian Cup five years later.[46]

Ownership and sponsorships were the most visible manifestations of the Emirati and Qatari moves into football. High-profile acquisitions included Manchester City by Sheikh Mansour bin Zayed's Abu Dhabi United Group in September 2008 and Paris Saint-Germain by Qatar Sports Investment in 2011, especially as each team went on to dominate the English Premier League and Ligue 1, respectively.[47] A 2009 interview with Khaldoun Al Mubarak, the Emirati Chairman of Manchester City, highlighted the perceived soft power benefit for Abu Dhabi, as he stated that "There is an appreciation of the association the club have with Abu Dhabi that we hold very dearly (...) We are acknowledging that how we are handling this project is telling a lot to the world about how we are (...) This is showing the world the true essence of who Abu Dhabi is and what Abu Dhabi is about."[48] Similarly, the chief commercial officer at Etihad, Abu Dhabi's newly-established airline (in the 2000s) and Manchester City's stadium and shirt sponsor, stated that "developing Man City's global reputation (...) in turn helps us to build our reputation."[49] Acquiring the naming rights to the Arsenal and Manchester City stadiums took brand recognition to a whole new level as "going to the Emirates" and "going to the Etihad" entered the vernacular of football fans everywhere.[50]

Dubai, Abu Dhabi, and Qatar also took the regional lead in using sponsorships as tools of branding to raise their international profile by harnessing the global appeal of sport to reach new audiences worldwide. This was especially apparent in the competition among the three major Gulf airlines—Etihad, Emirates, and Qatar Airways—as they competed for routes and passengers. Gulf Air, then the region-wide airline for Bahrain, Oman, Qatar, and the UAE, had become

Chelsea's first shirt sponsor as far back as 1983, but first the UAE (in the mid-1980s), then Qatar (in the mid-1990s), and Oman (in the mid-2000s) left Gulf Air and established their own carriers, leaving Bahrain the sole national shareholder.[51] It was into this void that Emirates was established in 1985 by the Government of Dubai, Qatar Airways in 1994, and Etihad in 2003 by the Government of Abu Dhabi (the Dubai and Abu Dhabi cases being emirate- rather than UAE-specific). In 2004, Emirates fired the starting-gun in the sponsorship stakes when they signed their first shirt agreement, ironically with Chelsea, but this tie-up was quickly surpassed by a rights-naming agreement with Arsenal, who have played at the Emirates Stadium in London since 2006. Etihad similarly acquired the naming rights to the City of Manchester Stadium in 2011, while Qatar Airways became FC Barcelona's first commercial shirt sponsor in 2013, replacing the state-linked yet non-profit Qatar Foundation.[52]

Clubs in Saudi Arabia also signed aging international stars in the 2000s but eschewed the Emirati and Qatari approach of using sponsorship or ownership to raise the Kingdom's profile abroad. (Indeed, as later chapters detail, the post-2020 PIF-led strategy of moving into ownership, of Newcastle United, and sponsorship is essentially a replication of these earlier strategies which predated by nearly two decades the Saudi approach, using in some cases the same figures, such as in the leadership of Riyadh Air.) English media reports in 1996 raised the possibility of an approach by Prince Alwaleed bin Talal Al Saud, one of the most prominent Saudi "royal businessmen," for Manchester City, but nothing ultimately came of it.[53]

In the 2000s, there were periodic rumors of a Saudi-linked bid for Manchester United, but such commercial ties-ups as did occur took the form of a sponsorship agreement with Saudi Telecom in 2008 and the announcement of a strategic partnership with the General Sports Authority in 2017, rather than an attempt to acquire the club itself. Notably, however, the 2017 agreement was specifically intended to assist with the development of the football sector in the Kingdom, a move United's then-managing director, Richard Arnold, claimed was consistent with the club's "long-standing relationship with Saudi Arabia."[54] In 2008, the Manchester United squad traveled to Riyadh midseason to face Al-Hilal in a testimonial match for Sami Al Jaber, one of the greatest strikers in Al-Hilal's history who also scored in three World Cups for Saudi Arabia. A 22-year-old Cristiano Ronaldo was one of the scorers for Manchester United but Al-Hilal went on to defeat the then-English champions 3–2 in front of a full house of 67,000.[55]

Especially by comparison with the Qatar Stars League, fewer international stars played for Saudi clubs. In 1998, Hristo Stoichkov, the Bulgarian striker who made his name as part of Johan Cruyff's "dream team" at Barcelona in the early 1990s and was the joint top scorer in the 1994 World Cup, signed a two-match deal with Al-Nassr to play in the semifinal and final of the 1997–98 Asian Cup Winners' Cup, whereupon he scored the only goal in the final to give Al-Nassr victory over Suwon Samsung Bluewings of South Korea. In the 2000s, the biggest names to arrive in the Saudi Premier League were Roberto Donadoni and Bebeto, who both played for Al-Ittihad, in Bebeto's case only five times.[56] Al-Ittihad also tried to sign Roy Keane when he left Manchester United in acrimony in November 2005, as they sought a big-name player ahead of their participation in the FIFA Club World Championship as the AFC Champions League winners.[57] Just over a year later, in early 2007, Al-Ittihad were left fuming in embarrassment after calling a news conference in Dubai to announce the signing of Luis Figo only for it to emerge that Figo had used their approach as a bargaining chip in a contract negotiation with his existing club, Inter Milan.[58]

Consolidation and inertia

The success of Al-Ittihad in the 2000s, which included four Saudi Premier League titles, back-to-back victories in the AFC Champions League in 2004 and 2005, and a narrow defeat to Sao Paulo in the semifinal of the FIFA Club World Championship in 2005, highlighted the role that individuals could play in ostensibly state-funded clubs. In this case, the key figure was Mansour Al Balawi, a prominent businessman from Jeddah who, a decade later, in 2017, was among the many individuals held in extrajudicial circumstances at the Ritz-Carlton in Riyadh before being released.[59] Al Balawi served as Chairman of Al-Ittihad between 2003 and 2007, when he was forced to resign after accusations from Al-Hilal's chairman, Prince Mohammed bin Faisal Al

Saud, that he had tried to poach the Sierra Leonean striker Mohammed Kallon.[60] Amid an acrimonious war of words between the clubs, Al-Hilal filed a police complaint against Kallon, who was temporarily unable to leave Saudi Arabia and banned from playing in the Kingdom for three years.[61]

Al Balawi's resignation in 2007 sparked heated debate across the Saudi football community, not least because the Kallon affair appeared for many to be symptomatic of a broader approach that had caused considerable anger among supporters (and officials) of rival teams. The passions generated by football and fandom constituted one of the few spaces where feelings could be expressed, individually as well as collectively, and pressure exerted on the authorities, whether at club or national level. This phenomenon is not unique to Saudi Arabia, and has been observed across the world, with prominent regional examples in recent years seen in Egypt, Jordan, Turkey, and Iran, and further afield, such as in Indonesia.[62] In 2004, trouble between Arab and Kurdish football fans at a game in Syria expanded into "a full-scale revolt" in Qamishli as the local headquarters of the Ba'ath Party was burned and a statue of former president Hafez Al Assad torn down, recalling the toppling of Saddam Hussein's statue in Baghdad the year before.[63]

Especially in authoritarian settings with controlled or restricted spaces for political expression, the relative anonymity of large crowds at football games provided a veneer of security for collective action at times.[64] Stadiums and football crowds in Iran have long functioned as "public spheres [that] can become safety valves for social tension and defiance where spectators challenge the authority of the state" and as sites of political and ideological contestation, including mass appeals for the right of women to attend games.[65] In early 2011, organized "ultras" played an important role in the revolutionary upheaval in Egypt, where they drew upon "the skills and techniques of breaking through concentrated police forces to get into stadiums" to take over Tahrir Square in Cairo and overcome attacks from pro-regime camel-borne forces.[66] Two years later, football fans were prominent in the 2013 Gezi Park protests in Istanbul, to the extent that members of a Besiktas supporter group were accused of "attempting a coup d'état against the elected government" of Recep Tayyip

A BRIEF HISTORY OF FOOTBALL IN SAUDI ARABIA

Erdogan.[67] Alarmingly for the authorities, fans of bitter rivals Galatasaray and Fenerbahce expressed solidarity with their Besiktas counterparts and joined the demonstrations.[68] In Libya, in the 2000s, and in Algeria during the uprising in 2019, football stadiums functioned as sites of organized action against the Qaddafi regime (in Benghazi) and the gerontocratic Algerian political elite.[69]

As a Saudi professor, speaking anonymously to *The Economist* magazine put it in 2012, "Football has emerged as a rare area for free speech."[70] That year, the head of the football federation, Prince Nawaf bin Faisal Al Saud, stepped down after a supporter backlash following the Kingdom's failure to qualify for the 2010 World Cup. His replacement, Ahmed Eid Al Harbi, not only became the first non-royal to lead the federation but was also elected to the position (with Saudi Arabia permitting elections in many associations, such as chambers of commerce).[71] Fans of Al-Nassr also tried, unsuccessfully, to oust their president, Prince Faisal bin Turki Al Saud, after a poor run, with the issue assuming delicate proportions after a Facebook page appeared calling for a "revolution" at the club.[72] During this post-Arab Spring period, the role that organized football supporters played in some of the political upheaval, notably in Egypt, caused the authorities in Riyadh to consider focusing more on individual rather than team sports.[73]

While Saudi clubs continued to perform strongly in continental competitions, with Al-Hilal becoming the most successful side in the history of the AFC Champions League, both in the number of wins (four) and finals (nine), a degree of drift held back domestic developments in the 2010s. The sense of inertia was evident in the repeated announcement of plans to privatize clubs and wean them off state funding (which were revived again in 2023, as detailed in Chapter Five). In April 2013, the General Presidency for Youth Welfare unveiled a plan to sell the fourteen clubs in the Saudi Pro League and use the proceeds to invest in new stadiums and create a new entity, modeled on the Premier League, to market the league and secure more lucrative broadcast rights. An advisory committee on privatization was formed, led by Prince Abdullah bin Mosaad Al Saud, who hoped that the plan would have "a similar effect on Saudi soccer as the creation of the Premier League in 1992 had on the English game."[74]

Prince Abdullah later reached the Premier League in his own right with Sheffield United, a club he bought into in 2013, the same year as he spearheaded the privatization drive, when the Blades were struggling in League One, the third tier of English football.[75]

Three years later, by which time the national team had failed to qualify for a second successive World Cup and Mohammed bin Salman had emerged as a powerbroker in a restructured Saudi government, the Council of Economic and Development Affairs (CEDA), a new sub-Cabinet entity chaired by MBS, revived the privatization plan, which became known as the Sports Clubs Investment and Privatization Project. In 2016, the Saudi government commissioned Deloitte to prepare a feasibility study, and in November the CEDA set up a supervisory committee to oversee the process of transferring the clubs into private control.[76] The plan won the approval of the Council of Ministers, the Saudi cabinet, and was one of the responsibilities handed to the revamped General Sports Authority, which assumed oversight over Saudi football from its predecessor, the General Presidency of Youth Welfare.[77] Another, unrelated outcome of Mohammed bin Salman's rise was a curbing of clerical influence, including a stripping of the power of arrest from the religious police.[78] This removed an impediment to the accelerated modernization of aspects of Saudi society, as seen in an undated *fatwa* that had permitted the playing of football but not sporting competitions, a ruling that was judiciously ignored by successive Saudi governments.[79]

In February 2017, Jadwa Investment, a leading Riyadh-based financial entity co-founded by Prince Faisal bin Salman, an older half-brother of Mohammed bin Salman, was appointed to advise on the privatization of up to five clubs.[80] By then, it appeared that the push to privatize would be focused on the elite layer of teams in Riyadh and Jeddah only, and that the likeliest buyers would be wealthy Saudi individuals rather than foreign investors.[81] The General Sports Authority created a Sports Development Fund to assist with the process of preparing clubs for private ownership, and worked with the Ministry of Commerce and Investment to examine ways to generate new revenue streams based on more professional business practices.[82] However, in January 2019, it was reported that the plan was delayed, and the head of the Saudi Arabian Football Federation told a sports

A BRIEF HISTORY OF FOOTBALL IN SAUDI ARABIA

conference in Dubai that uncertainty remained over how many clubs would be involved in the process: "Nothing is seriously happening so far (…) Until we get a full plan, we can't tell whether it's the five clubs or full 16" in the Saudi Pro League at the time.[83]

The difficulties in agreeing on a procedure for privatizing Saudi football clubs mirrored some of the challenges facing the authorities as they initially struggled to meet the ambitious goals laid out in Vision 2030.[84] Whereas the transfer of state assets to the private sector was a key element in the economic reform agenda drawn up by Mohammed bin Salman in 2016, early progress was piecemeal and halting, with deadlines missed and lower than expected foreign investor interest.[85] An assessment in 2018 by a leading corporate law firm in the Gulf, Al Tamimi & Co., acknowledged that the privatization of Saudi Pro League (SPL) clubs "has become a bellwether project to showcase KSA's progressive economic and social reforms, with the expectation that the SPL will become a powerful marketing tool for KSA to attract international brands and investors."[86] To that end, measures designed to increase the audience and the marketability of the Saudi Pro League (as well as its attractiveness to foreign investors) included the lifting of the ban on women attending games and participating in football (in January 2018) and the announcement the following month of a new broadcast deal with the Saudi Telecommunications Company, which was itself 70 percent majority owned by the Public Investment Fund (PIF).[87]

However, even with the pace of change picking up and with the backing of high-level political support through Vision 2030 programs, the PIF, and its many subsidiaries, challenges remained. A perennial problem was the high rate of cases involving Saudi teams and claims for breach of contract heard at FIFA's Dispute Resolution Chamber. This resulted in heavy fines for Saudi teams, sanctions on clubs perceived to be repeat offenders, and a warning in 2022 by FIFPro, the international players' union, advising its members against signing for clubs in Saudi Arabia (as well as China, Algeria, Romania, and Turkey).[88] Among the clubs affected were Al-Ahli, which faced a claim from former Nottingham Forest captain Lewis Grabban, Al-Hilal, which was under a transfer ban in 2022 which prevented the club from trying to sign Cristiano Ronaldo in August that year, four

25

months before he joined Al-Nassr, and Al-Nassr themselves, banned in summer 2023 from registering new players for three transfer windows for failing to pay performance-related add-ons to Leicester City relating to the Nigerian striker Ahmed Musa.[89] Al-Nassr and Al-Ittihad had earlier been denied licenses to compete in the AFC Champions League in 2018, leaving Saudi Arabia with two, rather than four, entrants in the 2018–19 competition, an embarrassing rebuff to the General Sports Authority a year into its leadership by a close confidant of Mohammed bin Salman.[90]

Into the 2020s

Football in Saudi Arabia was therefore at a crossroads as the 2010s gave way to a new decade which began with a global pandemic that wrought havoc on the sport, leisure, tourism, and entertainment sectors worldwide, which were, in the Saudi case, integral elements of Vision 2030. The domestic game had developed into a multi-tier pyramid, and the elite teams were among the best in Asia with a record of success in continental competitions. The number of teams in the Saudi Pro League rose steadily, from 12 to 14 in 2010 and from 14 to 16 in 2018 before the most recent expansion to 18 in 2023, as did the number of foreign players, from nine in 2003–4 to 23 in 2008–9 and then a jump to more than 40 in the 2017–8 season and thereafter, when clubs were permitted to sign seven non-Saudis rather than two.[91] Indeed, in 2018, Saudi clubs spent more than anyone outside the top five European leagues and China as spending rose by more than 440% from 2017, in an indication of the financial muscle beginning to be flexed.[92] There was also a significant level of public passion for football, as seen at the 2022 World Cup in Qatar, even if this did not translate into higher attendances for domestic games, which remained stubbornly low.

Progress was also evident in the women's game in Saudi Arabia, albeit from one of the most restricted starting points in world football. This was rooted in the lack of opportunities for women in public life and society at large, as Saudi Arabia was the last country to send female athletes to the Olympic Games in 2012 (together with Qatar and Brunei, and admittedly just four years after the United Arab

A BRIEF HISTORY OF FOOTBALL IN SAUDI ARABIA

Emirates and Oman sent their first female athletes to the Beijing Olympics in 2008).[93] Two women represented the Kingdom in the London Olympics, in judo and track and field, and the number rose to four at the games in Rio de Janeiro in 2016 with a second track and field participant as well as a fencer.[94] 2007 saw female students at Al-Yamamah university in Riyadh start a football team, the first organized (albeit unofficial) one in the Kingdom, and the Norwegian academic Charlotte Lysa used field research and participant interviews to establish that eight teams participated in a league system that began play in 2008.[95] In March 2009, the *Al-Watan* newspaper covered a game between two teams of women, "University" and "Barcelona," in front of 400 female spectators that raised money for people with disabilities.[96] However, it was only in 2018 that women were permitted to enter Saudi stadia as spectators, 2019 when a domestic league for women was officially created, 2021 when a national women's football team followed suit, and 2022 when the league was rebranded into the Saudi Women's Premier League, with Al-Nassr becoming its first champion, finishing ahead of Al-Hilal in the eight-team competition.[97]

The optimistic outlook was offset by several issues which cast a shadow over Saudi football in the late-2010s as the Kingdom was buffeted by crosswinds generated by Mohammed bin Salman's turbulent rise toward power (see Chapter Two). Close ties to state-led initiatives exposed football to external pressures. One of the highest-profile cases of blowback (and unintended consequences) concerned the emergence of beoutQ during the blockade of Qatar by Saudi Arabia, Bahrain, the UAE, and Egypt, which began in June 2017 and lasted until January 2021. BeoutQ, a jibe at beIN Sports, the Qatari network which held regional broadcasting rights for a wide array of events, including the FIFA World Cup and the Premier League, appeared several months after the blockade began, and soon comprised ten channels engaged in what the *New York Times* called "the brazen bootlegging of a multibillion-dollar sports network."[98] By 2018, the illicit activity, which included televising every game at the World Cup in Russia, led one sports-focused publication to ask, rhetorically, "what happens when the scale of a piracy operation is so sophisticated that it can no longer be contained?"[99]

Although beoutQ claimed to have Cuban and Columbian backing, investigators from beIN traced its signal to Arabsat, a Riyadh-based pan-Arab satellite operator, noted that the signal was geo-locked so that only users in Saudi Arabia could access it, and that annual subscription packages offered "access to hundreds of channels from around the world, providing valuable sports and entertainment events for a fraction of the price that legitimate rights holders charge for the same content."[100] In 2020, a panel formed by the World Trade Organization (WTO) to adjudicate the dispute reported that there was "evidence that beoutQ was promoted by prominent individuals and newspapers within Saudi Arabia."[101] Among the individuals named was Saud Al Qahtani, one of Mohammed bin Salman's closest aides, later implicated by US officials in the killing of Jamal Khashoggi inside the Saudi Consulate in Istanbul in October 2018.[102] The WTO panel largely ruled in favor of Qatar in June 2020 as it found that "beoutQ is operated by individuals or entities under the jurisdiction of Saudi Arabia" and that the Kingdom had "taken measures" that failed to establish penalties for beoutQ and which prevented beIN from enforcing its rights in Saudi Arabia.[103]

The beoutQ affair had consequences for Saudi Arabia's football breakout. One high-profile casualty was the attempt by the Public Investment Fund to acquire a majority stake in Newcastle United.[104] First mooted in January 2020, the bid was made public in April, as documents filed at Companies House in the U.K. listed a senior PIF official as director of NCUK Investment Ltd, a company established by PIF Governor Yasir Al Rumayyan.[105] However, a delay in the next phase of the takeover, the Premier League's Owners and Directors Test, which had been introduced by the Premier League in 2004 as the "Fit and Proper Persons Test" before evolving into its current guise in 2011, led the PIF-led consortium to withdraw from the bid process in July 2020, due in part to a challenge by beIN, the league's regional broadcast partner.[106]

It was only when beIN's access to Saudi Arabia was restored eleven months later, in October 2021, that the takeover was revived, whereupon it received Premier League approval within 24 hours after "legally binding assurances" were received that the Kingdom of Saudi Arabia would not control Newcastle.[107] Chapter Six will examine in

A BRIEF HISTORY OF FOOTBALL IN SAUDI ARABIA

detail the Saudi ownership of Newcastle, which is closest to the "sportswashing" narrative that has taken root in media and public discourse in Europe. The sight of thousands of jubilant Newcastle supporters celebrating the takeover outside St James' Park certainly sent a symbolic message that Saudi investment and involvement was welcome in at least parts of Britain, despite the post-Khashoggi isolation of Mohammed bin Salman by Western leaders, including President Joe Biden, who had vowed, in 2019 (when campaigning for the presidency) to turn Saudi Arabia into a "pariah" state.[108]

The Kingdom's relationships with national and international bodies also suffered as a result of the pirating of broadcast content, although ties with FIFA were noticeably less affected. During the 2018 World Cup in Russia, a tense exchange on Twitter between Turki Al Sheikh, the then Chairman of the General Sports Authority, and an unnamed UEFA official suggested a breakdown in relations on both sides. Al Sheikh sent a ten-tweet thread in which he claimed, among other things, that UEFA's president, Aleksandar Ceferin, "is trying to meet me, but I am telling him that I do not like to meet men of many faces," and added that "If you want to meet, you should have a clear stance on fair issues, including the monopoly and politicization of sports by beIN SPORTS, which you force us to watch without taking into account the feelings of 30 million Saudi citizens" (tellingly, Al Sheikh went on to describe FIFA President Gianni Infantino, who had sat between Mohammed bin Salman and Vladimir Putin at the World Cup's opening game a week earlier, as "a dear friend for whom the Kingdom and I hold great respect.")[109] In response, UEFA tweeted an expression of surprise at Al Sheikh's comments, "as the UEFA President has never heard of this person and he therefore would have no reason to meet with him.[110] As the beoutQ standoff continued, in September 2019 FIFA, UEFA, the Asian Football Confederation, and the Bundesliga, La Liga, Serie A, and the Premier League issued a joint statement which drew attention to the lack of legal remedies available to them in the Kingdom, including an inability to obtain or instruct legal counsel.[111]

Saudi fingerprints were also rumored to be on an apparent offer by an unnamed consortium, which reportedly was led by SoftBank from Japan, to invest US$25 billion in FIFA in 2018 to create new global tournaments, including a significantly expanded Club World Cup. At this time, SoftBank had a close working relationship with the PIF, which had invested heavily in SoftBank's Vision Fund, and Saudi, Emirati, Chinese, and American investors were said to be involved, although specific details were scarce.[112] While Infantino had hoped to railroad the pledge through FIFA, he was met with strong opposition from UEFA, whose president, Ceferin, stated in May 2018 that "I cannot accept that some people who are blinded by the pursuit of profit are considering to sell the soul of football tournaments to nebulous private funds."[113] Also in 2018, Infantino pushed to bring the planned expansion of the men's World Cup (from 32 to 48 teams) forward from the 2026 tournament, played across North America in the United States, Canada, and Mexico, to the 2022 edition, in Qatar.[114] In the context of the ruptured Saudi-Qatari relationship at the time, some in Doha saw the move as part of a covert attempt to force the small state to spread the hosting rights for an expanded tournament among its neighbors, including Saudi Arabia.[115]

By 2020, Saudi football was therefore at a fork in the road as Covid-19 rapidly spread its tentacles across the world and hit hardest the economic sectors that were at the forefront of the "giga-projects" associated with Vision 2030, as Chapter Three documents. The disruptive impact of the pandemic began to dissipate in 2021 as vaccines became widely available, and largely disappeared in 2022 as global public health restrictions eased and international travel revived. For Mohammed bin Salman, the pandemic functioned as a timeout that drew a line under the volatility associated with his startling emergence, both domestically and on the regional and global stage. By the time the world began to fully reopen, following the final pandemic-related Omicron spasm at the end of 2021, the international situation had changed markedly. After the full-scale Russian invasion of Ukraine in February 2022, Saudi Arabia's geopolitical and energy significance forced Western leaders to re-engage with the Crown Prince following his post-Khashoggi diplomatic isolation. A perhaps-unintended side-effect of the isolation of Vladimir Putin in 2022 was the international rehabilitation of Mohammed bin Salman, and it is to him that this book now turns.

2

MOHAMMED BIN SALMAN, A PRINCE IN A HURRY

In a lengthy special report on succession politics and scenarios in Saudi Arabia, published in 2010 by *Gulf States Newsletter*, an industry newsletter released fortnightly since 1974, Mohammed bin Salman merited three lines on page 45 of a 52-page document.[1] Even if they had noticed his inclusion, this would not have seemed surprising to Saudi-watchers at the time, given that the then-25-year-old Mohammed bin Salman was a much younger son of Prince Salman, then the long-serving Governor of Riyadh but not in the line of succession to the Saudi throne, had several much older and professionally accomplished half-brothers, and virtually no public or international profile. Greater focus was paid in the report to Salman's sons by his first wife, namely Sultan, who had become the first Arab astronaut in space in 1985 (the year Mohammed bin Salman was born), Abdulaziz, who started a lifelong career in the Ministry of Petroleum in 1987 (which culminated in his appointment as Minister of Energy in 2019), and Faisal, who headed the influential Saudi Research and Marketing Group which owned staple titles of Saudi and pan-Arab media.[2]

Within three years of the *Gulf States Newsletter* report, Prince Salman had, by virtue of the death of two of his older brothers, Crown Prince Sultan (in October 2011) and his successor as Crown Prince, Nayef (in June 2012) become Crown Prince himself, and his millennial son Mohammed was appointed head of his royal court with ministerial rank in March 2013.³ One year after that, Mohammed bin Salman was appointed a Minister of State in May 2014 with Cabinet rank, by which time he was increasingly being described as a "gatekeeper" who controlled access to his father in the final months of King Abdullah's ten-year reign.⁴ Eight months later, Abdullah passed away on 23 January 2015, after being hospitalized for pneumonia, and Salman duly acceded as the sixth (and, as it turned out, the last) of Ibn Saud's sons to serve as King following the founder's passing in 1953.⁵ Salman became King of Saudi Arabia at a turbulent time, on the same day that the Saudi- and Gulf-backed government in neighboring Yemen was forced to flee into exile (in Saudi Arabia) as Houthi forces threatened to take complete control of the country.⁶

The startling rise of Mohammed bin Salman is integral to the study of contemporary Saudi Arabia, a state in the process of being reshaped to such an extent that the processes of governance established by Ibn Saud and maintained since his death in 1953 by his sons are being subject to fundamental change. Rulership in Saudi Arabia after 1953 was rooted in circles of power clustered around senior members of the royal family who remained in their ministerial positions for decades and could not easily be bypassed or dislodged. This introduced informal checks and balances and required successive Kings to seek and achieve a degree of consensus before any major policy decision was taken. As a result, decision-making was frequently slow and ponderous rather than fast and decisive, an exception being King Fahd's decision in August 1990 to accept a U.S. offer of military support days after Iraqi forces invaded Kuwait.⁷ This departure from the norm proved to be consequential, as it contributed to the radicalization of Osama bin Laden and was a major element of Al Qaeda's messaging and mobilizing appeal throughout the 1990s.⁸

Reshaping governance in Saudi Arabia

Writing in the early 2000s, the Saudi historian Madawi Al-Rasheed identified five main circles of power among the Al Saud, around King Fahd, Crown Prince Abdullah, and Princes Sultan (Minister of Defense), Nayef (Minister of Interior), and Salman (Governor of Riyadh), each consisting of a senior prince (and his sons) "anchored in a ministerial office, which forms its social, military, economic and bureaucratic basis."⁹ King Fahd gradually withdrew from public life after a stroke in the mid-1990s and died in 2005, and the other key figures passed away between 2011 and 2015, meaning that, by the time Salman became King, their departure from the scene had opened up significant spaces in the decision-making landscape. As a former member of the Shura (Consultative) Council told the journalist Karen Elliott House in 2016, "Salman can do anything he wants to (…) He is the only King who could. Power is concentrated now."¹⁰ The fact that Salman had, for years, served as head of the royal family council, and functioned effectively as a chief whip who maintained discipline, placed him at the heart of the rebalancing of power and control.¹¹

On 23 January 2015, Salman, as King, appointed Mohammed bin Salman as his successor as Minister of Defense, a position Salman had held since Crown Prince Sultan's death in October 2011. Aged 29, Mohammed bin Salman was five years younger than Sultan had been upon his appointment, in 1963, to the Ministry of Defense, a post he would hold for the next 48 years. Six days later, Salman oversaw a restructuring of the Council of Ministers as he abolished eleven councils and committees created under King Abdullah, and streamlined the decision-making process in two "supercommittees," a Council of Political and Security Affairs (CPSA) and a Council of Economic and Development Affairs (CEDA).¹² In view of what followed, it was significant that while the CPSA was chaired by Mohammed bin Nayef, the Minister of Interior whose appointment as Deputy Crown Prince in January 2015 put him into the line of succession, and the CEDA was chaired by Mohammed bin Salman, only Mohammed bin Salman sat on both committees, thereby marking him as distinct from the beginning of his father's reign.¹³ A senior Saudi energy official observed that the CEDA quickly asserted control over the decision-making process, as "Any suggestion, policy, development, or guideline had to be debated and approved by the economic council."¹⁴

Mohammed bin Salman quickly began to accumulate responsibilities over key areas of economic decision-making, and a series of developments between March and May 2015 established the parameters for his subsequent consolidation of political authority across the key pillars of the Saudi state. On 23 March, oversight over the Public

Investment Fund, hitherto a relatively low-profile and largely domestic-focused entity, was transferred from the Ministry of Finance to the Royal Court, and Mohammed bin Salman became Chair of its Board of Governors. On 29 April, King Salman replaced Crown Prince Muqrin with Mohammed bin Nayef and appointed Mohammed bin Salman Deputy Crown Prince, bringing him directly into the succession in a decision which caused surprise among analysts of Saudi Arabia. On 1 May, a new Supreme Council for Saudi Aramco, the state oil company, was established, again under the chairmanship of Mohammed bin Salman, which meant he now had oversight over Saudi oil policy (through Aramco) and investment decisions (through the Public Investment Fund).[15] In-between, Saudi Arabia also intervened militarily in Yemen, on 26 March, with Mohammed bin Salman, as Minister of Defense, heavily involved in initial policymaking when a swift victory was, at first, expected, from *Operation Decisive Storm*.[16]

The appointment of Mohammed bin Salman as Deputy Crown Prince, a position that had not existed in Saudi Arabia until King Abdullah named Muqrin to the post in 2014, upended dynastic politics within the royal family as well as assumptions among external observers. It was accepted that, at some point, succession would have to move down to the grandsons of Ibn Saud as his sons aged and passed away, with Muqrin being the youngest brother left in the line. A generational transition had not occurred since the death of Ibn Saud (Abdulaziz bin Abdulrahman Al Saud), the founder of the modern Kingdom of Saudi Arabia, in 1953, and there appeared to be little, if any, consensus as to whom among the hundreds of eligible grandsons should become the heir. To the extent that qualifications existed, these were often thought to revolve around age, seniority, experience, and more intangible qualities related to the exercise of effective and strong leadership.[17] An Allegiance Council, consisting of surviving sons of Ibn Saud as well as grandsons of the founder, was also created by King Abdullah in 2006 in an attempt to regularize the process of succession and generate royal consensus around the eventual choice of next generation heir.[18]

Twenty-six years older than Mohammed bin Salman, Mohammed bin Nayef possessed many of the qualities that positioned him as the

MOHAMMED BIN SALMAN, A PRINCE IN A HURRY

candidate for eventual succession. These included more than two decades' experience in increasingly senior portfolios at the Ministry of Interior (alongside his father, Prince Nayef, who served as the Minister between 1975 and 2012 and briefly as Crown Prince in 2011–12). During this period, Mohammed bin Nayef was seen by many in western circles as the architect of Saudi Arabia's counter-terrorism and deradicalization programs, especially after a spate of Al Qaeda-linked attacks between 2003 and 2006, and he survived an assassination attempt in August 2009 when he received a member of Al Qaeda who ostensibly wished to recant but instead detonated a bomb hidden in his rectum during their meeting.[19] In October 2010, it was Mohammed bin Nayef who supplied the U.S. and other partners with intelligence that led to the successful interdiction of two bombs hidden in printer cartridges that had originated in Yemen and been placed on cargo planes bound for destinations in the U.S.[20]

King Salman's decision in April 2015 to replace the Crown Prince (switching Muqrin with Mohammed bin Nayef) was the first time this had happened in Saudi Arabia. Every Crown Prince from Saud in 1953 to Abdullah in 2005 had duly become King upon the death (or, in Saud's case, removal) of the incumbent, but in April 1992 King Fahd issued decrees establishing a Basic Law of Governance and a Consultative Council and amending the succession process. While most international attention focused on the creation of the council and the drawing up of a constitution-type document, the third decree annulled the automatic right of the Crown Prince to accede and gave the monarch the right to appoint and dismiss the heir.[21] In 2011, however, Crown Prince Sultan predeceased King Abdullah, as did his successor as Crown Prince, Nayef, in 2012. It was only in 2015 that the replacement of Muqrin established the precedent that a living Crown Prince could in practice be replaced, which was to assume greater significance two years later, in 2017.

Internal and external challenges

The Saudi leadership faced regional and internal challenges in 2015 that shaped early decisions associated with Mohammed bin Salman as he gained political and economic authority. Military intervention in

Yemen provided an indication of a more assertive policy stance, as well as greater unpredictability in decision-making, as the Saudis reportedly gave their Arab coalition partners only 24 hours' notice. As a Western official said of the UAE, a close Saudi ally, "They were not quite as surprised as us, but it still took them aback that they were suddenly part of this military coalition."[22] *Operation Decisive Storm* gave way to *Operation Restoring Hope* three weeks into the campaign, but the relabeling could not hide the failure of the coalition to subdue the Houthis or the fact that the most significant military successes, recapturing key areas in southern Yemen from Houthi and Al Qaeda control, were achieved by Emirati rather than Saudi forces.[23] As the war ground on, and prospects of victory receded, Mohammed bin Salman became less prominent in public associations with the military campaign, after being highly visible in its early stages.[24]

Internal challenges revolved around the sharp decline in oil prices, which began to fall in June 2014, in the final months of Abdullah's rule, and hit government revenues, in Saudi Arabia and in the other Gulf States, hard. The price of oil crashed from a peak of US$107/barrel in June 2014 to US$44/barrel by January 2015, when Salman became King, continued to trend downward throughout his first year in power, and reached a low of US$28/barrel in January 2016, by which time oil had fallen to 2004 price levels.[25] This was the backdrop that faced Mohammed bin Salman as the newly-appointed Chair of the Council of Economic and Development Affairs, as the budget fell into deficit for the first time since 2009, the currency peg with the dollar came under pressure, and foreign assets were being rapidly drawn down.[26] A US$97.9 billion budget deficit in 2015 necessitated steep cost-cutting measures across the board, which included the scaling back of a plan to build a series of new football stadiums across the country.[27]

In April 2016, on the eve of launching his Vision 2030 program of economic reform, Mohammed bin Salman gave an interview to *Bloomberg Businessweek* that contained remarkable details about the depth of the economic malaise that faced Saudi Arabia when his father became King. Given that Salman as King moved swiftly to oust relatives of and officials linked to the late King Abdullah, the interview may be read as a new regime seeking to differentiate itself from a predecessor by playing up the difficult legacy it inherited. The interview made headlines globally for the claim that "the prince's team discovered the kingdom was rapidly becoming insolvent. At last April's spending levels, Saudi Arabia would have gone "completely broke" within just two years, by early 2017."[28] Additional eyebrows were raised by the following exchange between Mohammed bin Salman and a key financial advisor, Mohammed Al-Sheikh:

> During the oil boom from 2010 to 2014, Saudi spending went berserk. Prior requirements that the king approve all contracts over 100 million riyals ($26.7 million) got looser and looser—first to 200 million, then to 300 million, then to 500 million, and then, Al-Sheikh says, the government suspended the rule altogether.
>
> A journalist asks: How much was wasted?
>
> Al-Sheikh eyes a running recorder on the table. "Can I turn this off?" he says.
>
> "No, you can say it on record," Prince Mohammed says.
>
> "My best guess," says Al-Sheikh, "is that there was roughly between 80 to 100 billion dollars of inefficient spending" every year, about a quarter of the entire Saudi budget.
>
> Prince Mohammed picks up the questioning: "How close is Saudi Arabia to a financial crisis?"
>
> Today it's much better, Al-Sheikh says. But "if you'd asked me exactly a year ago, I was probably on the verge of having a nervous breakdown."[29]

While Chapter Three focuses on Vision 2030 and the rise of the Public Investment Fund as the entity tasked by Mohammed bin Salman with turning his vision into (some form of) reality for major projects, the prospect of wide-ranging reforms generated considerable and initially very positive international media coverage for Mohammed bin Salman. A prime example was a *New York Times* profile of the newly-appointed Crown Prince written by the paper's celebrated Pulitzer Prize-winning columnist, Thomas Friedman, in November 2017. Entitled, somewhat incongruously in view of the uprisings against authoritarian misrule that had swept across the

Middle East and North Africa in 2011, "Saudi Arabia's Arab Spring, at Last," Friedman argued that "the country is going through its own Arab Spring, Saudi style," and that "Unlike the other Arab Springs—all of which emerged bottom up and failed miserably, except in Tunisia—this one is led from the top down by the country's 32-year-old crown prince."[30]

A four-hour interview left Friedman marveling that "It's been a long time (…) since any Arab leader wore me out with a fire hose of new ideas about transforming his country," and quoting Mohammed bin Salman as telling him that "I fear that the day I die I am going to die without accomplishing what I have in my mind. Life is too short and a lot of things can happen, and I am really keen to see it with my own eyes—and that is why I am in a hurry."[31] The gushing nature of the interview led the *Middle East Research and Information Project*, a collective of scholars who study the region, to respond with an open letter which expressed "amazement, concern, and anger" at Friedman's analogy with the Arab Spring, his failure to mention the war in Yemen or the significant increase in repression of dissenting voices inside Saudi Arabia, and, they charged, his "ignorance of the history, religious, and political dynamics" in the Kingdom as well as his "complicity in a completely false narrative of what is really happening on the ground."[32]

As 2016 gave way to 2017, observers of Saudi politics began to closely track the relationship between the Crown Prince (Mohammed bin Nayef) and the Deputy Crown Prince (Mohammed bin Salman), especially since the Deputy Crown Prince appeared to be the driving force behind so many of the new initiatives. During this period, Mohammed bin Salman made high profile visits to Russia and China as well as to the United States, both in June 2016, when he met with Facebook founder Mark Zuckerberg in California, and in March 2017, when he had lunch with President Donald Trump at the White House.[33] These international trips contributed to the global profile the Deputy Crown Prince was building, while regionally he grew close to the Crown Prince of Abu Dhabi (and *de facto* ruler of the UAE until his accession as president in 2022), Sheikh Mohammed bin Zayed Al Nahyan.[34] As a figure of standing, Mohammed bin Zayed's support for, and confidence in, Mohammed bin Salman raised the

MOHAMMED BIN SALMAN, A PRINCE IN A HURRY

latter's credibility, especially in the U.S., at a time when he was relatively little-known outside Saudi Arabia, especially in comparison with Mohammed bin Nayef, with whom international officials had a long working relationship.[35]

Observers also noted that Mohammed bin Salman and Jared Kushner, President Trump's son-in-law, and advisor on Middle East issues, were developing a working relationship based on regular conversations between two millennials who shared a fondness for action and who brought a business background to policymaking. This extended to uncannily similar nicknames bestowed (entirely separately) on the pair by U.S. journalists—"Mr Everything" for Mohammed bin Salman and the "Secretary of Everything" for Kushner.[36] In 2018, an anonymous former U.S. official, who had remained in contact with Mohammed bin Salman, told Dexter Filkins of the *New Yorker* that Kushner and the (by then) Crown Prince "became close very fast. They see the world in the same way—they see themselves as being in the same tech-savvy world."[37] It was Kushner who reportedly organized Mohammed bin Salman's lunch with Trump in the Oval Office, in an apparent breach of protocol given he was not a visiting head of state or government, and the *New York Times* went so far as to suggest, in 2018, that Kushner had, in spring 2017, been "enquiring about the Saudi royal succession process and whether the United States could influence it."[38]

Rise to Crown Prince

Months of rumor and counter-rumor came to a head on the night of 20–21 June 2017 when Mohammed bin Nayef was summoned to meet King Salman at a palace in Mecca and persuaded to step aside in favor of his 31-year-old cousin. Reports in Western media outlets alleged that an element of coercion was involved in inducing the Crown Prince to stand down, along with suggestions that a reliance on painkillers arising out of injuries sustained during the 2009 assassination attempt played a role.[39] The Allegiance Council, the body of senior members of the royal family established by King Abdullah in 2006 to regulate matters of succession, met the following day and selected Mohammed bin Salman as the heir apparent, with 31 of the

34 members voting in favor.[40] Two of the three princes who did not support Mohammed bin Salman's appointment were later reported to have been detained, in March 2020, in one of the several roundups of perceived critics and opponents as the new Crown Prince consolidated authority.[41]

By the time Mohammed bin Salman became Crown Prince, he had gained a reputation for unpredictable and, at times, seemingly reckless decisions with an apparent disregard for consequences. On the domestic level, an early example was his announcement, in January 2016, that a sale of shares in Saudi Aramco was being considered, a declaration (made in the midst of a five-hour interview with *The Economist*) which generated a degree of surprise at the company itself.[42] Another was the detention in November 2017 of dozens of senior businesspeople, royal family members, and government officials at the Ritz-Carlton hotel in Riyadh while allegations of corrupt activity were investigated. Among the detainees were Prince Miteb bin Abdullah, the Minister for the Saudi Arabian National Guard and son of King Abdullah, Prince Alwaleed bin Talal, the most prominent "royal businessman" in the Kingdom, heads of major media groups, a long-serving Minister of Finance (who became Foreign Minister after his release), and the Minister of Economy and Planning who had been entrusted with a key role in the initial rollout of Vision 2030.[43]

The Ritz-Carlton affair was described variously as a "purge" and a power grab by Mohammed bin Salman as well as a "shakedown" of the business elite, although it was also a populist move that appealed to many Saudis who had long chafed at the perceived difficulties of breaking through deep-rooted vested economic interests.[44] The events at the Ritz-Carlton (and at detention centers once those detainees who did not come to financial settlements were transferred into more conventional custody) nevertheless shook international investor confidence in Saudi Arabia, and levels of inward investment slumped in the aftermath.[45] Concerns focused on the opacity and seeming lack of due process in the detentions, the subsequent negotiations and agreements, and the eventual decisions to release or charge those involved.[46] In January 2019, the Royal Court stated that US$106 billion in cash, real estate, and other assets had been seized from the detainees, which, in Prince Alwaleed bin Talal's case, reportedly involved an undisclosed financial settlement after 83 days at the Ritz-Carlton.[47] At least one detainee was said to have died in custody and several appear never to have been released.

On the regional level, Saudi policymaking became more volatile, although this was also a response to the political uncertainties triggered by the Arab Spring in 2011 and its messy aftermath, and thus did not begin with Mohammed bin Salman but originated instead in the waning years of the King Abdullah era. In September 2013, for example, the Kingdom abruptly declined to take up the "Arab seat" on the United Nations Security Council, to which it had just been elected. The decision stunned the Saudi diplomatic corps both in New York and in Riyadh who had celebrated the achievement, with the Saudi Ambassador to the U.N. initially telling the *New York Times* that "Our election today is a reflection of a longstanding policy in support of moderation and in support of resolving disputes by peaceful means."[48] The volte-face was seen as an expression of the anger felt by King Abdullah at the failure of the Security Council (and the U.S.) to enact measures to hold the Bashar Al Assad regime in Syria to account, especially after its use of chemical weapons at Ghouta in August 2013 and President Obama's failure to enforce his "red line."[49]

The Saudi intervention in the Yemeni conflict, in March 2015, did not go as planned, as noted above. The fact that the military campaign was launched just as international and Iranian negotiators were finalizing what became the Joint Comprehensive Plan of Action illustrated Saudi (and Emirati) displeasure with the notion that a deal could be struck on Iran's nuclear program but not address Teheran's regional activities.[50] 2017 saw two additional regional missteps that reinforced an impression held by many observers that the "old" dictums of Saudi decision-making had given way to something totally new and unknown. The first was the blockade of Qatar in June 2017 by Saudi Arabia in tandem with the UAE, Bahrain, and Egypt, just two weeks after the Kingdom hosted Donald Trump on his first foreign visit as U.S. president. Although Saudi Arabia, Bahrain, and the UAE had acted in concert in 2014 to withdraw their Ambassadors from Doha for nine months (toward the end of King Abdullah's reign), the action in 2017, which lasted 43 months until the crisis was resolved in January 2021, was far more serious both in scope and scale.[51]

Five months after the blockade of Qatar, with the Gulf rift still in full swing, came the second instance of Saudi action which caused analysts of regional politics to stop and catch their breath. On 4 November 2017, the day of the Ritz-Carlton roundup, the visiting Lebanese Prime Minister, Saad Hariri, who also happened to hold Saudi citizenship and whose family owned a major construction company in the Kingdom (Saudi Oger), made a shock announcement, from Riyadh, that he was resigning as premier. Media reports alleged that Hariri had been presented with his resignation speech after a meeting with Mohammed bin Salman and speculated that he was kept in a form of house arrest in the Saudi capital, where his family had long conducted business.[52] While initial suggestions that Hariri may have been detained as part of the Ritz-Carlton operation proved unfounded, it took the intervention of French President Emmanuel Macron to secure his return to Lebanon whereupon Hariri withdrew his resignation and subsequently resumed office where he remained Prime Minister until 2020.[53]

Other foreign policy missteps also marred Mohammed bin Salman's rise to international prominence. A sharp standoff with Canada erupted in August 2018 after Saudi officials reacted with fury to tweets from the Canadian foreign ministry which called for the release of jailed activists. Canada's Ambassador in Riyadh was expelled, the Saudi Ambassador to Canada was recalled, and economic sanctions were imposed which primarily affected thousands of Saudi students at Canadian universities.[54] As the war of words escalated, a pro-Saudi account tweeted a digitally-altered photograph of an airplane flying toward the CN Tower in Toronto, a reference many took to be to 9/11, alongside the caption "Sticking one's nose where it doesn't belong! As the Arabic saying goes: 'He who interferes with what doesn't concern him finds what doesn't please him.'"[55] Although the tweet was soon removed, diplomatic relations between Saudi Arabia and Canada were not fully restored until new Ambassadors were exchanged in May 2023.[56]

By September 2018, critics of Mohammed bin Salman, primarily outside Saudi Arabia, could point to a pattern which appeared to give credence to an assessment, made by Germany's foreign intelligence agency in December 2015, that "The careful diplomatic stance of older members of the Saudi royal family has been replaced by an impulsive policy of intervention."⁵⁷ The German Foreign Ministry issued an unusual rebuke of the Federal Intelligence Service (BND) after the memorandum made its way into the media, especially as the assessment also warned that

> (...) The concentration of economic and foreign policy power on Mohammed bin Salman contains the latent danger that, in an attempt to establish himself in the royal succession while his father was still alive, he could overreach with expensive measures or reforms that would unsettle other members of the royal family and the population.⁵⁸

Two letters which circulated online in September 2015, three months before the German intelligence memo, hinted at pockets of disquiet within the royal family at the new dispensation of power around the King and Mohammed bin Salman. Published against the backdrop of the worsening economic situation, the war in Yemen, and a pair of public safety failings which killed hundreds of people in Mecca, the letters were attributed to an unnamed grandson of Ibn Saud but their provenance was never authenticated.⁵⁹

The Khashoggi threat

One close observer of the trajectory of change in Saudi Arabia was Jamal Khashoggi, a longtime "insider" who had worked for more than three decades as a newspaper editor and sometime advisor to members of the Al Saud, with occasional setbacks along the way. In 2003, and again in 2010, Khashoggi lost his job as editor of *Al-Watan* newspaper after he fell foul of Saudi Arabia's carefully controlled media landscape.⁶⁰ 2015 saw Khashoggi involved, as general manager, in the establishment of *Al Arab*, a new Saudi-backed media group (with Prince Alwaleed bin Talal said to be among the backers⁶¹) that was based in Bahrain and intended to compete with Qatar's *Al Jazeera*. However, the channel was taken off the air, never to return, on its first day after a program ran an interview with a former member of Bahrain's parliament who had been elected on an opposition ticket and resigned in protest at the Arab Spring crackdown in 2011.⁶²

In November 2016, days after the election of Donald Trump to the U.S. presidency stunned the world, Khashoggi criticized the president-elect at a think-tank event and in his column for a Saudi newspaper. As a result, Khashoggi claimed that his column was cancelled and he was de facto banned from writing and public speaking.[63] The restrictions led Khashoggi to relocate from Saudi Arabia to the U.S. in June 2017 where he took up residence in Virginia and began to write a regular column for the *Washington Post*.[64] This provided him with a platform to express views on the process of change in Saudi Arabia which were often very critical of Mohammed bin Salman, even as he welcomed the prospect of economic reform, and focused in particular on the crackdowns in the Kingdom, with Khashoggi's first *Washington Post* article (in September 2017) entitled "Saudi Arabia wasn't always this repressive. Now it's unbearable."[65] Another, published the day after the Ritz-Carlton detentions, accused Mohammed bin Salman of "acting like Putin" as Khashoggi kept up a running commentary (to a receptive Beltway audience) on Saudi Arabia.[66]

Khashoggi's presence in Washington, D.C. posed a threat to the Saudi narrative, especially as he used his columns to counter statements made by Mohammed bin Salman at a time when officials sought to portray a message of change and renewal to U.S. audiences. Thus, after Mohammed bin Salman told *CBS News* that "Women were driving cars, there were movie theaters in Saudi Arabia, women worked everywhere. We were normal people developing like any other country in the world until the events of 1979" (referring to the Islamic revolution in Iran and the siege of the Grand Mosque in Mecca), Khashoggi accused the Crown Prince of "peddling revisionist history" as he recounted his own memories of Saudi Arabia before 1979, which he had lived through as a teenager and young adult, unlike Mohammed bin Salman, who grew up in the 1990s and 2000s and had no personal experience of the period.[67] Responding directly to the Crown Prince in a manner few in Saudi Arabia have since dared to replicate, Khashoggi wrote that "My own memories of those years (…) are quite different" as "Women weren't driving cars. I didn't see a woman drive until I visited my sister and brother-in-law in Tempe, Arizona (…) In the 1970s, the only places on the Arabian Peninsula where women were working outside the home or school were Kuwait and Bahrain."[68]

MOHAMMED BIN SALMAN, A PRINCE IN A HURRY

The presence in D.C. of a high-profile, well-informed critic able to challenge the official Saudi narrative mattered because Mohammed bin Salman embarked on a long trip to the U.S. in March and April 2018, where he met with President Trump and Congressional leaders in D.C., Mike Bloomberg and Bill Clinton in New York, George H.W. and George W. Bush in Houston, and Bill Gates and Jeff Bezos in Seattle.[69] A meeting with Lloyd Blankfein captured the mood of modernization and expectation generated by the Crown Prince, as the then CEO of Goldman Sachs tweeted that "The Crown Prince is always impressive when he sets out his vision for the KSA. Can't remember WHEN my beard turned white, but I remember WHY. MBS is much younger and I'm sure handles stress better!"[70] Khashoggi kept a spotlight trained on issues such as the several rounds of arrests in which Saudis of diverse backgrounds, including women who had long advocated for the right to drive, were detained in 2017 and into 2018.[71]

The brutal circumstances of Khashoggi's death, in which he was dismembered by a 15-strong squad in the Saudi Consulate in Istanbul in October 2018, and his body never recovered or returned to his family, made global headlines and abruptly punctured the aura of Mohammed bin Salman in Western circles. U.S. intelligence agencies assessed that Mohammed bin Salman approved the operation to capture or kill Khashoggi, based on "the Crown Prince's control of decision-making in the Kingdom since 2017, the direct involvement of a key adviser and members of Muhammad bin Salman's protective detail in the operation, and the Crown Prince's support for using violent measures to silence dissidents abroad."[72] While Donald Trump appeared to be more exercised that "They had a very bad original concept, it was carried out poorly, and the cover-up was one of the worst in the history of cover-ups," other more informed observers noted that Khashoggi was likely silenced because of his visibility, his reach, and his incipient attempts to connect the various (hitherto largely separate) communities of Saudi dissidents around the world.[73]

It took years for Mohammed bin Salman to recover from the Khashoggi killing and for the stain on Saudi Arabia's international image to be removed. Many of the would-be investors in the Vision 2030 projects stayed away from the second Future Investment

Initiative, which happened to take place three weeks after the murder.[74] Their absence compounded the challenge of anemic levels of foreign investment in Saudi Arabia as figures plunged in 2017 (after the shock to investor confidence of the Ritz-Carlton affair) and did not reach 2016 levels again until 2021.[75] Net inflows of foreign direct investment had in fact been in steep decline for a decade, down from US$39.5 billion in 2008 to just US$4.2 billion in 2018, and the Future Investment Initiatives were intended to reverse the trend and generate investor interest.[76] The struggle to attract foreign investment, even into the "giga-projects" linked to Vision 2030, meant that more of the financing burden would be placed on the Public Investment Fund, as Chapter Three details.[77]

The trajectory of the early years of the Foreign Investment Initiative (FII) is a microcosm of the multiple roadblocks that appeared between 2017 and 2020 and threatened to derail the Saudi project. Organized by an FII Institute chaired by Yasir Al Rumayyan, the Governor of the Public Investment Fund, the inaugural FII in October 2017 made headlines as much for the bestowing of citizenship upon a robot named Sophia as for Mohammed bin Salman's launch of Neom, a development project the size of Belgium.[78] However, the unexpected repurposing of the FII's venue, the Ritz-Carlton in Riyadh, into a makeshift detention center less than two weeks after the conference hit foreign investor sentiment hard. The second FII in October 2018 took place under the cloud of Khashoggi's death while the third, in October 2019, was followed within months by the global pandemic shutdown which also affected the fourth FII in 2020. A myriad of difficulties, self-inflicted as well as unplanned, thus affected the rollout of Mohammed bin Salman's vision.

Trump and Biden

By 2020, circumstances seemed bleak for Mohammed bin Salman. Internally, the Saudi economy was badly hit, not only by Covid-19 but also by oil prices which plunged due to cutbacks in demand and an oversupplied market which led futures prices at one point to trade negatively for the first time in history.[79] The imbalance was magnified by a Saudi decision in March 2020, just as global demand for oil cratered, to ramp up production in a bid to gain market share, after negotiations with Russia for a coordinated OPEC+ price agreement to reduce supply broke down.[80] As Trump faced calls from lawmakers in mainly Republican-voting oil-producing states to stem the market meltdown in the U.S. election year, with Senator Ted Cruz telling the Saudi Ambassador to the U.S. that "You are waging economic warfare on Texas," he reportedly threatened the Crown Prince that he would not veto Congressional attempts to withdraw U.S. military support from Saudi Arabia if the Kingdom did not reverse the increase in output.[81]

The spat with Trump notwithstanding (in which tensions eased after Trump claimed credit for a Saudi-Russian production agreement[82]), by the end of 2020 the Saudi leadership faced the prospect of an incoming U.S. president who had pledged to make the Kingdom "pay the price" for the death of Khashoggi. Joe Biden made the comments during a debate of Democratic presidential hopefuls in November 2019, during which he vowed to "make them in fact the pariah that they are" and added, for good measure, that he saw "very little social redeeming value in the present government" in Riyadh.[83] When Biden took office in January 2021, he initially refused to engage with Mohammed bin Salman who, when asked in 2022 his opinion of what Biden thought of him, responded "Simply, I do not care."[84] The Biden administration also authorized the declassification of an intelligence assessment into Khashoggi's death and announced the suspension of arms sales that could assist the Saudis in the conduct of offensive operations in Yemen.[85]

It was the buildup of forces along the Russia-Ukraine border in 2021 and the full-scale Russian invasion of Ukraine in February 2022 that altered the geopolitical and energy-economic landscape for Saudi Arabia. Oil prices recovered strongly in 2021 and rose over US$100/barrel in 2022 as the post-pandemic economic rebound intersected with the spike in geopolitical tensions in Eastern Europe. Saudi Aramco announced a record financial performance in 2022 with net income of US$161.1 billion and the Saudi budget returned to surplus after nearly a decade of deficits of varying sizes.[86] The economic tailwinds supercharged state spending which surged in 2022 and continued into 2023 as oil prices and public revenues remained at an elevated level, and provided backdrop and context for the new projects and initiatives, including in sport.[87]

Higher oil prices were among the factors which contributed to inflationary pressures as world economies reopened following the easing of pandemic (and travel) restrictions. As prices spiked, the scruples over whether to engage with Mohammed bin Salman fell away. In December 2021, French President Emmanuel Macron became the first Western leader to meet in Saudi Arabia with the Crown Prince post-Khashoggi for talks on regional security issues.[88] The pace of visits quickened after February 2022 when German Chancellor Olaf Scholz, Macron again, and British Prime Minister Boris Johnson all sought Saudi support for measures to bring down oil prices (to fight inflation and hit Russian energy revenues). Johnson's visit in March 2022 came four days after 81 people were put to death in the largest mass execution in Saudi modern history, surpassing even the 63 executed in January 1980 in the wake of the Grand Mosque siege at the end of 1979.[89] The executions indicated confidence in the Saudi leadership at the lack of international pushback, and assertiveness borne of the Kingdom's centrality to world events.[90]

The aftermath of President Biden's brief stopover in Jeddah in July 2022, during which he exchanged an awkward fist-bump with Mohammed bin Salman, was illustrative of the evolving relational dynamics. Biden administration officials touted oil cooperation and progress toward a normalization of Saudi-Israeli relations as key reasons for the trip, but came away largely empty-handed.[91] A senior White House official returned to Washington, D.C. in the apparent belief that Saudi Arabia and the UAE would significantly increase oil production to bring down prices, but this did not happen.[92] A marginal rise in output in the immediate aftermath of the visit was followed by a steep cut in October 2022, in close coordination with Russian officials, a decision which caused anger in Washington, D.C.[93] The Jeddah trip also indicated evidence of friction between the U.S. and the UAE, as Emirati officials publicly pushed back at an invitation by Biden for UAE President Mohammed bin Zayed Al Nahyan to visit the U.S. before the end of the year.[94]

By the end of 2022, the Saudi leadership had weathered the storms that had buffeted the Kingdom between 2015 and 2020.

MOHAMMED BIN SALMAN, A PRINCE IN A HURRY

Mohammed bin Salman was recasting himself as a regional statesman, playing a visible role in the Gulf Cooperation Council summit at Al Ula in January 2021 that ended the 43-month long blockade of Qatar.[95] The sight of leaders beating a path to Saudi Arabia after the Russian invasion of Ukraine in 2022 had the effect of restating the Kingdom's centrality to energy security and geopolitical considerations. Meanwhile, the national team's astonishing 2–1 victory over eventual champions Argentina in their opening game at the World Cup in Qatar arguably did more than anything in boosting Saudi soft power and generating international goodwill, demonstrating the enduring ability of football to reach mass global audiences and tell its own powerful story. An evolving Saudi nationalism and a reinventing of narratives added to the changing sense of state-led identities in the "new" Saudi Arabia taking shape under the ever-watchful eye of MBS.[96]

In November 2017, Mohammed bin Salman had explained to Thomas Friedman and readers of the *New York Times* that he was a prince in a hurry. Just over four years later, he used another interview with an American publication to return to the analogy of a race. In March 2022, the Crown Prince told *The Atlantic* magazine that "The finish line is something distant. You just keep running, and keep running faster. And keep creating more finish lines and just keep running. Our aim is to be faster than the rest and achieve more than the rest."[97] The next chapter picks up with Vision 2030 and the empowerment of the Public Investment Fund as the key engines of transformation that provided the context as well as the tools for the Kingdom's surge into the landscape and consciousness of global sport in such a rapid and major way.

3

VISION 2030 AND THE PUBLIC INVESTMENT FUND

Vision 2030 and its associated giga-projects provided the context for Saudi Arabia's moves into international sport, including football, and the Public Investment Fund (PIF) was catapulted to global prominence, becoming one of the most recognizable and central entities in this process. From Newcastle Utd to LIV Golf to world tennis and the acquisition of majority stakes in four of the leading Saudi football clubs in 2023, PIF has become synonymous with Saudi Arabia's sporting ambitions, whether as owner, disruptor, investor, or sponsor through the many PIF subsidiary companies. Given that the giga-projects are predicated on the arrival of tens of millions of new residents and visitors by 2030, sport has emerged as a pivotal tool in the framing of a new set of reference points for a fast-changing Kingdom, not least in creating a sense of momentum and excitement about the reforms underway in Saudi Arabia.

On 25 April 2016, nearly a year to the day since Mohammed bin Salman became Deputy Crown Prince, the Council of Economic and Development Affairs (CEDA) unveiled Vision 2030, a blueprint for a wide array of targets designed to diversify the Saudi economy. To accompany the launch of the roadmap, MBS, as Chair of CEDA, gave his first televised interview, to *Al Arabiya*, to outline and explain the rationale for the Vision. The Deputy Crown Prince pushed back, at times forcefully, against a skeptical line of questioning over the need for such far-reaching changes, as he made the case for treating oil as an investment and transforming the Public Investment Fund. In response to questions from Turki Al Dakhil, Mohammed bin Salman talked about the need to move beyond the "quick fix" approach to economic management, and at one point appeared to suggest that "in 2020, we can live without oil."[1]

In the years that followed, a series of realization programs provided structure and depth to Vision 2030, as did related initiatives such as a National Transformation Plan and a Fiscal Balance Program which laid out more specific, shorter-term plans.[2] The process unfolded in fits and starts, with the National Transformation Program being revised in 2017 and the Fiscal Balance Program subjected to the volatile swings in oil prices which still accounted for most government revenues.[3] Legal and judicial reforms sought to create a more predictable business climate and build upon reforms begun under King Abdullah to codify and update laws and practices.[4] Other measures, which curbed the powers of the religious police and eased many of the restrictions on women, fostered a narrative of social as well as economic change, albeit strictly on the state's terms. However, progress was uneven, as seen in the detention of female activists in May 2018, just as women were allowed to drive, or that one of the first high-profile cases of a new anti-harassment law concerned a female concert-goer in Taif who went on stage to embrace the male singer.[5]

Vision 2030 has become so closely intertwined with the rise and political fortune of Mohammed bin Salman that it has effectively become his calling card to power on the basis that only he can deliver the reforms needed to reboot the Saudi economy for the challenges of the mid-twenty-first century. So, too, has the PIF, a hitherto largely domestic-focused entity with little international profile, evolved into Mohammed bin Salman's declared "engine for economic diversification."[6] The onus to meet and exceed expectations may explain some of the more grandiose aspects of the "giga-projects" that, over time, have become so associated with Vision 2030 and with PIF and its subsidiaries. An uneasy balance has arisen between the more practical and workable elements of Vision 2030, with a clear domestic focus, and the giga-projects, which appear to be aimed at a global and more exclusive audience.[7]

VISION 2030 AND THE PUBLIC INVESTMENT FUND

Top-down processes of change

There is a long record of state-led attempts to overhaul economic structures in Saudi Arabia and in the other five states in the Gulf Cooperation Council. In some respects, Mohammed bin Salman is not doing anything not seen before, although its sheer scale marks Vision 2030 as distinct. Top-down projects of reform have long been a feature of the political-economic landscape in the Gulf States, as have multi-decadal national "visions."[8] Oman launched a Vision 2020 as early as 1995 which ran its course and proved hard to translate from plan to practice, and has moved onto Vision 2040.[9] Abu Dhabi, Bahrain, and Qatar all unveiled their own Vision 2030s in 2008, while Kuwait launched Vision 2035, developed by Tony Blair Associates, in 2010, a plan which received "widespread criticism for its vast public expense, gained no policymaking traction, and was abandoned at the end of 2011."[10] The UAE also has a Centennial Plan that aims to future-proof a diversified post-oil economy by 2071, and an even more long-range plan to establish a human settlement, a city reportedly set to be the size of Chicago, on Mars by 2117.[11]

While no two plans were the same, they generally aimed to diversify the economic base and move beyond oil and public sector/state spending as the main drivers of growth. Common features included measures to strengthen the private sector and expand non-oil economic activity, support the development of human capital through educational and labor market reforms, and, over time, build competitive economies that did not rely primarily upon a comparative advantage in natural resources. Many of the plans were developed by Western management consultancies, which accounted for their frequently generic policy assessments and proscriptions.[12] Plans drawn up by external consultants often downplayed or failed to consider vested political and economic interests which could hold back their implementation.[13] At times, consultants sought to import concepts with little regard for local knowledge, as when a British town planner tasked in the 1950s with remodeling Kuwait City drew up an urban design based on the model of garden cities then in vogue in England but quite unsuited to conditions in Kuwait.[14]

From the start, development planning in Saudi Arabia was closely intertwined with international, primarily American, expertise. In

1958, an Economic Development Committee was established on the advice of the International Monetary Fund, and in 1965 it expanded into the Central Planning Organization, but financial constraints limited its remit.[15] Both the Arabian American Oil Company (Aramco) and the Ford Foundation helped the Saudi government to establish a civil service in the 1960s, and in 1970 the newly-appointed head of the Central Planning Organization, Hisham Nazer, inaugurated the first of a series of five-year development plans. Nazer contracted the Stanford Research Institute (SRI), an American firm, to draw up the first (1970–75) and second (1975–80) plans, and the cycles continued until the Ninth Development Plan, which ran from 2010 until 2014.[16] A fan of Al-Ittihad, Nazer bonded with Crown Prince (later King) Fahd, who supported Al-Hilal, as "endless banter about football increased the depth of their relationship." This extended to Nazer's appointment as Minister of Petroleum in 1986, as he related how "King Fahd phoned me and talked about many issues including football games. At the end of the phone call, he told me that he would call me at one o'clock in the morning to give me a new assignment."[17]

Vision 2030 is not the first long-range strategic plan drawn up by the Saudi authorities. In 2005, just as oil prices began their decade-long boom that lasted until 2014, the Kingdom unveiled a Long-Term Strategic Plan to cover development through to 2024. Unveiled as part of the Eighth five-year plan (for 2005–9), the Long-Term Strategic Plan sought to transform Saudi Arabia into a global industrial nation by 2024, develop the services sector, with banking and tourism identified as priorities, and create six new economic cities, rooted in a guiding vision that "By the will of Allah, the Saudi economy in 2024 will be a developed, thriving and prosperous economy based on sustainable foundations."[18] Tim Niblock, a leading academic expert on the modern development of Saudi Arabia, noted at the time that, unlike the succession of five-year development plans since 1970, the private sector appeared to have a key role in the Long-Term Strategic Plan and that, for the first time, "The role of government was portrayed more as the facilitator of transformation than the sole instrument through which transformation could be achieved."[19]

One of the centerpieces of the Long-Term Strategic Plan in the mid-2000s involved the creation of six large new economic cities by

2020, but only one, the King Abdullah Economic City (KAEC), saw any significant progress as the projects struggled to get off the ground, still less move toward reality.[20] However, by 2018, by which time attention had turned to the new slate of giga-projects associated with Vision 2030, KAEC had attracted only 7000 residents against an initial target of two million, and the other five planned cities had failed to see any real development at all. The projects struggled to generate "buy-in" from stakeholders across the bureaucratic apparatus. Progress was held back by a lack of cross-state support from the various agencies involved, as observers noted that "Other parts of the Saudi government clearly were unhappy with the project, and refused to be drafted into cooperating or providing services."[21]

From the outset, KAEC struggled to attract investors and residents, did not develop as intended into a hub for manufacturing and logistics, and raised questions about the viability of the "build it and they will come" approach to development. McKinsey released a critical assessment of KAEC in 2016 which drew attention to the risk of creating a "ghost city" by "building for long-term use without an economic base. Facilities that lie idle until the population expands to support them are expensive to maintain. In a private-sector model, however, facilities must be economically viable almost from the outset to mitigate maintenance costs."[22] Two years later, a report in the *Financial Times* described the fate of the economic cities as a "cautionary tale" as Vision 2030 gathered steam, and cited an unnamed former government advisor who acknowledged that "If KAEC was viable the city would have taken off a long time ago. Their marketing was amazing but the whole concept behind it was flawed. The economic base was never there."[23]

Drawing on the KAEC experience and applying it to the massive planned development at Neom, a 2019 assessment of the initial phase of Vision 2030 concluded that "For a country like Saudi Arabia, which has faced high rates of youth unemployment, it is not clear how this high-tech, capital-intensive economic city will contribute to creating adequate job opportunities for the Kingdom's young population," and that "it makes more sense to first complete the KAEC project, which is extremely underutilized, rather than proceed with Neom."[24] The Vision 2030 document itself acknowledged that "the economic cities of the last decade did not realize their potential. Work has halted in several cities, and others face challenges that threaten their viability."[25] Vision 2030 singled out another flagship initiative from the pre-2015 era for particular criticism, as it recorded how "works started at the King Abdullah Financial District, without consideration of its economic feasibility," and the financial district eventually came under PIF control.[26]

The mention in the Vision 2030 document of the fate encountered by the economic cities and the King Abdullah Financial District indicated that the authorities in 2016 were fully aware of the difficulties which had so undermined previous reform efforts. Chapter Two described how Mohammed bin Salman began concentrating political authority and economic decision-making and centralizing control in the Royal Court to a degree unseen in the modern history of Saudi Arabia. This alone meant that the broader context within which Vision 2030 unfolded was distinct from the pre-2015 initiatives which had to contend with a segmented institutional structure which did not always pull in the same direction and could delay the implementation of policies. Ibrahim Almuhanna has provided multiple examples of pre-2015 decisions undermined by factional struggle in his fascinating memoir of three decades' experience in the Ministry of Petroleum/Energy.[27] Under Mohammed bin Salman, the ability of bureaucratic structures (and individuals) to undercut or maneuver around difficult or unpopular decisions was sharply curtailed, in part by the arrest or detention of perceived laggards or opponents.[28]

Vision 2030 and the giga-projects

Vision 2030 is best viewed as a roadmap for an ongoing process of economic reform than a static plan with a rigid or specific end-goal. Similar to several of the visions drawn up by other Gulf States in the preceding decade, Vision 2030 was influenced by a report drawn up in December 2015 by the McKinsey Global Institute, entitled "Moving Saudi Arabia's Economy Beyond Oil."[29] It argued that the Kingdom would need to "accelerate the shift from its current government-led economic model to a more market-based approach."[30] McKinsey had, in the 2000s, been tasked by Bahrain's Crown Prince to develop recommendations for their own Vision 2030 which sought a "productive, globally competitive economy, shaped by the government and driven by a pioneering private sector."[31] Some in Riyadh took to referring to the Ministry of Economy and Planning as the "ministry of McKinsey" in early 2016, such was the company's visibility.[32] That year, the company reportedly was involved in 137 projects in the Kingdom.[33] In 2018, however, the *Wall Street Journal* reported that a Saudi partner of McKinsey had been detained in the Ritz-Carlton roundup, as was the Minister of Economy and Planning, Adel Fakeih.[34]

The core of Vision 2030 and the associated National Transformation Plan is to map out a path toward a diversified economy using Saudi Arabia's resource revenues as a catalyst for change—in the words of Khalid Al Falih, the newly appointed Minister of Energy, Industry and National Resources and Chairman of Saudi Aramco (in 2016), "Saudi Aramco will be a bridge for a transition away from itself."[35] Macro level targets included a tripling of non-oil revenue by 2020, the creation of 450,000 jobs outside the government sector, and reducing the share of public sector wages from 45 percent of the budget to 40 percent. Both the Vision and the National Transformation Plan envisaged a program of thorough economic (and social) transformation to take place without any corresponding political change, seemingly with the Singapore (or East Asian) model of the developmental state in mind (or Dubai, closer to home).[36]

Three overarching pillars of Vision 2030 sought to develop a "thriving economy," a "vibrant society," and an "ambitious nation" through a series of economic, governance, and cultural and social changes. The document contained "more than 30 specific targets from the size of the non-oil economy to the proportion of Saudis who take regular exercise."[37] A "Character Enrichment Program" set out to shape a new national and Islamic identity "to shepherd Saudis no longer guided by the harsh discipline of the religious police," and the Council of Ministers (the Saudi Cabinet) issued new regulations that stripped the religious police of many of their powers on 11 April 2016, two weeks before Vision 2030 was unveiled.[38] Somewhat incongruously for a roadmap to strengthen the non-oil and private sectors in an economy long reliant on oil revenues and public sector spending, Vision 2030 envisaged a pivotal role for state-led entities and projects to diversify and expand the economic base of Saudi Arabia. This later became evident in the centrality of the PIF in the national transformation of oil revenues (through the sale of shares in and transfers from Saudi Aramco) and as the developer of every key domestic initiative launched by MBS.

Sport, entertainment, and tourism all feature heavily in Vision 2030 and are key to positioning Saudi Arabia as a destination, as will be examined in Chapter Four. Another key area of focus is the mining sector, in light of the Kingdom's untapped resources of many of the critical minerals which Saudi leaders believe will form part of evolving global supply chains associated with the various energy transitions around the world.[39] Comments in 2024 by Khalid Al Mudaifer, the Vice Minister for Mining and former head of the Saudi Arabian Mining Company (Ma'aden) that "We are in the middle of the world. Saudi Arabia is location-wise between three continents (…) we think we connect the whole world all together" illustrated the sense among policymakers in Riyadh of the connectivity that aimed to cement the Kingdom as a critical link in the "new" chain of economic and political hubs as the world moves toward midcentury.[40] The scale of ambition is such that officials want the mining sector to increase its value from US$17 billion in 2023 to US$75 billion by 2035, with one industry analyst noting that "The Saudis are so palpably ambitious: even if they achieve 60 per cent of what they are after, then it will be enormous."[41]

Many of Vision 2030's objectives, such as raising women's participation in the labor force from 22 to 30 percent or reducing the unemployment rate from 12 to seven percent, are realistic and, in the case of female participation in the workforce, the 2030 target was surpassed years ahead of schedule.[42] It is these policies that are likely to resonate most strongly among the domestic audience of young Saudi citizens coming of age and entering the labor market, and for whom the "social contract" with the government needs to be updated. The degree to which Vision 2030 (and PIF investment ventures) can develop and diversify the domestic economic and industrial base and create sufficient new jobs for Saudi citizens as they enter the labor market will be the ultimate test of its success. A pent-up desire for change after years of stasis meant that Vision 2030 was popular among many young Saudis of the Crown Prince's generation.[43] However, the

VISION 2030 AND THE PUBLIC INVESTMENT FUND

pragmatic, and much needed, elements of Vision 2030 coexist alongside the series of "giga-projects" announced since 2017 which have dominated the policy focus, media attention, and funding streams even as their economic utility, and viability, remains largely untested.

The six "giga-projects" launched by Mohammed bin Salman and handed to PIF for delivery have come to synonymize Vision 2030 for many people, even as new initiatives continue to be added. These include Qiddiya, a large-scale entertainment, sports, and cultural complex near Riyadh that was launched by the Crown Prince in 2017, and the far better-known Neom and other large-scale developments along the Kingdom's hitherto largely underutilized Red Sea coastline.[44] The idea for Neom reportedly began when Mohammed bin Salman "pulled up a map of his country on Google Earth and saw its northwest quadrant was a blank slate."[45] Media reports in the *Wall Street Journal* nevertheless painted a picture of a fractious working environment, rapid turnover of personnel, and culture of micromanagement in some of the "giga-projects" as they got underway.[46] *Gulf States Newsletter* suggested in 2021 that Mohammed bin Salman "is intensely focused on even minor details in these projects." especially at Neom, and cited a "Kingdom-based consultant" who, in a nod to the ultraluxury tourism focus of many of the projects, acknowledged that "the gap between the haves and have-nots is increasing and a lot of these projects are marketed at the haves." A similar tone was struck by a Saudi-based academic who cautioned (in 2021) that "If we are only going to see jet-setters, the impact will be superficial. If, on the other hand, middle class Saudis will consider having second homes along the Red Sea—especially to escape Riyadh's hot summers—then our assessments will need to be re-evaluated."[47]

In addition to being projects of staggeringly grandiose and arguably utopian ambition, with Neom initially incorporating a planned 100-mile-long linear city (The Line) and even a slimmed-down plan for 10 miles amounting to "constructing the equivalent of all the office buildings in Midtown Manhattan three times over," and an enormous cube planned as the centerpiece of the redevelopment of Riyadh's downtown reportedly set to be large enough "to fit 20 Empire State buildings" within it, the giga-projects highlighted the critical PIF role in delivering them.[48] The transformation of PIF's scope of activities is fundamental to the success of Vision 2030 and, by extension, to Mohammed bin Salman himself. When he launched Vision 2030, Mohammed bin Salman stated that the Public Investment Fund "will own more than 3% of the assets on earth" once its transformation into a US$2 trillion fund was complete, by which time, he forecast (in 2016), "There will be no investment, movement, or development in any region of the world without the vote of the Saudi sovereign fund."[49]

Remaking the Public Investment Fund

Since 2015, the Public Investment Fund (PIF) has been globally recognized, seemingly omnipresent, and thoroughly intertwined with Mohammed bin Salman and Vision 2030. A full appreciation of the scale of change in PIF only becomes clear from a look at its pre-2014 history, covering the opening four decades of an organization founded by royal decree back in 1971. PIF was mandated to "finance commercial projects belonging to the government, to industrial institutions associated with the government and to public institutions."[50] PIF began to fund local projects in sectors such as petrochemicals, oil refining, fertilizer, and electricity, and "For the next 44 years, approximately 99 percent of the fund's investments were domestic."[51] PIF also became one of the main shareholders in Saudia, the national airline, in the 1970s and 1980s.[52] In 2013, a book about the political economy of Gulf States' sovereign wealth funds contained barely a mention of PIF, such was its obscurity, and as late as 2015 it did not have a website.[53]

David Rundell, an American diplomat who served in various postings, including as Commercial Attaché and Chief of Mission at the U.S. Embassy in Riyadh, recalled how, prior to 2015, "the PIF functioned for many years as a domestic development bank" and "held the government's share in many largely state-owned enterprises," such as the Saudi Basic Industries Corporation (SABIC).[54] In this period, PIF worked as "the government investment arm" to develop domestic industry, and was overshadowed by the Saudi Arabian Monetary Agency (SAMA), which managed the Kingdom's assets.[55] As examples, PIF provided loans to SABIC, which was a notable success story

VISION 2030 AND THE PUBLIC INVESTMENT FUND

of diversification, as well as to Ma'aden, another successful entity (in mining), but also to Petromin, a Saudi oil company which was intended to be a national alternative to the Arabian American Oil Company (Aramco) but which was plagued by poor performance and political interference and was wound down in the 1990s and dissolved in 2005.[56] In one of the first academic studies of PIF, in 2022, Alexis Montambault Trudelle observed that "the contrasting PIF ventures in Petromin and SABIC reveal how earlier investments were intertwined with rivalries and coalitions among high-level elite players, technocrats and a network of key merchant families."[57]

Despite managing less than $100 billion in assets and having only about 40 staff in the early 2010s, two decisions made in King Abdullah's reign, predating the transition of power to King Salman and the subsequent ascent of Mohammed bin Salman, had a significance that paved the way for the shift PIF would take in 2015. First, in 2008, in the midst of the post-2003 oil boom, the authorities established a sovereign wealth fund, Sanabil Investments (formally the Saudi Arabian Investment Company), as a wholly-owned entity of PIF, although it took a further five years for Sanabil to make its first investment.[58] Second, in July 2014, the Council of Ministers issued a royal decree which permitted PIF to fund and establish new companies, inside and outside Saudi Arabia, "either independently or in cooperation with the public and private sectors."[59] While they were unrelated to Mohammed bin Salman, these two decisions meant that PIF was beginning to acquire the means and mandate to evolve in scope and activity.

Everything changed after King Salman's accession on 23 January 2015. Precisely two months later, on 23 March, a resolution of the Council of Ministers transferred the oversight of PIF from the Ministry of Finance, under whose control PIF had operated since 1971, to the Council of Economic and Development Affairs, chaired by Mohammed bin Salman, as noted in Chapter Two.[60] Mohammed bin Salman became Chairman of the Board of PIF and Yasir bin Othman Al Rumayyan, a close confidant, was appointed Governor. Al Rumayyan had worked at the Capital Markets Authority and as chief executive of Saudi Fransi Capital before becoming an advisor to the Royal Court in 2015, whereupon he was tasked by Mohammed bin Salman with identifying a CEO for PIF. In Al Rumayyan's own telling, Mohammed bin Salman

> asked me to hire a CEO for the fund. I requested the names of CEOs in the investment sector, got the files and everything. I was traveling with the prince on a plane and we were going through each one. He wasn't fully satisfied with the majority. "No, bring me someone else," he said. Then it clicked. The decision was made to make me the supervisor of PIF.[61]

Building on the July 2014 royal decree, the March 2015 transfer to CEDA "broadened PIF's mandate and expanded its scope" to play "a strategic national role" in Vision 2030.[62] Whereas the "old" PIF had been a mostly silent financing partner in state-owned companies, the "new" PIF was given a far more active remit to establish and invest in new entities and sectors in Saudi Arabia, create strategic international partnerships, support domestic programs, and deliver the giga-projects and other state initiatives.[63] Al Rumayyan established himself as one of the most important non-royal technocrats in Saudi Arabia, a status reflected in his appointment, in 2016, to chair the Decision Support Center within the Royal Court to coordinate Vision 2030 decision-making, and, in 2019, his appointment as Chairman of Saudi Aramco.[64]

Al Rumayyan's accumulation of technocratic authority complemented, and to an extent mirrored, Mohammed bin Salman's concentration of political and economic power, albeit at the level of policy implementation rather than national decision-making. Together, the two men were able to leverage the hitherto-disparate organs of the Saudi state in ways that eluded their pre-2015 predecessors, in pursuit of Mohammed bin Salman's desire to treat oil as an investment, "nothing more, nothing less."[65] It was this centralization of power and authority which led Al Rumayyan to reject concerns that the giga-projects associated with Vision 2030 would go the way of KAEC and the economic cities of the 2000s. David Ottaway, a veteran journalist who has covered Saudi Arabia for decades, recorded how, at a briefing in Washington, D.C. in 2017, Al Rumayyan "dismissed any parallel, noting that KAEC had depended totally on private investors, whereas the PIF he headed stood behind Neom. In other words, the government would not allow Neom to fail, and the PIF had the billions to ensure it didn't."[66]

The ability to shift and shuffle resources became evident in 2019 when, as Chairman of Aramco as well as Governor of PIF, Al Rumayyan oversaw Aramco's acquisition of PIF's 70 percent shareholding in SABIC, which transferred US$69.1 billion to PIF, and the listing of 1.5 percent of Aramco shares on the Saudi Stock Exchange, which raised US$25.6 billion for PIF deployment.[67] Notably, the outgoing Minister of Energy and Chairman of Aramco, Khalid Al Falih, reportedly expressed reservations about both the SABIC deal and the sale of Aramco shares, as well as about a PIF tie-up with SoftBank of Japan on solar projects which seemingly took ministry officials by surprise.[68] Officials in the Saudi energy sector offered "passive resistance" and drew up alternative proposals to channel resources to PIF.[69] After his removal, an Aramco advisor observed that Al Falih "advocated a more considered path, not understanding that the boss wanted to move faster. The boss wants a listing—it is foot to the floor now."[70]

PIF therefore became central to Vision 2030 and to Mohammed bin Salman's plans for Saudi Arabia. This had both positive and negative effects. In September 2019, a "person close to the government" told the *Financial Times* that "PIF is the vehicle for everything. All the money has to go through it (…) It will be moulded and shaped in any way that is required to help deliver his highness's orders."[71] Speaking in April 2021, the five-year mark of Vision 2030, Mohammed bin Salman acknowledged that "The Public Investment Fund motivates the economy of Saudi more than the budget, and this will continue."[72] By the end of 2023, the PIF had become the seventh-largest sovereign wealth fund in the world with US$720 billion of assets under management. However, as Tim Callen has noted, 32 percent of the growth in the PIF portfolio of assets came from the government's transfer of eight percent of Aramco shares (in two tranches of four percent) to PIF in 2021 and 2022.[73] An additional allocation of another eight percent of shares in Aramco to PIF in March 2024 added further value onto PIF's books and was in line with the Crown Prince's desire to see the fund hold US$1 trillion in assets by the end of 2025.[74] By August 2024, the volume of assets under management reached US$925 billion as PIF closed on the target.[75]

Unlike many of the sovereign wealth funds in other Gulf States, which focus most of their activity on international investments, the PIF has an outsized domestic presence.[76] In part, this reflects the PIF's pre-2015 mandate and is a trend that has continued under Mohammed bin Salman, who directed the fund to invest a minimum of US$40 billion into the Saudi economy each year between 2021 and 2025.[77] The proportion of assets held in the local economy rose from 51 percent in 2021 to 68 percent in 2022 and 76 percent in 2023.[78] In addition, each of the giga-projects was handed to PIF to oversee, either directly or through wholly-owned subsidiaries, and PIF was tasked with developing Saudi Arabian Military Industries (SAMI). Launched with immaculate timing in May 2017, days before Donald Trump made Saudi Arabia the destination for his first foreign visit as president and boasted of securing US$110 billion in arms sales, SAMI laid out plans to become one of the world's largest defense companies by 2030 and create 40,000 new jobs.[79] However, the aim to localize defense spending drew criticism from Anthony Cordesman, the veteran national security analyst at the Center for Strategic and International Studies, who labeled it "the silliest and least convincing aspect" of Vision 2030" with "so few real-world benefits in job creation."[80]

PIF has thus become the most important cog in the contemporary state apparatus of Saudi Arabia, with a ubiquitous presence in the domestic economy and initiatives abroad. Virtually every big new development since 2017 has had a connection to PIF, and, in the words of Karen Young, an analyst of energy and economic trends in the Gulf, "Feeding the PIF is still a national economic and security priority. And the PIF gets what it wants."[81] This has led to concerns that the PIF might crowd out or muscle into the private sector as a new phase of centralized state-led development ("state capitalism" as a Saudi analyst told the *Financial Times* in 2023) takes root.[82] In 2022, the PIF acquired minority stakes in four family-owned construction conglomerates and in 2024 outlined plans to take a 36 percent stake in the Binladin Group as well, bringing the companies under closer state control.[83] The fund has also established dozens of new domestic companies in sectors that range from ecotourism and electric vehicles to shipbuilding and space development, with the aim that some will become national champions.[84] Doing business with PIF, and PIF-associated entities, also became a way for foreign investors to hedge risk, especially after the Ritz-Carlton detentions in 2017 and Khashoggi killing in 2018, when at least some potential entrants to Saudi Arabia took the view that "the political risks of investing in the Kingdom needed to be mitigated by co-investment" with PIF, given its close association with the inner circles of power in Saudi Arabia.[85]

As 2022 gave way to 2023 in the afterglow generated by the Saudi national team's victory over eventual champions Argentina, Vision 2030 reached the midpoint in the chronological timespan between its unveiling in 2016 and its projected end. Few of the giga-projects had yet delivered tangible outcomes, with the Six Flags amusement park set to form the core of the Qiddiya complex outside Riyadh missing an initial target to open in 2023 and aiming for 2025 instead.[86] At Neom, satellite images showed largely empty patches of desert save for an airport, which opened in 2019, a film studio, and "a sprawling new royal complex that boasts giant palaces, a golf course and at least 10 helipads."[87] Cranes were beginning to loom around the site of the planned giant cube in Riyadh, while in Jeddah, the attempt to redevelop the city center there (by a PIF subsidiary) sparked a public backlash as more than 60 neighborhoods were set to be demolished and up to half a million residents displaced.[88] As several of the Red Sea resorts moved toward opening in 2024, it became apparent that they would be at the ultraluxury end of the market that consultants in 2021 had cautioned against.[89]

Building and developing the giga-projects and turning vision into reality was only one half of the equation, and once the surge in oil prices and government revenues in 2022 and early 2023 began to abate, challenging financial realities started to bite, as Chapter Seven explores. In addition to the "supply" side of delivering the projects, the onus of which falls on the Saudi authorities, officials in Riyadh needed to generate a "demand" for the millions of new residents and tourist arrivals that would populate the projects, once they were opened, and meet the ambitious targets set by Mohammed bin Salman himself. Engaging with global sport, at first tentatively in the post-Khashoggi shadow and then at an accelerated pace after the upheaval of the pandemic subsided in 2021–22, provided an opportunity to address several different objectives at once. These included utilizing the mass appeal of sport as a platform to publicize the changes taking place in Saudi Arabia, albeit on regime-friendly terms, and to generate worldwide awareness of the giga-projects along with a sense of anticipation for the developments underway. Using sport to create new narratives and, in the Saudi case, position the Kingdom as a destination after decades of being largely closed to (non-Muslim) visitors, will be examined more fully in the next chapter, before Chapter Five examines the sweet spot of 2023 and Chapter Six explores the debates over sportswashing.

4

REBRANDING SAUDI ARABIA AS A DESTINATION

The speed and scale of Saudi investments into sport is consistent with the focus in Vision 2030 on creating new areas of comparative advantage for the Kingdom, such as tourism. A key part of the narrative of change is implanting the notion that the Saudi Arabia people thought they knew is not the Saudi Arabia of the 2020s, and that issues such as the September 11, 2001 attacks and the reputation of being an ultra-conservative and off limits country are now a thing of the past as the country opens up (the reality, of course, is messier). While those accusing the Saudis of sportswashing would argue that using sport to alter the conversation about a country is precisely the point of the label, the Saudi case is motivated by a need to target and mobilize the prospective residents, visitors, and investors if the giga-projects are to succeed.

In June 2023, the *Discovery Channel* aired a documentary about Neom and The Line which featured an interview with Mohammed bin Salman, in which the Crown Prince projected that the population of Saudi Arabia would rise to between 50 and 55 million by 2030, up from 33 million at the time of broadcast.[1] Three months later, the Ministry of Tourism raised its target of attracting 100 million visits a year by 2030 to 150 million as the original figure was deemed to be too low (for comparison, France had 30 million visits in 2019, directly before the pandemic intervened).[2] Such statements put pressure on Saudi officials to deliver, especially when they came directly from the Crown Prince himself, as with the expectation that the Kingdom would attract around twenty million new residents in a seven-year timespan. For good measure, Mohammed bin Salman told the *Discovery Channel* that the plan for The Line "sounds very doable and the idea is amazing, so it's massive, it's huge, I wish I can explain it in a smaller way."[3]

This chapter examines the use (by Saudis and many others) of sport as a tool of national rebranding. It begins with a comparative section that explores how sport has been utilized by countries for a variety of reasons, from telegraphing national power to facilitating political rehabilitation. The Saudi authorities are not the first, and will not be the last, to seek to harness the unique reach of sport and its ability to go far beyond conventional branding campaigns or soft power projection. Section two returns the focus to Saudi Arabia and analyzes the importance to the success of Vision 2030 of positioning the Kingdom as an essential destination for all manner of flows of people, goods, and services. The final section pivots to the many investments into sports, as well as esports, since the late-2010s, that preceded the "big bang" into football in 2023 and which, taken together, have placed Saudi Arabia firmly on the global sporting map.

Using sport for political purposes

Sport and politics have long been intertwined, going back to the tradition of a truce associated with the ancient Olympic ceremonies intended to ensure that participants from across the Hellenic world could safely travel to Olympia to partake in the games.[4] The emergence of "modern" codes of football (including rugby league and union as well as soccer) in the late-nineteenth century also reflected the outcome of fundamentally political considerations, not least over whether players should be paid.[5] In 1883, Blackburn Olympic became the first team from northern England and from a working-class background to win the prestigious FA Cup as they defeated the two previous winners, the solidly amateur and public school based Old Carthusians in the semifinal and Old Etonians in the final. The Rubicon had been well and truly crossed as the dominance of amateur clubs was shattered and football became the preserve of professional teams.[6] Something similar happened in the Hijaz five decades later as Al-Ittihad defeated the more exclusive (and elite-rooted) Hijazi Sports Club in 1931, "with enthusiastic support by young men of the different quarters" of Jeddah, which helped to ensure that their broader approach to participation was the one that endured, as football rapidly grew in popularity among male Hijazi youth.[7]

Scholars have identified multiple reasons why nations and their political leaders engage in sport, to accrue soft power, engage in branding campaigns, or as tools of public diplomacy. History is replete with examples of countries which have turned to sport to push national narratives or engage in image rehabilitation after times of turmoil. The Nazis' use of the 1936 Summer Olympics in Berlin (as well as the Winter Olympics that year in Bavaria) for propaganda purposes remains infamous for the public spectacles they produced, and may be considered the first "sports mega-event."[8] Leni Riefenstahl documented the 1936 Olympics in a film, *Olympia*, that maximized the propaganda value of the Games and won numerous international awards for its groundbreaking cinematic techniques for the time.[9] In football, the 1978 World Cup in Argentina saw the military junta aggressively control media coverage of the tournament and use the tournament "to promote nationalism and a better image of the country abroad," while FIFA ignored a report from Amnesty International on the grounds that it did not engage in politics.[10] On a more positive note, the 2006 World Cup in Germany drew two million foreign visitors and is now regarded as "one of the most successful recent uses of elite sport to improve a nation's image abroad."[11]

In other instances, countries have used the hosting of sports megaevents (SMEs) to either announce their arrival on the global stage (as, for example, South Korea and the 1988 Summer Olympics in Seoul or China and the 2008 Summer Olympics in Beijing[12]) or their reacceptance. Examples of the latter include the 1960, 1964, and 1972 Summer Olympics which took place in Italy, Japan, and West Germany, and functioned as unofficial yet powerful seals of postwar reconciliation.[13] Japanese politicians, in particular, emphasized "how hosting the Tokyo Olympics in 1964 contributed greatly to Japan's developing economy and raised the pride of Japanese citizens after the experience of the Second World War."[14] More recently, the 1995 Rugby World Cup symbolized South Africa's re-integration into the international community after apartheid and presented an image to the world of a dynamic and changing society.[15] An indelible image from the 1995 Rugby World Cup final was President Nelson Mandela clad in a Springboks jersey as he celebrated with the (overwhelmingly white) team that defeated New Zealand to win the Webb Ellis trophy.[16] In a speech he made to open the tournament, Mandela linked the hosting of the Rugby World Cup to "our nation-building effort" in "our young democracy," and after the final his predecessor as president, F.W. de Klerk, who oversaw the dismantling of apartheid, stated that the Springboks' victory "has united the nation and solidified the reconciliation spirit which exists in the country."[17]

Political leaders around the world have also used sport for specific domestic and foreign policy purposes. Officials in Japan, including Crown Prince (and future Emperor) Akihito, used sports diplomacy to re-set relations with the United States during the postwar Allied occupation that lasted from 1945 to 1952, with a shared love of baseball playing a key role in a high-profile "friendship tour" of Japan by the San Francisco Seals in 1949.[18] At the end of the tour, which saw nearly a million people greet the arriving American players and enormous crowds of spectators attend the games, General Douglas MacArthur, the Allied supreme commander and *de facto* ruler of occupied Japan, was moved to declare that "This trip is the greatest piece of diplomacy ever. All the diplomats put together would not have been able to do this."[19] A generation later, table tennis was used to create tentative openings between the US and China in the "ping-pong diplomacy" of 1971 which helped to pave the way for expanded sporting, cultural, and political exchanges, including President Richard Nixon's path-breaking week-long visit to China in February 1972.[20]

Local leaders in Nigeria in the 1970s and in Yemen in the 1990s promoted sport (and specifically football in the Yemeni case) to try and overcome deep internal fissures after periods of civil conflict, and achieve greater national cohesion.[21] East Germany used sport as a way to overcome political and diplomatic isolation in the 1970s and 1980s and develop a national consciousness separate from that of

West Germany. Erick Honecker, the chief secretary of the ruling Socialist Unity Party between 1971 and 1989, had earlier, in the 1960s, acknowledged that "Sport is not an end to itself, but rather the means to an end."[22] Sporting success, especially at the Olympic Games (albeit overshadowed by claims of systematic and state-sanctioned doping programs), was a source of national pride for East Germans, and Honecker later wrote that the star athletes, whom officials called "sports-diplomats in track-suits," had contributed "to the prestige of our socialist state and gained us more than a little recognition in other countries."[23]

Finally, in terms of public diplomacy, which often overlaps with national branding campaigns, host nations have become more proactive in tapping into the hyper-commercialization of modern sports mega-events, which began in earnest with the 1984 Summer Olympics in Los Angeles.[24] One example was the creation of *Brand Australia* in 1995, two years after Sydney was named the host of the 2000 Summer Olympics, followed in 1998 by a three-year campaign that straddled the runup to and hosting of the games.[25] The Commonwealth Games in Kuala Lumpur in 1998 were heavily marketed by host authorities who promoted Malaysia as a model Muslim state and explicitly began to tie sports events to the promotion of tourism.[26] A year before the 2012 Summer Olympics in London, Prime Minister David Cameron launched the GREAT Britain campaign designed to improve the United Kingdom's image abroad. While the posters which formed the basis of the campaign were visually striking, their effectiveness was tempered as Brexit and the tortured process of leaving the European Union undid much of the gains to U.K. soft power from 2012.

How to measure the specific impact of engaging with sport has proven difficult in practice to quantify, just as it has been for assessing the legacy of hosting a mega-event or sponsoring tournaments or teams.[27] Target audiences do not always respond in the manner expected (or hoped for), and as early as 2004 a special issue of a journal that examined the interplay between sport and international relations, just as major sporting events began to take place beyond Europe and the Americas, noted "the powerful role of the Western media, in particular, in determining the degree to which hosting a mega-event amplifies or effectively diminishes the host's international reputation."[28] The crescendo of criticism in Western media coverage of Qatar ahead of and during the 2022 men's World Cup proved that hosting a sports mega-event could function instead as an exercise in "soft disempowerment" that inflicts reputational harm.[29]

What, then, lies behind the Saudi strategy of engaging with sport, especially internationally? Chapter Six will address in detail the discourse on "sportswashing" that has arisen since the mid-2010s and taken root in much Western media coverage of the Gulf States and global sport. A 2023 study of Saudi sports diplomacy by Aaron Ettinger, a Canada-based academic, made the point that Riyadh is neither seeking international prestige as, for example, China or Brazil have done, nor looking to announce its rehabilitation in the manner of West Germany or Japan after 1945, the stain of the Khashoggi shadow notwithstanding.[30] The one exception appears to be the hosting of the inaugural Islamic Solidarity Games in Mecca in April 2005 as a means of portraying the Kingdom as "a modern Muslim country open to change, progress and modern technology" in the aftermath of the September 11, 2001 terrorist attacks on the U.S., in which 15 of the 19 hijackers were Saudi nationals, as was the Al Qaeda founder, Osama bin Laden.[31] The brainchild of Prince Faisal bin Fahd, a son of King Fahd who played a critical role in developing Saudi football in the 1970s and 1980s as the president of the Saudi Arabian Football Federation, the Islamic Solidarity Games were closely associated with the Jeddah-based Organization of Islamic Cooperation. However, the two subsequent Solidarity Games were cancelled as Iran withdrew as host in 2009 after a row about the naming of the Persian/Arabian Gulf, and Syria pulled out in 2013 as the Assad regime found itself a regional and international pariah as the civil war raged.[32]

The reach of international sport means it can provide a platform for states to signal to a wide audience, external as well as internal, that key changes or developments are underway.[33] This aligns with elements of the sportswashing narrative, but the Saudi authorities' increased engagement with global sport after 2017 is rooted in internal and external policy objectives. Chief among these drivers are the need to generate a sense of momentum around the giga-projects (and Vision 2030 more broadly) and to spread the message of a rapidly changing

REBRANDING SAUDI ARABIA AS A DESTINATION

Saudi Arabia to an audience of prospective investors and eventual visitors and residents, once the projects are open and operational. To the extent that improving the Kingdom's image is a factor, it is linked to promoting and advertising a "new" Saudi Arabia and thus a means to an end, rather than constituting a specific end-goal in itself.

Positioning Saudi Arabia as a destination

Tourism, together with the hospitality and entertainment sectors, has emerged as a key feature of Vision 2030 and the push to diversify the Saudi economy, and is a core element of many of the giga-projects as they move forward, albeit at a slower pace than originally anticipated. Aside from religious tourism for Muslims performing Hajj or Umrah in Mecca, the tourist sector in Saudi Arabia barely existed until tourist visas began to be issued in 2019.[34] Prior to that, most visitors had to procure a business visa which involved securing a letter of invitation from a host entity and providing an employment verification letter from their workplace. In February 2020, a revamping of Cabinet portfolios (within the Council of Ministers) saw the creation of dedicated Ministries of Tourism, Sports, and Investment for the first time, but Covid-19 and pandemic lockdowns intervened almost immediately.[35] In October 2021, the Minister of Tourism unveiled a strategy that envisaged investing US$1 trillion over ten years with the aim of creating one million new jobs in the sector and attracting 100 million visits a year by 2030. However, it emerged that the authorities were using an unconventional metric of "visits" rather than "visitors" or "arrivals," such that "a person who visits 10 destinations in the country during a trip will count for 10 visits."[36]

That said, Saudi Arabia registered the highest year-on-year increase in international arrivals among G-20 countries in 2022 as borders reopened.[37] Saudia, the national carrier, launched weekly scheduled flights from the newly-completed Neom Bay Airport to Dubai and London Heathrow, although passenger numbers to a destination still largely in varying phases of construction remain unclear.[38] Huge new art and heritage projects, many centered around the pre-Islamic oasis settlement of Al-Ula in the northwest of the Kingdom, created their own momentum and drew accusations of "art-washing."[39] So, too, did the arrival of music festivals which generated favorable international headlines owing both to the caliber of the global stars who performed as well as the size of the crowds which attended. In December 2022, 600,000 people attended a three-day music festival near Riyadh featuring Saudi and international DJs and artists, a figure actually down from the 732,000 attendees the year before albeit over four days.[40]

The campaign to promote Saudi tourism additionally enlisted the two most famous male footballers on the planet and tapped into their unparalleled name recognition and global appeal. Lionel Messi, the Barcelona legend who captained Argentina to victory in the 2022 World Cup in Qatar, was signed as a tourism ambassador in 2021 and featured heavily in advertising for the Riyadh Season in 2022.[41] Messi's great rival, Cristiano Ronaldo, reportedly turned down an offer to become "the face of Saudi Arabian tourism" in 2021, but after the Portuguese superstar signed for Al-Nassr in January 2023, his social media accounts filled up with laudatory and very positive impressions of his life and lifestyle in the Kingdom.[42] Just as Ronaldo's unveiling in Riyadh in 2023 took place against the backdrop of the "Saudi, Welcome to Arabia" tagline that has become the cornerstone of the Kingdom's global marketing campaign, in January 2024 the tourism authorities launched another campaign, starring Messi, entitled "Go Beyond What You Think," which aimed "to dispel stereotypes about the Kingdom".[43]

While there was also a push to expand local tourism, to ensure that spending on leisure remained in the Kingdom rather than in nearby Bahrain or Dubai, as well as to boost non-religious tourism by developing domestic tourist destinations, many of the initiatives in the giga-projects appeared to be geared toward the highest end of the market, raising questions about their accessibility to many Saudis.[44] So, too, did the Riyadh Season of events during the winter months, which included concerts and festivals that would have seemed unimaginable in the Kingdom prior to 2015, but which led one Saudi commentator to tweet that the "cost of events and restaurants during the Riyadh Season highlight a stark class divide, which seems to confirm that such entrainment options are targeting the rich and middle-class families."[45]

The formation of Riyadh Air as a new flag carrier for Saudi Arabia drew together numerous strands. Launched by Mohammed bin

REBRANDING SAUDI ARABIA AS A DESTINATION

Salman in March 2023 and owned by PIF, the objective is for Riyadh Air to connect Saudi Arabia to the world and be based in Riyadh, with the existing carrier, Saudia, focusing on Jeddah and religious travel to Mecca.[46] Riyadh Air, and the planned redevelopment of the city's airport into one of the largest in the world with six runways, moved the Kingdom into a crowded regional market, though the planned focus on point-to-point rather than transfer traffic suggests the airline will rival Emirates and Dubai more than Qatar Airways and Doha.[47] Tony Douglas, the former Etihad CEO appointed to the same position at Riyadh Air, noted in June 2023 that

> (…) I can't think of a start-up on this scale for decades and decades, and because we don't have a legacy in terms of systems or things that were inherited, we genuinely have an opportunity with a clean sheet of paper to build something really exciting going forward (…) Because we don't have a legacy, we haven't got 40 years of good reasons why you had to do certain things, certain ways. You are starting from ground zero, a clean sheet of paper.[48]

These comments were remarkably similar in tone to those made by James Hogan, the then chief executive of Etihad during its own start-up phase in Abu Dhabi in the 2000s

> (…) I don't have to tackle the union issues of these other carriers (…) When it comes to other carriers, we are both similar service airlines, but they are bound by agreements, employment agreements, 15, 20, 30, or 40 years old that are very hard to renegotiate. They are bound by infrastructure—facilities and bases that were right for them 30 years ago or even 20 years ago, but aren't today. I am fortunate that I have a clean sheet of paper.[49]

The Etihad comparison is a cautionary tale for Riyadh Air, given that missteps after Abu Dhabi's creation in 2003 of a national carrier to take on Emirates in Dubai nearly bankrupted the airline and necessitated a four-year restructuring program overseen by Douglas himself before he joined Riyadh Air.[50] Away from the aviation context, notions of a "clean sheet of paper" and lack of inherited legacy constraints would be observable in the spending patterns of Saudi football clubs in 2023 as they operated beyond financial fair play regulations imposed by UEFA and European leagues on their member teams.⁵¹ A further point of similarity was Riyadh Air's adoption of a "tease and reveal" strategy of using social media to build their domestic brand among what Douglas labeled a generation who "want to engage pretty much everything they do—including their new national carrier—as a true digital native."⁵² This, too, was mirrored in the nature of the Kingdom's forays into sport as they developed in earnest after the pandemic.

Given the heavy use of football sponsorship by other Gulf airlines since the 2000s, it was little surprise that, within five months of launching, Riyadh Air became the main sponsor and official airline partner of Atletico Madrid, the third most successful club in Spain with 11 La Liga titles between 1940 and 2021.⁵³ The appearance of the airline's logo on Atleti's famous red-and-white shirts in domestic and UEFA Champions League play in the 2023–24 season was a marketing boon, given that Riyadh Air was not expected to start flying until 2025, and undoubtedly helped to raise the start-up carrier's profile. A statement from MBS on Riyadh Air's launch captured the ambitious plans for the airline and its role within wider development plans, as the Crown Prince stated that he expected "Riyadh to become a gateway to the world and a global destination for transportation, trade, and tourism."⁵⁴ One year later, in October 2024, as the launch date for Riyadh Air's first commercial flight neared, the airline also secured a nine-year agreement for the naming rights to Atletico Madrid's Metropolitano stadium.⁵⁵

The role of sport

In the second half of this book, the spotlight turns to the role of football in the project to transform Saudi Arabia and to generate external awareness of and internal support for the process of change. On the domestic level, sport has been earmarked as one of four priority sectors (alongside mining, tourism, and entertainment) in which, in the words of Saudi commentator Ali Shihabi, the Kingdom either has "a clear global competitive advantage or else there is substantial pent-up domestic and regional demand."⁵⁶ Two of the eleven "vision realization programs" to translate Vision 2030 into deliverable reality include a focus on sport (the PIF Program and the Quality of Life

Program) while the impact of a third, the Privatization Program, is evident in the plans to wean Saudi Pro League teams off state funding.[57] This is evident in the implementation of projects. Qiddiya, the large-scale entertainment complex outside Riyadh, was redesigned to include districts for esports and gaming as well as sporting venues, while the Sports Boulevard project in Riyadh set out to redevelop outdoor spaces for sport and recreation.[58]

Focus now turns to how Vision 2030 and its associated initiatives became a centerpiece of the approach to sport by Saudi officials as well as the investments made by the Public Investment Fund. Just as the narrative around the rollout of the giga-projects was based on a breakneck pace in their early days, so have the authorities been as expansive in their ambition for sport, at least until fiscal realities began to bite in 2024 and prompt a reconsideration and partial scaling back. Officials briefed journalists in 2023 that the Kingdom aimed to host 25 world championships across multiple sports by 2030.[59] One which gained global attention was the October 2022 announcement by the Olympic Council of Asia that the 2029 Asian Winter Games would take place at Trojena, an as-yet unbuilt "mountain destination" part of Neom, with 36 kilometers of slopes planned and "snowmaking technicians" already testing artificial snow.[60]

Under Mohammed bin Salman, Saudi Arabia became active in seeking to harness the power of culture and sport to burnish its international image and change the narrative about the Kingdom away from focus on such issues as human rights violations and the war in Yemen. Much of the initial Saudi engagement with international sport was driven by an advisor to MBS, Turki Al Sheikh, in both his professional capacity as Chairman of the General Entertainment Authority since 2018 (and, for a year before that, as Chairman of the General Sports Authority) and his private capacity as an investor in football clubs in Egypt, Sudan, and Spain and a major figure in the hitherto-fractured landscape of men's boxing.[61]

The scale and intensity of Saudi involvement in sporting initiatives, as a host and a participant, quickened considerably after 2018, the year of Khashoggi's death but also as the Vision 2030 initiatives kicked into gear. That year, the General Entertainment Authority signed a ten-year agreement with World Wrestling Entertainment (WWE) to host two "Crown Jewel" events each year in the Kingdom, and the first one took place only a month after Khashoggi's murder.[62] Multi-year deals were also signed with the Italian and Spanish soccer federations to host each country's Super Cup in Saudi Arabia in 2018 and 2019 (Italy) and 2020 and 2022 (Spain) which were later extended, major boxing bouts took place at Diriyah, the "ancestral home" of the Al Saud family just outside Riyadh, and the inaugural Saudi Arabian Grand Prix was organized on a street circuit along the Jeddah Corniche in 2021 as part of a ten-year deal with Formula One.[63]

Writing in August 2023 during a reporting trip to Saudi Arabia ahead of the start of the much-anticipated Saudi Pro League season, Paul MacInnes of the *Guardian* observed that "Every corner of the Saudi state, it seems, is moving into sport." In his report from Jeddah, MacInnes quoted an (unnamed) executive who had been briefed on the Kingdom's plans for sport who stated that

> This is a sports strategy that is as comprehensive and more detailed than any other in the world. It is not a fad, this is not just some rich man's whim. This has been planned, it is a real approach to what sport can do to change a nation in relation to health, wellbeing and active participation. It's a really detailed plan and it's been based on the best sports strategies in the world. This is a very coordinated approach.[64]

One contact who went on the record for MacInnes was Andrea Sartori, a sports consultant who had also worked on Qatar's sports strategy, and who looked at the bigger picture as

> Sport, with the massive emotional component attached to it, and extensive media coverage, can benefit investment in other sectors of the economy (…) it is an opportunity for Saudi Arabia, at a relatively low cost, to quickly reposition the country on the international market (…) You shouldn't just look at the amounts of money invested, you should also look at the speed with which people's opinions change. In the next four or five years they will change our mindset and perception of the country—something others have taken decades to achieve.[65]

Simon Chadwick, a professor of sport and geopolitical economy who has long worked on the Gulf States, observed that "Saudi Arabia is now shaping the commercial, industrial and geopolitical networks of sport" and that "It's beginning to test the limits of rules and governance."[66] Speaking to the BBC in December 2023, Saudi Arabia's Minister of Sport, Prince Abdulaziz bin Turki Al Faisal, stated that "We want to attract the world through sports" and added that "Twenty million of our population are below the age of 30, so we need to get them engaged."[67] For these reasons, any attempt to view Saudi engagement with sport solely through a sportswashing lens is overly restrictive and misses the bigger picture at play.

Boxing was particularly successful in generating a worldwide buzz and spreading awareness of a "new" Saudi Arabia which, in the words of promoter Eddie Hearn, was "trying to showcase to people that their country is changing. Every country has problems. But from what I see, I believe they are trying to make a change."[68] Seemingly without realizing the import of his choice of wording, heavyweight champion Anthony Joshua labeled Saudi Arabia "the Mecca of boxing" ahead of his rematch fight with Andy Ruiz in Diriyah in December 2019, a breakthrough moment in the Kingdom's ability to attract the highest caliber events and sportspeople.[69] Four years later, Tommy Fury defeated Jake Paul in Diriyah, the ringside featuring former champions Mike Tyson and a thobe-wearing Deontay Wilder as well as Cristiano Ronaldo. Fury stated that "Saudi Arabia is an amazing place" and thanked the organizers for treating "me and my team like kings the whole way through," while Mike Tyson added that "I'm interested in being part of the success of Prince Khalid [bin Abdulaziz, owner of a sports and entertainment agency which co-promoted the fight]", and Wilder announced that "We're in Saudi Arabia, baby. And if you ain't here, you should've been!"[70] Tyson Fury, the British heavyweight boxing champion and older brother of Tommy Fury, told ESPN in 2024 that "I'm being paid a s---ton of money from Saudi not to turn up and do a boxing fight, but to put a show on and put Saudi on the map, So that's what I'm gonna do, what I'm being paid for. Put on a show."[71]

PIF also began to invest significantly in gaming and esports in 2022 through a subsidiary, the Savvy Games Group, established as part of PIF's new 2021–2025 strategy, building on a string of investments into various esports and gaming platforms and companies in 2020 and 2021.[72] Savvy, in particular, was consistent with the PIF's launching of national champions capable of transforming the Kingdom into a central hub of an emerging sector, in this case the global gaming market.[73] The group quickly began to invest heavily in taking stakes in gaming companies across the world as Mohammed bin Salman announced that his aim was for Saudi Arabia to become "the ultimate global hub for the games and esports sector" by 2030. The speed and scale of Savvy's activity led one market analyst to state that "It's a bulldozer approach" as "The industry in Saudi Arabia is nascent; they have to build it literally from the ground up." Savvy's CEO explained the investments by stating that "The region is populated with demographics that are favorable to us (…) When you fold in the national strategy (…) and the desire to diversify the economy away from oil and gas, it's a natural assumption to be making a lot of investments in Saudi Arabia towards games."[74]

Esports and gaming provide a conventional example of PIF investment in sport in terms of compatibility with the need to contribute to the economic development and diversification of the Kingdom. Aside from media reports that Mohammed bin Salman himself is an avid gamer, this emerging and rapidly growing sector is consistent with PIF's mandate, as laid out by Yasir Al Rumayyan at the launch of the new PIF plan for 2021–25, namely to "enable the private sector" by working with "innovative, transformative, and disruptive companies around the world" to develop "the industries and opportunities of the future."[75] Establishing leadership in the new economy and positioning the Kingdom as a "growth engine" for market disruptors and technological innovators explains the targeting of such companies for PIF investment, and this has become evident in the way Saudi Arabia has come to dominate the fast-growing esports sector.[76] Thus, the inaugural Esports World Cup took place in Riyadh across seven weeks in July–August 2024, and during the competition the International Olympic Committee announced a twelve year partnership with the National Olympic Committee of Saudi Arabia to host the first Olympic Esports Games in 2025.[77]

A separate PIF investment made in 2021, the acquisition of a minority stake in the McLaren Group (which was sold in 2023), was followed in 2022 by a "strategic title partnership" that saw Neom brand itself on McLaren's Formula E and Extreme E racing cars and

McLaren become a founding partner in an advanced and clean industries initiative to be based at a research and innovation campus in Neom itself.[78] The Neom/McLaren tie-up was thus a combination of soft power/branding and an example of a PIF investment intended to support the development of research and investment capacity in Saudi Arabia. In this regard, it was similar to a (non-sports-related) PIF investment into the electric vehicle manufacturer, Lucid Motors, in 2019, which was followed by an announcement in 2022 that Lucid would open an assembly plant in Saudi Arabia and produce between 50,000 and 100,000 locally-produced electric cars for the Saudi market over a ten-year period, thereby contributing to job creation and the manufacturing base.[79]

Less conventional returns on investment may explain the PIF's investment in Newcastle United (which is examined in greater detail in Chapter Six) and LIV Golf which appear to be more about the projection of soft power and the use of sport to reach new constituencies beyond Saudi borders. Indeed, in August 2023, Joseph Nye, the Harvard academic who did more than anyone to conceptualize how states accrue and project soft power, observed that "If you are Saudi, trying to draw attention away from Khashoggi (…) a new golf tour can help," and added that sport is a potent tool of soft power because it "often creates a favorable environment and draws attention." Nye cautioned that the use of sport does not always work as intended and cited "British football fans in Europe" as an example, although he could also have noted the negative coverage of the 2022 FIFA men's World Cup in Qatar as another instance.[80]

If football, and the Premier League, reaches a massive global audience, professional golf holds more of a niche appeal to a distinct demographic of often affluent and politically engaged consumers. PIF's decision to associate itself with, and finance, LIV Golf not only reflects Al Rumayyan's passion but also amounts to a very different approach to Saudi Arabia's engagement in sport.[81] It is one thing to acquire one of 20 teams in the Premier League or organize one of two dozen grands prix in the Formula One World Championship but another to back a breakaway that positioned itself as a direct rival to the existing institutional structure, in this case the PGA and European Tours. An analogy would be PIF setting up a rival football league or motor racing championship and incentivizing teams to jump ship. Just as Al Rumayyan backed disruptive technologies for PIF investments, so disruption to the hidebound world of men's professional golf was a feature of "Project Wedge" as it took shape prior to the launch of LIV Golf in 2022.[82]

The Public Investment Fund's backing of LIV Golf in 2022 and the surprise agreement to combine commercial operations with the PGA and DP World Tour in June 2023 represented a striking breakthrough against the *status quo* in a notoriously conservative sport, and a signal that existing stakeholders could not simply ignore the PIF and the level of resources at its disposal.[83] The fact that two of the eight tournaments in the inaugural season took place at courses owned by former U.S. president Donald Trump also hinted that political motives could potentially be at play, given the PIF's decision—reportedly against the advice of its investment committee—to invest US$2 billion in Affinity Partners, a private equity firm established by Trump's son-in-law and former senior adviser, Jared Kushner.[84] Trump himself told reporters who attended the inaugural LIV event at his club in Bedminister, New Jersey in July 2022 that

> I've known these people for a long time in Saudi Arabia and they've been friends of mine for a long time. They've invested in many American companies. They own big percentages of many, many American companies and frankly, what they are doing for golf is so great, what they are doing for the players is so great. The salaries are going to go way up.[85]

Trump added that "LIV has been a great thing for Saudi Arabia, for the image of Saudi Arabia. The publicity they've gotten is worth billions," while a "Saudi consultant close to the government" told the *New Yorker* magazine that "You can't deny that even the controversy has inserted the Saudi name into golf. I think they're getting exactly what they hoped for."[86] Earlier, the PGA Tour's initial rebuff to PIF outreach in 2021 led an advisor to Golf Saudi to tell the journalist Alan Shipnuck that "There are heads of state who will turn their schedules upside down to get a few minutes of Yasir's [Al Rumayyan's] time. The Saudis are used to getting their own way. They are not used to being told no."[87] Once LIV Golf was up and running, Al Rumayyan was photographed wearing a "Make America Great Again" hat while talking to Trump.[88] Moreover, a LIV Golf executive told Shipnuck that whereas "left-leaning [media] outlets" were "obsessed" with "the Saudi/Khashoggi narrative" and "don't even mention the actual golf (…) conservative platforms are a more friendly audience and they're willing to talk about golf and what we're trying to accomplish."[89]

One of the distinctive features of LIV Golf which carried into the PIF's investment into Saudi football clubs in 2023 was the development of franchises, based around teams of four pro golfers each, with ownership rights and individual branding that could be monetized to generate new revenue streams.[90] Teams duly appeared with names such as Crushers, Fireballs, Iron Heads, Ripper, and Smash, but after the opening seasons of the LIV Invitational Series (2022) and LIV Golf League (2023) the teams have struggled to break into the wider consciousness of a sport known for its crusty adherence to tradition.[91] Part of the rationale for the PIF's acquisition of 75 percent stakes in Al-Hilal, Al-Nassr, Al-Ahli, and Al-Ittihad in 2023 was "to build up the brands of those clubs, then bring in private investors to buy them," which explains why the move, which appeared to bring them under closer state control, was labeled a process of privatization.[92]

The degree to which the Saudi move into global sport disrupts or moves into existing structures and dynamics of power remains to be seen. In tennis and cricket, Aramco has engaged with the International Cricket Council, and the PIF with the existing ATP and WTA Tours (in men's and women's professional tennis), first as sponsor and later as host, rather than as a disruptor and a rival to the existing competitive structure in each sport.[93] In March 2025, the PIF also reached an agreement with the WTA to provide twelve months of paid maternity leave through the PIF WTA Maternity Fund Program. The WTA's CEO, Portia Archer, acknowledged that "We wouldn't have been able to provide the benefits were it not for this relationship and the funding that PIF provides" but the WTA did not disclose the value of the fund and others noted that the leave period far exceeded that granted to working women in Saudi Arabia.[94]

With regards to golf, while much was made of the PIF and the PGA Tour's June 2023 framework agreement to combine resources, an end-of-year deadline to finalize the nature of the arrangement was missed, and a breakthrough in the negotiations remained elusive as of the end of December 2024, a full year later.⁹⁵ Amid the limbo, the PGA Tour reached a US$3 billion deal with the Strategic Sports Group, a consortium of American investors led by John Henry, the owner of Liverpool FC, and LIV continued to recruit star golfers, including Jon Rahm, the defending Masters champion and former world number one, "for what is believed to be more money than the PGA Tour's entire prize fund," meaning that the 2024 LIV Golf League would feature the winners of eight of the previous fourteen Masters.⁹⁶

Men's cricket offers a mixed experience of the legacy of disruptors which may yet prove comparable to the Saudi engagement with sport in the medium- to longer-term. Kerry Packer's World Series Cricket only lasted for two years before a reconciliation with the Australian Cricket Board in 1979, but the breakaway competition did spur innovations, especially in the way the game was marketed and valued, as well as far greater television coverage, the introduction of floodlit night games, and higher wages.⁹⁷ A generation later, the launch of Twenty20 cricket in 2003 was a gamechanger which transformed cricket as it created a new format configured for television that held mass appeal, and the formation of the Indian Premier League in 2008 took the game to a completely different level.⁹⁸ The relocation of the International Cricket Council from its traditional headquarters at Lord's in London to Dubai in 2005 was also an early harbinger of the impact of globalizing forces on a hitherto Western-centric architecture of sports governance.

The end of 2022 thus saw the Saudis basking in the reflected glory of having defeated Argentina at the World Cup and visibly demonstrating the depth of their passion for football on the streets of Doha. Meanwhile, after a year of high oil prices following the full-scale Russian invasion of Ukraine, the Kingdom generated a record level of revenue as Saudi Aramco reported a net income of US$161.1 billion for the year.⁹⁹ Flush with cash and needing to make progress on Vision 2030, the pump was primed for the acceleration of the gigaprojects and associated initiatives as the halfway stage of the timescale announced in 2016 arrived. Having used the convening power of sport to signal to sports fans around the world that the Kingdom was changing, 2023 was the breakthrough year as Saudi Arabia announced its arrival on the global football stage as the sports- and non-sports related aspects of policy converged. In addition, the PIF established a dedicated sports investment company, SRJ Sports Investments, to give greater structure to the PIF's investments in sport, with the first deal made being in mixed martial arts.[100]

5

THE 2023 BREAKTHROUGH

The British Marxist historian Eric Hobsbawm popularized the term "the long nineteenth century" to refer to the period between the French Revolution in 1789 and the outbreak of the First World War in 1914 as a unit of study that did not neatly fit into temporal frames.[1] Saudi Arabia can be said to have experienced "a long 2023" in its engagement with world football, spanning the 14 months between 22 November 2022 and 18 January 2024. On 22 November 2022, tens of thousands of young Saudis celebrated the defeat of Argentina in the stadium, around Doha, and in public spaces across the Kingdom, arguably doing more for Saudi Arabia's soft power globally than anything else, as the images of a fun-loving, football-mad nation challenged conventional stereotypes of the country.[2] 18 January 2024 marked the end of Jordan Henderson's brief sojourn at Al-Ettifaq as the former England captain terminated his contract and moved to Ajax less than six months after his arrival from Liverpool. As rumors swirled that other big names might also depart, and no new stars arrived in the midseason transfer window, the durability of the Saudi football project came in for questioning and scrutiny.[3]

Although the Green Falcons lost their next two games in Qatar, 2–0 to Poland and 2–1 to Mexico, to finish bottom of Group C, the enthusiasm generated by the win over Argentina and the enormous contingent of Saudi fans who traveled across the border for the tournament, left a lasting impression.⁴ Less than two weeks after Argentina and France produced the most pulsating men's final in living memory came the news, on 30 December 2022, that Cristiano Ronaldo would join Al-Nassr.⁵ The Portuguese superstar had seen his contract with Manchester United terminated following the release of an eve of World Cup interview Ronaldo had given to Piers Morgan which was deeply critical of the club.⁶ Three months earlier, Ronaldo had rebuffed an offer from Al-Hilal, and in his interview with Morgan he indicated that he wished to play at the highest level rather than (as Morgan put it) "be in Saudi Arabia earning a king's ransom."⁷

Ronaldo's move to Saudi Arabia was announced while the football world was in mourning for Pele, the legendary Brazilian three-time World Cup winner, who had died the previous day. Pele had moved to the New York Cosmos in 1975 in a blockbuster deal that saw him earn an annual wage "twice the sum of the combined salary of every other player" in the North American Soccer League (NASL).⁸ The Cosmos were owned by Warner Communications and the media giant contributed US$2.5 million of the US$7 million package that brought Pele out of semi-retirement in a bid to kickstart the professional game in the U.S. Such was the impact of his arrival that home attendances for Cosmos games more than trebled and the team moved into the 76,000 capacity Giants Stadium in 1977, Pele's swansong year in New York.⁹

Echoes of Pele's move to the U.S. could be seen in Ronaldo's arrival in Saudi Arabia. In both cases, an aging star who had been the defining player of his era (shared, in Ronaldo's case, with Lionel Messi) was meant to supercharge an existing league infrastructure. Just as Clive Toye, the former chief sportswriter for the *Daily Express* in Britain who became the General Manager of the New York Cosmos, recalled that, in the 1970s, "we had decided that we had two major things to do to draw attention to all the minor things that were being done: we had to sign Pele and we had to host a World Cup," so Saudi officials made a similar calculation in the 2020s.¹⁰ Yasser Almisehal, the president of the Saudi Arabian Football Federation, told *The Athletic* in September 2022 that "we would love to see a player like Cristiano Ronaldo playing in the Saudi league (…) It would bring a huge positive feedback (…) it wouldn't be an easy transaction for a Saudi club or even for him, but we would love to see him or even some other top players of the same level."[11]

The unveiling of Ronaldo at a packed Mrsool Park, Al-Nassr's stadium, in January 2023 was significant for several reasons. One was the prominence given to the promotion of Saudi Arabia as a destination, with Visit Saudi (for whom Messi is a brand ambassador) on prominent display at the press conference. Another was the comingling of funds to make the transfer happen, just as Warner had assisted the Cosmos with the signing of Pele, with state-led tourism- and media-related entities reportedly supporting Ronaldo's $210 million/year salary.[12] Ronaldo was effusive in his praise of Saudi Arabia and became something of a fixture at sporting and social events in Riyadh, which he described to his half-billion social media followers as "one of the best places I have ever seen, with the most quality restaurants. With what the country is building for the future—I like to see different things, try different things. This is why I am here."[13]

Football as entertainment

If Saudi officials are to meet the targets of attracting 150 million visits a year and realize Mohammed bin Salman's prediction that the population of Saudi Arabia would rise from 33 million to more than 50 million in 2030, international awareness of (and excitement about) the narrative of change will be essential. It is here that the mobilizational appeal of elite football is unparalleled in its truly global reach, its impact magnified by generational and technological changes to the concept of "fandom."[14] The exponential rise of social media (such as Facebook and Instagram) and microblogging platforms (such as Twitter) since the mid-2000s has changed the ways that fans and teams engage and interact with each other.[15] In 2012, the Summer Olympics in London were labeled "the first truly social and digital Olympic Games" and more tweets were sent during the Opening Ceremony in London than during the entire two weeks of the Beijing Olympics four years earlier, while the pace of engagement has only accelerated in the years since.[16]

A shift in preference among younger Millennials and Gen Z worldwide from choosing and sticking with supporting teams to following individual players as they moved from club to club was also consequential. This became especially evident in the late-2010s and early-2020s as Cristiano Ronaldo and Lionel Messi left their long-time teams (Real Madrid and Barcelona, respectively) and became more transient figures as they moved around with greater regularity as their club careers waned.[17] Research conducted by the European Club Association in 2020 found that 53 percent of respondents who said they followed a player (over a team) were aged between 13 and 34, and that there was significant country variation, with 31 percent of fans in India supporting a player compared to just six percent in the U.K.[18] Such figures track developments in other sports, such as the NBA, where more than a quarter of fans profess more loyalty to a player (such as LeBron James) than a franchise, and are products of the social media age where players are brands and frequently have far greater personal followings than the teams they represent.[19]

An additional trend that originated internationally but became a core feature of the Saudi approach in 2023 was the coming together of sport and entertainment into a new product, both in content and delivery. To an extent, this was an evolution of an existing practice, just as the rise of ESPN in the U.S. in the 1980s and 1990s had transformed "how people accessed sport content across multiple platforms and converted sports fans with ever-shortening attention spans from game watchers to highlight watchers."[20] Changes to viewing patterns and the desire to target younger demographics led even the crustiest sports and event organizers to take a new approach. Ussama Al-Qassab, the marketing and commercial director at the All England Club which runs the Wimbledon tennis championship, captured the mood as he told the *Financial Times* in 2024 about the need to attract younger fans: "You've got to fish where the fishes are. If the first thing they're switching on is their PlayStation, or they're looking at their mobile phone, you've got to be able to interact with that [technology] first and foremost and use that as an on-ramp."[21]

This occurred as "legacy" and "new" media grappled with the impact of digital platforms and streaming services in the 2010s and generational changes in the ways younger audiences engage with the sector.[22] During the 2024 Summer games in Paris, Gary Zenkel, the president of NBC Olympics, drew attention to the rise of influencer marketing, and the importance of content "creators," as he stated that "There are certainly audiences, especially among younger generations, who spend more time on short-form content than they do on longer, more traditional programing. We will reach them through these platforms."[23] It could be said that Ronaldo and Messi are ultra-elite influencers each time they post on their Instagram and other social media accounts about their overwhelmingly positive impressions of the Kingdom.

Key to the changing pattern of content creation was the success of the *Drive to Survive* series on Netflix in creating relatable storylines based around the human element and "giving audiences the chance to emotionally invest in the drivers, teams, and the personal rivalries" in Formula One, with two metrics of its success being a surge in television ratings for the races and a significant fall in the average age of Formula One viewers from 44 to 32.[24] Other sports, such as golf and tennis, jumped onto the bandwagon with their own Netflix series, while the *All or Nothing* series on Amazon Prime focused initially on the NFL in American football and later branched into soccer, ice hockey, and rugby union.[25] A report on *Drive to Survive* noted the role of Liberty Media, the company which acquired Formula One in 2017

> (…) while the print media still has a role, much greater importance is given to what emerges online—whether that's through social media, on podcasts and YouTube, or on Netflix. It is those channels which provide the chatter which in turn drives interest in Formula One.
>
> Liberty Media understand this because they are not in the sports business in the way that organizations like Fenway Sports Group (current owners of Liverpool FC) are. Liberty Media is in the entertainment industry, and it wants to entertain.[26]

The appeal of *Welcome to Wrexham* and its transformative effect in generating worldwide support for a club then in the fifth (non-league) tier of English football, albeit one with an average attendance which exceeded that of the Saudi Pro League, provided further illustration of the sport-entertainment nexus.[27] From a leading industry voice, a similar point was made by Ferran Soriano, the former vice-chairman of Barcelona who became the CEO of Manchester City in 2012 and oversaw the creation of the Abu Dhabi-backed City Football Group.

In 2020, Soriano observed that "The business of entertainment will grow and sport is a fundamental part of entertainment and football is the number one sport, no question."²⁸

Football officials in Saudi Arabia identified and sought to appropriate these trends in the "new" landscape of the Saudi Pro League in 2023, which appeared at times to be designed as if the past was an irrelevant blank slate. The sense that the authorities had *carte blanche* to transform the SPL also reflected a freedom of action simply not applicable in leagues with autonomous and deeply-embedded existing stakeholders, as seen in the pushback to the European Super League in 2021. In an age of digital strategies designed to reach the relentlessly online communities of youth, both in Saudi Arabia and around the world, the crafting of narratives has been at the heart of the rebranding of the SPL. Speaking as the new season kicked off to a wave of global interest in August 2023, Carlo Nohra, the chief operating officer, described the SPL as "experiential" in which the stars who had arrived in the summer transfer window, were figures "in a world of digital entertainment" that "many sports struggle to understand."²⁹ It was thus little surprise when a Netflix series, entitled *Saudi Pro League: Kickoff*, was released in November 2024, in the runup to the confirmation of the Kingdom as host of the 2034 FIFA World Cup. Six episodes charted the "new dawn" in 2023 and documented the season that followed in 2023–24.³⁰

As the way fans consumed sport evolved, the celebrity-led approach taken by the Saudi Pro League was, for the *New York Times*, "much quicker, and much easier, to use a competition to generate digestible, fun-size content, the sort that can be quickly and easily shared on Instagram and TikTok."³¹ This was evident in the narrative arc of the Netflix series, as individual episodes followed each of the "PIF-4" clubs, plus Steven Gerrard's Al-Ettifaq, and focused on an international star and an up-and-coming Saudi player. Separately, in 2023, *The Athletic* reported that "One person close to the SPL believes that getting players with large social-media followings (…) to post positive messages about Saudi Arabia and its league is far more powerful than getting people in other countries to watch their games live."³² Indeed, the Ronaldo effect lifted Al-Nassr's Instagram following from 823,000 in December 2022 to 22.4 million a year later, a following that Oliver Kay of *The Athletic* noted was "more than all but five clubs in the Premier League" and nearly as many as Aston Villa, Newcastle, and Tottenham put together.[33] By contrast, international ratings for SPL games were "anemic" and tiny in comparison to social media reach, with one televised game in 2024 involving Al-Nassr and Ronaldo reportedly attracting a French viewership of around 4000.[34]

Lionel Messi, Ronaldo's great rival, was already a brand ambassador for Visit Saudi with an agreement, signed in 2021, which included spending time in the Kingdom with his family, promoting Saudi Arabia on his social media accounts, especially to his half-billion-strong following on Instagram, and participating in annual tourism campaigns.[35] Messi's arrangement with Visit Saudi became newsworthy in May 2023 when he made a trip to the Kingdom that was unauthorized by his club, Paris Saint-Germain, which led to a two-week suspension and was swiftly followed by the news that he would depart at the end of the season.[36] The announcement of his impending departure from Paris triggered speculation that Messi would follow Ronaldo to Saudi Arabia, a move anticipated by many in the Kingdom as inevitable, but ultimately Messi chose to join Inter Miami in the U.S. with a tie-up to Apple part of the deal.[37] Messi later told a Spanish newspaper that "If it had been a question of money, I would have gone to Saudi Arabia or somewhere else, where they offered me a lot of money. My decision is not because of money."[38]

Rise of the PIF-4

Messi's choice of the U.S. over Saudi Arabia heightened the importance of signing additional high-profile players in the summer 2023 transfer window, to ensure that Ronaldo was not a one-off, as had been the case with Rivelino in 1978 when plans to sign Zico and other Brazilian stars fell through. Ahead of the opening of the window on 14 June came an announcement that the Public Investment Fund would acquire 75 percent ownership of Al-Hilal and Al-Nassr in Riyadh and Al-Ittihad and Al-Ahli in Jeddah. The remaining stake would be held by newly-created non-profit foundations, and the objective was to prepare the clubs for transfer to the private sector by unlocking new commercial and sponsorship opportunities, as well as new licensing and broadcasting agreements, including those in the digital domain.[39] For this reason, the move was described by Saudi officials as the first step in a multi-phased Sports Clubs Investment and Privatization Project (which was announced by Mohammed bin Salman), even though it appeared to many external observers to be more akin to an example of nationalization by bringing four of the biggest teams in Saudi Arabia under even closer state control, not least by giving them access to PIF's resources.[40]

By taking majority stakes in the four biggest clubs in Saudi Arabia, the PIF runs the risk of cementing a gap between the "big four" in the Saudi Pro League and the rest. Supporters of Al-Shabab, the third big club in Riyadh, responded with dismay that their team was not among those included in the PIF acquisition, despite being the fourth most successful side in Saudi history with their six titles, double the three of Al-Ahli. The fact that Al-Ahli had only just returned to the SPL after suffering a shock first relegation in 2021–22 compounded the sense of injustice felt by Al-Shabab fans, who expressed disappointment with the decision not to include the team on the PIF roster. However, there was a symmetry in acquiring two teams in Riyadh and two teams in Jeddah, as well as the historic inter-city "clasico" rivalry between Al-Hilal and Al-Ittihad which has been likened to the Saudi equivalent of the Real Madrid-Barcelona rivalry in Spain.[41]

The results of the new hierarchy of power in the SPL became clear in the 2023–24 season as Al-Hilal embarked upon a record-breaking run of 34 consecutive wins in an unbeaten domestic season, Al-Nassr and Al-Ahli finished in the top four, and only the defending champions, Al-Ittihad, underperformed, as they finished fifth, one place ahead of Steven Gerrard's Al-Ettifaq. The fact that Al-Shabab finished a distant eighth, 52 points behind Al-Hilal, gave credence to the frustration expressed by the club's president, Khalid Al Baltan, at the time of the PIF's exclusion of Al-Shabab from their majority acquisition of the "big four" in June 2023, when he had "wondered aloud how Al-Shabab was supposed to compete when Ronaldo's salary for one season is four times the size of his club's annual budget," and asked, rhetorically, "Am I expected to close that gap myself? My car is a small Japanese sedan, and I'm somehow expected to race against Lamborghinis and Ferraris. If I don't win then I'm bad? This is not logical."[42]

THE 2023 BREAKTHROUGH

In addition to the PIF's direct investment at the elite level of Saudi football, four other entities linked to PIF and the giga-projects invested in lower league clubs. Here, too, there was a discernible logic in matching the entities with the teams, as each appeared to be carefully planned around a geographical connection. Thus, Saudi Aramco acquired Al-Qadsiah, a Saudi First Division club from Al Khobar in the (oil-rich) Eastern Province, Al-Suqoor, a Saudi Second Division club from Tabuk in the northwest was taken over by and rebranded into Neom Sports Club, Al-Diriyah Club, also in the Saudi Second Division, were acquired by the Diriyah Gate Development Authority, while Al-Ula FC in the Saudi Third Division was transferred to the Royal Commission for Al-Ula. Performances on the pitch immediately improved, to the extent that the 2023–24 season that followed their transfer to key state-linked entities saw Al-Qadsiah, Neom, and Al-Ula crowned the champions of the Saudi First, Second, and Third Division, respectively.[43]

Neom, Diriyah, and Al Ula are central to tourism-related initiatives and linking them to local clubs is clever politics, especially as the teams began to ascend the league pyramid and, in the case of the heavy spending allocated to Al-Qadsiah for the 2024–25 season, attracted the former Borussia Dortmund and Arsenal star Pierre Emerick-Aubameyang as well as Nacho Fernandez, a Euro 2024 winner with Spain.[44] By the end of 2024, Al-Qadsiah were third in the SPL table, several points behind league leaders Al-Ittihad and Al-Hilal, but three points ahead of Ronaldo's Al-Nassr, and on track for their best season in three decades. Neom Sports Club, for its part, ended 2024 top of the First Division and looked poised (at the time of writing) to return to the top flight of Saudi football for only the second season in the club's (pre-rebrand) history. Meanwhile, Al-Diriyah Club bounced back from the disappointment of losing a promotion playoff at the end of the previous season to end 2024 eleven points ahead in Group B of the Second Division while Al-Ula lay in second place in Group A in a playoff spot against their Group B counterpart for promotion.[45]

Given the popularity of football and the strong allegiances that many fans develop for their teams, which is just as intense in Saudi Arabia as it is elsewhere, there is a risk that perceptions of a "two-tier" system, in which selective teams are favored with state resources, could become a source of grievance. The many arrests and lengthy terms of imprisonment meted out to critics since 2017 may blunt the impact of hard feelings and lead supporters to choose their words carefully, but the relative anonymity of crowd dynamics in mass gatherings could provide opportunities for the venting of frustrations, just as was seen in the criticism of senior football federation (and team) officials in the early 2010s. Elsewhere in the Middle East, stadiums and football crowds have become some of the few contested public spaces in the Arab world, particularly as state repression increased with the crushing of the Arab Spring uprisings in 2012.[46]

Evidence from another authoritarian setting, China, has shown the authorities to be concerned with tracking and pre-emptively blocking anything they judge to have the ability to spur collective action that could, if unchecked, bring people together and threaten the regime's hold on power.[47] In Saudi Arabia, the aftermath of a devastating flood in Jeddah in 2009, which left more than 100 people dead, showed the mobilizing ability of then-relatively-new forms of social media, as reports online contradicted official reports of the scale of the disaster and fueled growing public anger.[48] This is not to suggest that anything similar is necessarily likely to be triggered by disgruntled fans if footballing inequalities widen, not least because the penalties for speaking out are higher in the 2020s than they were in 2009. It is nevertheless an observation that Saudi Arabia is a country described (rightly so) as "football mad" and that passions kindled by the game may not always be bottled up, especially if they are seen to intersect with perceived fault-lines such as those between "haves" and "have-nots" or urban-rural and regional divides.[49]

Transfer window mayhem

The summer transfer window in 2023 ran from mid-June to early-September, and Saudi Arabia dominated the media coverage as virtually every big name seemed to be linked at one point or another with a move to the Kingdom. A combination of the rumor mill and the succession of players who decided to join the Saudi Pro League meant that Saudi Arabia became the great disruptor of European football during the window as clubs lost key players and had to rethink their plans for the new season. Although the biggest stars—Mohammed Salah of Liverpool and Kylian Mbappe of Paris Saint-Germain (as well as Messi) turned down eye-wateringly large offers from Saudi clubs, many others accepted. Among the highest profile were Karim Benzema, who left a glittering career at Real Madrid for Al-Ittihad; Riyad Mahrez, who moved from Champions League and serial Premier League winners Manchester City to Al-Ahli; and Neymar, the mercurial Brazilian who joined Al-Hilal from Paris Saint-Germain. Virtually every major team in Europe saw multiple first-team regulars move to Saudi Arabia, including Liverpool and Manchester City as well as Chelsea, for whom Saudi sales were a significant boost to the club's financial fair play return.[50]

Amid reports that the PIF-owned teams had a mandate to sign "a minimum of three world renowned players" per club on three-year contracts that would ensure they remained in the Kingdom until the 2026 World Cup, the frenetic activity established Saudi Arabia as the new destination in world football.[51] The case of Jordan Henderson, the Liverpool captain who left for Al-Ettifaq, stood out because his was the only the case of a marquee name moving to one of the non-PIF clubs outside the big four. Henderson also attracted significant criticism in the British media due to his high-profile support and advocacy for LGBTQ+ communities in (and beyond) football. In a lengthy interview with *The Athletic*, Henderson defended his decision to join Al-Ettifaq, managed by his former Liverpool teammate Steven Gerrard, by suggesting that "having someone with those views and values in Saudi Arabia is only a positive thing" and adding that "I felt as though, by myself not going, we can all bury our heads in the sand and criticize different cultures and different countries from afar. But then nothing's going to happen. Nothing's going to change."[52]

A rather blunter perspective was given by Michael Emenalo, the former technical director of Chelsea who oversaw the SPL's player recruitment strategy, who said of Henderson in August 2023, as the SPL season kicked off, that "I think he remains pro-gay rights" but went on to add that

> (…) I'm pro having a little bit of fun every once in a while but I'm also much more pro respecting the cultures of every country because

I have done that everywhere that I have lived and I have never seen one country with the same culture as the other, there's always something different. In some countries you can drink publicly but it has to be in a brown paper bag and in others you can do this inside your home or not at all. It is what it is.⁵³

Emenalo went on to add that "We have to demolish some of these very outrageous narratives out there that there is something wrong with the Saudi league or with the Kingdom of Saudi Arabia."⁵⁴ Somewhat bombastically, Emenalo also claimed that "The league would like to have all the top players. And I think it is something that will be at the heart of this strategy. In a couple of years, in a few short years, this will become a league for exceptional players only."⁵⁵ Emenalo had reportedly been the first choice for director of football at Newcastle after the PIF-led takeover in October 2021, and had traveled to Saudi Arabia for talks with the new ownership but rejected an offer "after the club could not match his ambitious plans."⁵⁶ Two years later, ensconced in his new role, Emenalo's confidence in the SPL project was matched by Ronaldo, who sought to take credit for the influx of talent, as he used a press conference while on international duty with the Portuguese national team in September 2023 to claim that "As I said six months ago—and back then everybody thought I was crazy—now it's normal to play in the Saudi league. I knew this was going to happen. I was the pioneer of all that and feel very proud of it."⁵⁷

Among the tasks entrusted to Emenalo was the Player Acquisition Center of Excellence (PACE) program which was launched by the SPL in July 2023. PACE was intended to connect the SPL with the clubs "through a step-by-step process for foreign player acquisition that includes squad mapping, budget allocations, negotiations, and transactions."⁵⁸ In May 2024, Saad Al Lazeez the Saudi executive who took over as (interim) CEO of the SPL from Garry Cook,⁵⁹ the former CEO of Manchester City who left the post in June 2023 after just five months, explained how the process of acquiring foreign players functioned in practice:

> (…) The process always starts ahead of every transfer window by allocating budget. I would like to stress two things: budget allocation

THE 2023 BREAKTHROUGH

depends on a lot of variables available to us, and all 18 clubs are notified in advance about the allocated budgets to them through their official representatives.

After that, we communicate with the clubs, sit with them to understand their needs and draw a road map identifying their technical requirements and priorities. The following step includes scouting targets and available players.

At PACE, we allow the clubs to get to know the players; we do not direct players to join any clubs and have never done that. The clubs choose the players and we document that through request forms signed by the clubs and both the technical and financial department of the SPL.

Once a player is selected and the green light was given to negotiate with them within the allocated budget, the club has the full freedom to negotiate the deal based on the player's market value and the assigned budget.[60]

A particular significance was attached to the recruitment of stars such as Benzema, Mahrez, and Sadio Mane, who all spoke of the religious significance to them as Muslims of playing in Saudi Arabia, custodian of the two holiest places in Islam in Mecca and Medina. On joining Al-Ittihad in Jeddah, the port-city that historically has been the "gateway to Mecca,"[61] Benzema stated that "because I am Muslim and it's a Muslim country, I've always wanted to live there. I've already been to Saudi Arabia. Most importantly, it's a Muslim country, it's beloved and it's beautiful."[62] For Mane, the Senegalese forward who scored the fastest hat-trick in Premier League history in 2015 when he was with Southampton and, with Liverpool, won the UEFA Champions League and the Golden Boot as top Premier League scorer in 2019, "my whole family was excited to come here, so it was not hard—it is important to my faith."[63] A senior Saudi football official explained the pursuit of Mohammed Salah "because he is overwhelmingly popular in the Arab world and in Europe" and the Egyptian superstar had performed Umrah in Mecca in 2019.[64]

Among them, the four clubs that were majority-owned by the PIF accounted for £680 million of the £750 million in transfer spending by Saudi teams during summer 2023 when Al-Hilal, Al-Ahli, and

Al-Nassr had three of the six highest net spends in the world, alongside Paris Saint-Germain, Chelsea, and Arsenal.[65] As Oliver Kay noted in *The Athletic*, this compared with Saudi teams' spending in the 2022 summer window, when the highest fee paid was £5.6 million for a Gabonese forward.[66] Deloitte's Sports Business Group tracked the spending of Saudi teams and concluded that the SPL had the second-highest net spend in the world after the English Premier League. Moreover, almost half the total transfer fees received by Premier League teams in 2023 came from sales to Saudi Arabia, and for two teams—Liverpool and Fulham—all their summer transfer receipts came from teams in the SPL.[67] Teams in Turkey also spent heavily in the summer of 2023 but attracted only a fraction of the attention paid to Saudi Arabia, in part because of the caliber of the players involved but also because of the wider Saudi moves into sport as a whole.[68]

The transfer activity in 2023 prompted comparisons to the NASL after Pele's arrival as well as the Chinese Super League in the mid-2010s, both of which provide cautionary examples which are examined in Chapter Seven. No fewer than 35 big name players moved to China between 2012 and 2019 on enormous salaries that, for a time in 2016 and 2017 had a similarly destabilizing impact on the European transfer market as Saudi Arabia had in 2023, when 37 of the 94 foreign arrivals in the SPL came from the "big five" European leagues of England, Spain, Italy, Germany, and France.[69] Chelsea manager Antonio Conte labeled China's strategy a "menace" after two of the team's players moved to China and a third, leading scorer Diego Costa, received an enormous offer, in a season, 2016–17, that saw Chelsea crowned Premier League champions for the second time in three years.[70] Arsene Wenger of Arsenal added that Chinese clubs "seem to have the financial power to lure every player from Europe" and added that "There is a very strong political desire in China to become a big player and we have to be worried."[71]

While Major League Soccer officials, flush with the success of luring Messi, dismissed the Saudi competition as little more than a repeat of the (by 2023 failed) Chinese experiment, the then coach of DC United, former Manchester United striker Wayne Rooney, was more circumspect as he said of the Saudi Pro League that "If it stands the test of time, it can grow. Or it can do what China did 10 years ago when they put big money in then faded away. It'll be really intriguing to see how it goes."⁷² Others observed that the SPL was replicating the early strategy of Premier League clubs in the mid-1990s in signing aging European stars such as Gianluca Vialli and Ruud Gullit, although players in their prime such as Jurgen Klinsmann and Dennis Bergkamp also moved to England at around the same time.⁷³ This was a theme picked up by Saudi Arabia's sports minister in his December 2023 interview with the BBC's sports editor, Dan Roan. Prince Abdulaziz bin Turki Al-Faisal noted pointedly that "the Premier League did that and that's how they started (…) nobody questioned them when they did it", although he acknowledged that "When we planned to develop the league we never thought that we would do it with such pace."⁷⁴

The 2023–24 Saudi Pro League kicked off on 11 August 2023 in a blaze of publicity as journalists and football fans around the world tuned in to see what all the fuss was about. Al-Ettifaq sprang a surprise as the team bounced back from an early goal from former Liverpool winger Sadio Mane to defeat a Ronaldo-less Al-Nassr 2–1 and give Steven Gerrard a win on his dugout debut. Ronaldo went on to break the league's scoring record with 35 goals, including four hat-tricks.⁷⁵ However, the gap between the big clubs and the rest of the league rapidly became apparent, in the quality of play and the numbers of spectators inside the stadiums. The biggest games attracted capacity crowds and produced memorable performances from the stars on offer, such as Al-Hilal's 4–3 win in Jeddah in the "Saudi clasico" against Al-Ittihad in October 2023, which saw £50 million striker Aleksandar Mitrovic net a hat-trick for the visitors.⁷⁶ Other games were far less well attended, with some attracting fewer than 1000 fans, including games featuring Henderson's Al-Ettifaq which were a far cry from the packed Anfield crowds he left behind. By the midway point of the season, average crowds across the SPL were under 10,000 per game, a figure comparable to English football's third tier, with two Al-Riyadh games attracting just 133 and 144 fans.⁷⁷

As the season progressed, signs emerged which suggested that the "experiential" element of the SPL was less than the sum of reality. Gestures such as getting the star players to don Saudi national dress for national day appeared somewhat contrived. While Karim Benzema bore a striking resemblance to Ibn Saud and Ronaldo appeared regal in his robes, Steven Gerrard looked like a character from the set of *Lawrence of Arabia*.[78] Playing conditions also proved a challenge in a season which ran from mid-August to late-May, with early- and end-of-season games taking place amid temperatures that approached 35 degrees centigrade and, especially for the teams on the east and west coasts, stifling humidity as well. In addition, facilities in some cases were sub-standard compared with those found in the major European leagues from which most of the foreign stars had become used to, although this was in part due to several stadiums undergoing renovation and expansion ahead of the hosting of the 2027 AFC Asian Cup.[79]

Other moves did not work out and were quickly reversed. Robbie Fowler, the talismanic former Liverpool striker who became manager of Aramco-owned Al-Qadsiah in the Saudi First Division, lasted barely three months and eight games before he was dismissed with the club unbeaten, and replaced by the ex-Real Madrid and Spain midfielder, Michel, a decision Fowler attributed to Al-Qadsiah having "a Spanish sporting director so I think the Spanish model sort of fits into what he wanted to do."[80] Regardless of the reasoning, the ability to attract managers of such profile, in Michel's case from Greek giants Olympiacos, spoke volumes about the ambition in Aramco's acquisition of a lower-league club. Fowler later used an interview with *The National* to claim that Al-Qadsiah had made "the wrong decision" in sacking him, and, recalling the quality of football, stated that "Not everyone's brilliant but the fact is that there's a little bit of greatness, a little bit of rawness I think is what makes the whole spectacle that little bit better."[81]

Henderson's abrupt departure from Al-Ettifaq during the midseason break in January 2024 was another indication that some of the arrivals were finding it difficult to adapt to their new surroundings, playing away from the limelight of the UEFA Champions League and often in stadiums barely half-full.[82] Reports in the British media suggested that Henderson had become disillusioned with the quality of play on the field as well as the life off it, despite the fact he was permitted to live in next-door Bahrain.[83] There was a considerable sense of *schadenfreude* in some of the coverage as well as an "I told you so" tone as, in the words of one journalist, "The money was overwhelming but he's been counting the cost ever since."[84] Elsewhere, Neymar

THE 2023 BREAKTHROUGH

played just five games for Al-Hilal before suffering a season-ending knee injury while playing for Brazil in a World Cup qualifier, while Benzema was reported to be unhappy at Al-Ittihad and caused fury when he returned 17 days late from a holiday break in Mauritius in January 2024, although speculation that he too would depart proved unfounded.[85] Another big summer arrival, Aymeric Laporte, was reported as telling Spanish media that many players were discontented, that the Saudis "have not made it easy for us", and that "Being honest, many of us have not only come here for the football," comments which the ex-Manchester City player claimed were mistranslated and taken out of context.[86]

2023 was the "big bang" that launched the Saudi Pro League onto the global football landscape and imprinted the Kingdom in the minds of football fans around the world. All the arrivals and speculation about who might be next generated an undeniable buzz that got people talking about Saudi Arabia in terms of football rather than human rights or the situation in Yemen after years of war. To an extent, such an outcome is consistent with the "sportswashing" label, and the following chapter examines the emergence of the term and its validity in the Saudi context. However, the evolution of the football project was deeper and more nuanced than critics suggested, and it is necessary to analyze the sharp uptick of Saudi engagement with football on their own terms, not only to put into context what happened in 2023 but also to chart the significance of developments going forward.

6

THE SPORTSWASHING DEBATE

The opening decades of the twenty-first century have seen a significant shift in the spread of hosts for major sporting events.[1] While the men's World Cup had alternated since its inception in 1930 between Europe and the Americas, 2002, 2010, and 2022 saw the tournament take place for the first time in Asia, Africa, and the Middle East, in Japan/South Korea, South Africa, and Qatar. Each of the so-called BRICS group of emerging powers hosted sports mega events in the decade after 2008 with Brazil hosting the 2014 World Cup and 2016 Summer Olympics, Russia the 2014 Winter Olympics and 2018 World Cup, and India the 2010 Commonwealth Games, in addition to China and the 2008 Summer Olympics (followed by the Winter Olympics in 2022) and South Africa's World Cup in 2010.[2] Following the successful 2024 Summer Olympics in Paris, the Games may not return to Europe until 2040 at the earliest, given the allocation of the 2028 and 2032 events to Los Angeles and Brisbane, respectively, and the likelihood of strong bids from Asian and Middle Eastern states, including Saudi Arabia and Qatar, for 2036.

Such variation reflected an interest in hosting mega events, in contrast to trends elsewhere where concerns over costs and disruption led cities in Europe and North America to withdraw from bidding processes after failing to gain public or political support or by losing citywide referenda.[3] Boston, Hamburg, and Budapest pulled bids for the 2024 Summer Olympics citing a lack of public backing, which Oslo and Munich had earlier done for the 2022 Winter Olympics for the same reason.[4] Back in 2013, FIFA's then Secretary-General, Jerome Valcke, controversially asserted that "less democracy is sometimes better for organizing a World Cup (…) When you have a very strong head of state who can decide, as maybe Putin can do in 2018 (…) that is easier for us organizers than a country such as Germany, where you have to negotiate at different levels."[5] That Valcke's comments contained more than a grain of truth was shown in October 2023 when FIFA President Gianni Infantino gave interested parties a little more than three weeks to register interest in bidding for the 2034 men's World Cup. Whereas Saudi officials immediately declared their intention to enter the race, it proved impossible for Football Australia to put all the various federal, state, and funding commitments in place on such an accelerated timeframe.[6]

A new term emerges

Sportswashing" is a comparatively new term and appears to have first been coined in a tweet in April 2012 in connection with a marathon in Jerusalem, before it resurfaced in 2015 ahead of Azerbaijan's hosting of the European Games. Often used pejoratively, the term was selected as "word of the year" in Norway in 2021.[7] The juxtaposition of the Winter Olympics in Beijing and the FIFA men's World Cup in Qatar at each end of the year meant that 2022 was labeled "the year of sportswashing" and "a great year for authoritarian regimes looking to cover up their atrocious human rights records."[8] In 2023, the Saudi-backed LIV Golf confrontation with the PGA Tour popularized the term in the U.S. and it featured prominently in a Senate Committee on Homeland Security and Government Affairs inquiry into the PGA Tour-LIV Golf agreement, with Senator Richard Blumenthal, a Democrat, declaring that "Today's hearing is about much more than a game of golf. It is about how a brutal, repressive regime can buy influence—indeed even take over—a cherished American institution simply to cleanse its public image."[9] A 2024 book by Miguel Delaney, chief football writer at the *Independent* newspaper in Britain (which, ironically, is part-owned by a Saudi investor[10]) is entitled *States of Play: How Sportswashing Took Over Football*.[11]

THE SPORTSWASHING DEBATE

An emerging academic literature has begun to critically examine the concept of sportswashing and go deeper than the often facile and casual way the phrase is used by critics of the globalization of sport in the twenty-first century, especially in the host locations of Olympic Games and World Cups. Jules Boykoff noted the "definitional imprecision" of a term "often applied solely to autocratic hosts" and observed that sportswashing "can emerge in both authoritarian and democratic political spaces" as officials "use mega-events to try to foment national prestige and to convey economic or political advancement."[12] Boykoff recalled how the George W. Bush administration used the 2002 Winter Olympics in Salt Lake City—the first mega-event after the 9/11 terrorist attacks on the U.S.—"to sportswash the terrorist attacks and to reassert technological and security dominance," with the American flag that had flown above the World Trade Center on 11 September 2001 solemnly carried into the stadium during the Opening Ceremony.[13]

Boykoff (and others) thus drew attention to the internal as well as external aspects of sports policy, and the importance of domestic (rather than purely international) audiences in certain circumstances. A key example was the 2014 Winter Olympics in Sochi, which "were designed above all as a source of domestic soft power rather than simply as an external 'signaling' exercise" by the Putin regime in Russia.[14] Putin used the Sochi Games to boost Russian nationalism, as well as his own popularity, and armed pro-Russian groups entered Crimea and seized government buildings just four days after the Games ended.[15] Almost exactly eight years later, an almost identical scenario unfolded, as Putin ordered the full-scale Russian invasion of Ukraine in February 2022, four days (again) after the close of the Beijing Winter Olympics.[16] A focus on both the internal/domestic and external/international components of sports-related decision-making is more relevant to the Saudi case than blanket accusations of sportswashing.

Other scholars have also found fault with sportswashing as a frame of analysis. Michael Skey noted that sport has long "been used to pursue government objectives, engage foreign publics or promote a country on a more global scale" and agreed that "sportswashing is rarely, if ever, used outside discussions of the activities of non-Western states."[17] Skey added that "if sportswashing is to become a useful analytical concept, it needs to be applied to other parts of the world as well," as he questioned whether "an event like the 2012 London Olympics could ever be labeled as sportswashing, given that it arguably involved a former imperial power looking to raise its profile abroad."[18] At best, Skey argued that the label was useful "because it highlights the growing significance of image and reputation management in an era defined by intensifying global flows and, above all, the impact of digital technologies."[19] Nearly 20 years earlier, a volume of essays on sport and international relations noted presciently "the crucial role played by the global media in constructing positive and/or negative images and narratives" of major sports events.[20]

Stephen Crossley and Adam Woolf argued that "The term is slippery, deployed casually and extensively, and is hard to pin down" and observed that "Originally used to describe hosting of mega-events, the term is also now used to describe ownership and sponsorship arrangements [...] The focus has largely remained on the investors, rather than on the relations between investor and recipient."[21] Ian Jones, Andrew Adams, and Joanne Mayoh called for further study of its impact as "we need to know more about who supports and who resists" to "develop a full understanding of the role of sportswashing in contemporary society."[22] Moving the focus onto Saudi Arabia, Aaron Ettinger observed that the Kingdom's sports strategy "puts hard economic and political objectives first, while gains in soft power come later" and that "Saudi policy is laid out clearly and the intentions of its leadership is not difficult to decipher. What remains to be seen is whether Saudi sports diplomacy will continue to be politically profitable."[23]

Along with others, Ettinger cautioned that looking at Saudi (and wider Gulf) involvement in sport solely or even primarily through the prism of sportswashing was not only reductionist but also missed the bigger picture. Tom Taylor, Daniel Burdsey, and Nigel Jarvis argued that the term is often embraced uncritically and that it fails to provide a nuanced explanation for why Saudi Arabia and other Gulf States are investing so heavily in sport. As an example of the complexities missed by the label, they pointed out that members of the diaspora Yemeni community in South Shields near Newcastle criticized the PIF-led takeover (in view of the Saudi role in the Yemen war since 2015) of the club in 2021 even as the majority of the fanbase celebrated the new ownership.²⁴ Ironically, South Shields FC, the local club which plays in National League North, the sixth tier of English football, went on to host training sessions for the Saudi national team when the Green Falcons, managed by Italian legend Roberto Mancini, played two games in Newcastle in 2023.²⁵

There are times when sportswashing is more openly acknowledged as an objective. One example, identified by Natalie Koch, a political geographer who has worked extensively on the intersection of sport, geopolitics, and the Gulf States, is the Bahraini pro cycling team set up by Prince Nasser bin Hamad Al Khalifa, a younger son of King Hamad, in 2017, six years after mass protests rocked the country.²⁶ Initially formed as Bahrain-Merida and racing since 2021 as Team Bahrain Victorious, the team has enjoyed less success than UAE Team Emirates, which also entered pro cycling in 2017 and has since won three Tours de France and many other major races with Tadej Pogacar, the top-ranked male cyclist in the world.²⁷

Speaking to *VeloNews*, a specialist cycling publication, in early 2017, as the team launched, Prince Nasser stated that "Bahrain went through a lot, especially in the previous years, facing a lot of accusations against Bahrain" and recalled that, when he approached potential Bahraini sponsors, the response he received was that "The name of Bahrain is more important than our company on the jersey" and that "people should first know about Bahrain and the real intentions, and then when they ask about the companies. They want the flag to be out there and showcase Bahrain to the whole world."²⁸ For good measure, Prince Nasser added

> Let me be blunt and straightforward with you. At first, the sponsors did not even understand, they were like, 'A cycling team? Why? But those people who think about the indirect benefit to Bahrain and saw the vision that we saw, actually stayed committed to us. Slowly with time, they will understand the importance of this sport, the outcome of this work for Bahrain.²⁹

Bahrain's international image and domestic situation has improved since 2017. However, the process of recovery from the political nadir of the 2011 uprising was likely related far more to non-sporting reasons than to the relatively modest achievements of the cycling team that bears the country's name. While the prince's comments in 2017 indicate his awareness of the value of using sport to spread a positive image of Bahrain, it is not easy to measure the specific impact of such publicity either internally or externally. This was, in part, because the regime suppressed almost all opposition movements and jailed their leaders, but also because the passage of time meant that Bahrain slipped out of media interest, especially when compared to the international furor over the Formula One Bahrain Grand Prix in 2011 and 2012.[30]

Finally, it is not only nations but also corporations which have sought to use the appeal and visibility of sport to spread awareness of their brand, as seen most recently in the many tie-ups by cryptocurrencies and other digital assets with football clubs and other sports. Socios, a company that offers "fan tokens" in a financial ecosystem, replaced Pirelli as Inter Milan's shirt sponsor in 2021, ending a 26-year-association between the Italian tire manufacturer and the three-times European Cup/Champions League winners.[31] FTX, the crypto exchange whose implosion in 2022 sent its founder, Sam Bankman-Fried, to prison for 25 years, was especially active in its use of sport to market its brand and target its audience, whether by purchasing the naming rights to the Miami Heat basketball arena, running high-profile Super Bowl commercials, or obtaining endorsements from superstars such as Tom Brady and Steph Curry (as well as from celebrities in the acting and music worlds).[32] Binance, the other major cryptocurrency exchange whose own founder also served jail time, worked with Cristiano Ronaldo to promote non-fungible tokens, which led to a class-action lawsuit against Ronaldo in 2023.[33] In other sectors and sports, the chemical giant INEOS arguably engaged in a form of "washing" when it took over the sponsorship of Britain's leading pro cycling team in 2019 and put their name to the INEOS Britannia sailing team in the America's Cup.[34]

Is it sportswashing?

The shadow of "sportswashing" has loomed large over much of the coverage in Western media of developments in Saudi Arabia, especially with the intensity of the Kingdom's emergence onto the global football landscape in 2023, capped by FIFA's sudden announcement, in October that year, that the Kingdom would be the sole bidder to host the 2034 men's World Cup (see Chapter Eight). Even Mohammed bin Salman himself was asked for his thoughts on the term during his first major English-language television broadcast, with *Fox News* in September 2023. In response, the Crown Prince told Bret Baier, Fox's chief political anchor, that "If sports washing [is] going to increase my GDP by way of one percent, then I will continue doing sports washing. I don't care. One percent of growth of GDP from sport and I'm aiming for another one-and-a-half percent—call it whatever you want, we're going to get that one-and-a-half percent."[35] Sport, for Mohammed bin Salman, is part of the Vision 2030 economic project.

It is against this backdrop of broader "macro-level" trends that the leadership in Saudi Arabia has used sport, and especially football with its universal appeal, to support national programs. The internal objectives of the focus on football, and sport in general, are to contribute to economic diversification and promote a healthier society, for women as well as men, through greater participation. Princess Reema bint Bandar Al Saud, since 2019 the Saudi Ambassador to the U.S. (and sister of Prince Khalid bin Bandar Al Saud, the Saudi Ambassador to the U.K., as well as Prince Faisal bin Bandar, the Chairman of the Saudi Esports Federation) has been especially prominent in efforts to support the inclusion and greater involvement of Saudi women in sport.[36] Prior to her appointment as the Kingdom's first female Ambassador, Princess Reema had served as president of the Mass Participation Federation, an entity established as one of the social initiatives linked with Vision 2030.[37] Her cousin, Prince Abdulaziz bin Turki Al-Faisal, the Minister of Sport, also highlighted the need to engage the 70 percent of the Saudi population below the age of 30 as he batted away suggestions of sportswashing. However, the fact that he went on, in the same interview, to state that "We want to attract the world through sports" illustrated the keen appreciation of the value of sport in changing perceptions and shifting narratives—precisely the sort of reputation and image management that lies at the heart of allegations of sportswashing.[38]

An additional domestic objective, albeit one that is more intangible and difficult to measure, is tied to the emergence of a narrative of

Saudi nationalism which predates the rise of Mohammed bin Salman but has acquired a distinctive (and not always constructive) form since 2015.[39] Across the Gulf States, debates on national identity began to sharpen in the 2000s with the more visible celebrations of national days (which, in Saudi Arabia, was first observed only in 2005) and the construction of national museums.[40] Multiple reasons account for the reticence in adopting national narratives, including the persistence of strong supra- (religious) and sub-state (tribal) identities as well as the focus on state-building up until the 1980s. Also salient in the Saudi case was that the modern Kingdom was put together through force between 1902 and 1932, with Ibn Saud stating in the early 1930s that "Do not forget that there is not one among you whose father or brother or cousin we have not slain (…) it was by the sword that we have conquered you. And that same sword is above your heads […] We took you by the sword, and we shall keep you within your bounds by the sword."[41] It was only with the passing of that period of conquest out of living memory in the 2000s and 2010s that a more assertive approach to shaping national belonging fully evolved.[42]

Writing in 2023, Eman Alhussein, a Saudi researcher, noted the role of football in cementing nationalism as "the support Saudi Arabia enjoyed during the World Cup demonstrated the far-reaching influence of football, which has the power to strengthen national pride at home and increase soft power abroad."[43] It is this dual function of internal and external audience (as well as the difference between cause and effect) that is essential to going beyond claims that Saudis are simply "doing sportswashing" for image management, and to appreciating the nuanced approaches at play. Generating pride in national achievements and promoting participation in activities that resonate strongly among the overwhelmingly youthful Saudi population are public policy objectives, as is framing Saudi Arabia as a critical hub of connectivity and new geopolitical center of gravity. Using sport to make audiences worldwide aware of the (government-sanctioned) messages about the process of "reform" may also contribute, over time, to tapping into the flows of residents and visitors to populate the "giga-projects" and meet tourism targets.

It is undeniable that a considerable effect of Saudi investment in sport is that an international constituency has at least a superficial awareness that the country is changing and that some of the most prominent global names in the sports and entertainment sectors are excited by what they see. Even if the intent is motivated more by domestic considerations, the effect externally has been to move conversations around Saudi Arabia away from contentious issues and onto friendlier terrain, just as proponents of the sportswashing label suggest would happen. The internal and external levels are clearly and closely linked, which is why it is necessary to examine where and how they engage and interact. It is also worthwhile to note, as this chapter has done, that the Saudi leadership is not doing anything that others, including in the west, have not done before, and that the difference is perhaps more an issue of sheer scale and level of investment. Returning from his first visit to Saudi Arabia in December 2024, Matt Slater, a senior football news reporter for *The Athletic*, attracted a significant reader (and online) backlash after he acknowledged that, following his trip, 'I am now convinced many of us in the West are wrong about Saudi Arabia's huge recent investments in sport and entertainment simply being exercises in "sportswashing."'[44]

Chapter Five opened by paraphrasing Eric Hobsbawm in identifying "a long 2023" to describe the suddenness of the Saudi move into world football. In many of his writings, Hobsbawm emphasized the importance of sport in creating "badges of membership" as "power elites within most, if not all, Western nations capitalized on sport's entrenched popular appeal by selectively inventing sporting traditions."[45] In his 1990 book, *Nations and Nationalism since 1870*, Hobsbawm observed how

> (…) What has made sport so uniquely effective a medium for inculcating national feelings, at all events for males, is the ease with which even the least political or public individuals can identify with the nation as symbolized by young persons excelling at what practically every man wants, or at one time in life has wanted, to be good at. The imagined community of millions seems more real as a team of eleven named people. The individual, even the one who only cheers, becomes a symbol of his nation himself.[46]

The mobilizing power of sport is real enough, and was on full display in Doha in 2022. However, the Saudi moves into sport have only conformed in part to the sportswashing narrative, in that they helped to shift narratives about the Kingdom onto more friendly ground. Harnessing the mass appeal of elite sport also alerted a global audience to the notion that change is afoot and that the Saudi Arabia taking shape in the 2020s was not the Saudi Arabia of old or the Kingdom people thought they knew—regardless of the situation inside the country as the suppression of dissent continued with little apparent check. Few, if any, of the international stars who moved to the SPL had anything to say on issues such as the sentencing of young Saudi women to decades-long prison sentences for innocuous social media activity.[47] For all that a practical outcome of engaging so heavily with global sport has been precisely the sort of positive coverage that is consistent with the charges of sportswashing, Christopher Davidson, a longtime analyst of Gulf affairs, observed in 2023 that "Sportswashing is largely irrelevant to Saudi Arabia—there is little concern in Riyadh of what the rest of the world thinks about its human rights record."[48] The Saudi case is more nuanced than many of the more ardent advocates of sportswashing often appear to suggest, and to assess what the Kingdom is doing, and why, primarily through a polemical lens is limiting.[49]

The Newcastle exception

The above notwithstanding, the chapter concludes by examining an example of a Saudi investment in football which most closely fits with the sportswashing narrative in that it has little apparent link to domestic economic objectives, and for which external considerations appear to have been important. Newcastle United were second-last in the English Premier League in October 2021 and heading toward relegation when the club was acquired by a consortium led by the Public Investment Fund after a takeover that had taken more than a year to gain approval. The delay was caused by the Owners' and Directors' Test applied by the Premier League to prospective club owners and directors, and revolved around issues of separation and control between the Saudi state and the PIF, which formed 80 percent of the consortium alongside PCP Capital Partners and RB Sports & Media.[50] A further point of contention was evidence that figures in the Saudi state had expressed support for the pirating of rights held by beIN

THE SPORTSWASHING DEBATE

Sports to broadcast the Premier League across the Middle East and North Africa, as documented in Chapter One.[51]

The roots of the Saudi interest in acquiring Newcastle, a historic club with one of the most passionate fanbases in England but without a league championship since 1927 and whose last major trophy came in 1969, began in 2019 when Amanda Staveley pitched the idea to PIF Governor Yasir Al Rumayyan, reportedly on board a mega-yacht belonging to Mohammed bin Salman.[52] Staveley had risen to prominence a decade earlier when PCP Capital Partners worked closely with Abu Dhabi partners to invest in Barclays Bank during the global financial crisis in 2008, as well as in the purchase of Manchester City the same year.[53] In January 2018, Staveley had been linked to a separate bid for Newcastle (one of a total of three bids she made), but advisers to the club's unpopular owner, Mike Ashley, dismissed her as a "time waster" and claimed that "Attempts to reach a deal with Amanda Staveley and PCP have proved exhausting, frustrating and a complete waste of time."[54] Outreach resumed the following year, and by early 2020 the outlines of the consortium were in place, with the PIF and Al Rumayyan playing a central role, but the takeover stalled at the Owners' and Directors' Test between April 2020 and October 2021.[55]

To the chagrin of many in the human rights community, and to Jamal Khashoggi's fiancée, Hatice Cengiz, who called for the takeover to be rejected, the holdup was related more to the piracy of broadcast rights by beoutQ, especially after a World Trade Organization panel ruled in June 2020 that "beoutQ is operated by individuals or entities under the jurisdiction of Saudi Arabia."[56] Since its inception in 1992, the Premier League has based the explosive growth of its value and its brand on broadcast rights, initially in the U.K. but latterly all around the world. Any activity that threatened the rightsholders was therefore a challenge to the integrity of the Premier League as a product, and beIN lobbied for the takeover to be rejected.[57] It may not have been a coincidence that one day after the restoration of beIN's access to Saudi Arabia in October 2021, the Premier League announced that the acquisition of Newcastle had been approved.[58] Results took time to improve, with Newcastle finishing the 2021–22 season in eleventh place, just one spot higher than the previous season under the ownership of Ashley, but in 2022–23 the team surged to fourth place and secured a spot in the lucrative UEFA Champions League for the first time in twenty years.[59]

Several issues arising from the Saudi acquisition of Newcastle support the notion that this deal was a close approximation to allegations of sportswashing. Unlike LIV Golf, which could be justified by generating awareness among a constituency of "middle America" and potential investors and visitors of the changes underway in Saudi Arabia, this appeared less directly connected with Newcastle. The LIV investment also came to a head in 2022 and 2023, by which time the full-scale Russian invasion of Ukraine had had the effect of rehabilitating Mohammed bin Salman and Saudi Arabia in western eyes. However, the image of the Crown Prince and the Kingdom during 2020 and 2021 was still overshadowed by the murder of Jamal Khashoggi and the diplomatic isolation which followed. The sight of local politicians in northeast England, as well as senior figures in the British government, calling for the takeover to proceed in 2020 (when it looked as if it might fail) and thousands of jubilant Newcastle fans pouring into the streets to celebrate the eventual Saudi arrival in 2021 sent strong signals of support for the Kingdom at a difficult time.[60]

The Saudi-led takeover appeared to collapse in August 2020 when the PIF withdrew from the process, citing frustration with the length of time the Owners' and Directors' test was taking. In response, 96.7 percent of fans polled by the Newcastle United Supporters Trust declared themselves in favor of the team's acquisition, and more than 100,000 fans signed a petition calling on the authorities to explain the delay.[61] Chi Onwurah, the MP for Newcastle upon Tyne Central, wrote to the Premier League to demand an investigation into the takeover process, displaying a level of tacit support of Saudi Arabia not normally associated with the Labour Party and a former member of Jeremy Corbyn's shadow cabinet.[62] In total, more than 80 MPs expressed support for the takeover, including the Prime Minister, Boris Johnson, who reportedly received a private message from MBS in June 2020 which stated that "We expect the Premier League to reconsider and correct its wrong conclusion" and allegedly warned that British-Saudi relations would be at risk if this did not happen.[63] Correspondence later obtained by *The Athletic* under freedom of information requests showed that British government officials also engaged behind the scenes to try to facilitate a positive outcome to the takeover.[64]

Once the takeover was approved, it quickly became apparent that the new ownership was embraced by the Newcastle fanbase with a passion that drew comparisons with Manchester City's relationship with its Abu Dhabi owners after their purchase by Sheikh Mansour bin Zayed Al Nahyan in September 2008 (interestingly, the Qatari owners of Paris Saint-Germain have derived fewer soft power benefits from a far less reflexively loyal fanbase, despite a similar level of on-field success to Manchester City since 2011). The dizzying transformation of Manchester City from a middling team to serial Premier League winners and European champions in 2023 raised expectations that Newcastle would follow a similar path, albeit that financial fair play regulations introduced in the early 2010s made it more difficult to achieve instant success. There are parallels with Abu Dhabi and Manchester City, not least in the narrative of investing in regions left behind by the British government, with the urban redevelopment of East Manchester an example of the wider secondary benefits of closer economic ties to state-linked Gulf investment.[65] This potential was noted by the Foreign Office in 2020 as a cable from the British Ambassador in Saudi Arabia stated that "the PIF bid to acquire Newcastle is at the heart of their plans to invest in the north east."[66]

At the end of their first season under Saudi ownership, Newcastle unveiled a third kit that was described as being "remarkably similar to the kit worn by the Saudi national team," in a green-and-white configuration not previously associated with the club's colors.[67] The frequency with which the green and white kit was subsequently worn during away matches belied its status as the third choice of jersey, and it came as little surprise when a year later a fully green shirt (which bore a striking resemblance to the Saudi national team's away kit) became the shirt for away games. This opened the club to charges of literal washing of sports jerseys, as did an agreement which saw Sela, an events company owned by PIF, replace the Chinese gambling company Fun88 as team sponsor.[68] The Saudi national team also played two friendlies at St James' Park in September 2023, losing to South Korea and Costa Rica, albeit in front of paltry crowds of 3,000 and 5,000 people in the 52,000 capacity Newcastle stadium at St James' Park.

Subsequent developments illustrated the reach of football in normalizing acceptance of Saudi Arabia, as protests against the new owners largely faded away after the opening two post-takeover games, when posters of Khashoggi were prominently displayed, especially at a match at Crystal Palace in London. In early-2023, filings in the U.S. in the court battle between LIV Golf and the PGA Tour prompted a flurry of media interest in the U.K. about the "legally binding assurances" the Premier League received when it approved the takeover (but which are not public). The notion of an arms-length relationship between the PIF and the Saudi state appeared questionable after a submission to the court by lawyers acting for the PIF which described PIF as a "sovereign instrumentality of the Kingdom of Saudi Arabia" and Al Rumayyan as "a sitting minister of the Saudi government."[69] A ruling by the presiding judge in the U.S. District Court for the Northern District of California, that the PIF and Al Rumayyan submit to a deposition and document disclosure, threatened to shed light on the relationship between the PIF and LIV Golf that could have reopened interest in the assurances given to the Premier League in 2021 that PIF was separate from the Saudi state and that the latter would not control Newcastle.[70] However, the legal action between the PGA Tour and LIV Golf was dropped as part of the 2023 agreement to combine business operations.[71]

By and large, the ownership of Newcastle has been accepted by the English football establishment and celebrated by the Toon Army. Very quickly, the voices of dissent in much of the British media were replaced by a focus on the football as the team's fortunes on the pitch revived, to the extent that, by 2024, the Saudi ownership of Newcastle barely featured as an issue in mainstream coverage in Britain, even as the PIF shareholding rose to 85 percent with the departure of Staveley from the consortium in July 2024.[72] Staveley's exit, along with her husband and co-owner Mehrdad Ghodoussi, shocked many in the Newcastle fanbase as well as the manager, Eddie Howe, as the couple had been the public faces of the takeover and heavily involved in day-to-day operations, given the many other responsibilities held by Al Rumayyan, the club's chairman.[73] In an emotional interview with *The Athletic*, Staveley later recalled how "when we first took over (…) we did pretty much every job (…) we were doing the commercial stuff, the director of football stuff, the buying, PR, fan engagement. We were doing the role of chief executive and the Premier League stuff, constantly fighting while trying to build a relationship with other clubs."[74]

In 2025, Newcastle broke a 56-year run without a major trophy as they defeated runaway Premier League leaders Liverpool to win the League Cup. Much coverage in the U.K. focused on the wild celebrations of the Toon Army as they packed out Wembley Stadium and public spaces across London, such as Trafalgar Square, rather than on Yasir Al Rumayyan parading around the pitch with the cup in his hands. Three years of Saudi investment in the squad had transformed the club, and the win had a coming of age feeling about it, similar to Manchester City's first trophy in their Abu Dhabi era in 2011.[75] A fortnight later, more than 300,000 people braved the wintry elements and gathered on the Town Moor in Newcastle to celebrate the cup triumph, an experience many long-suffering fans thought might never come. Sela, an entertainment and hospitality company owned by the PIF which became Newcastle's shirt sponsor in 2023, contributed to the festivities with a drone show that featured animations of the Wembley goals.[76]

7

WILL VISION BECOME REALITY?

The pace of player signings and new announcements in 2023 was dizzying, and made Saudi Arabia the hottest topic of conversation among football fans the world over. European club owners and supporters cast nervous glances over their shoulders throughout the summer transfer window, in the knowledge that bids from the Kingdom, unshackled by financial fair play regulations imposed by national leagues or by UEFA, could seriously disrupt team planning ahead of the new season. Six months later, as the winter transfer window in January 2024 opened amid a very different regional backdrop with war raging between Israel and Hamas in Gaza, and Houthi militants from Yemen attacking shipping in the Red Sea, the mood was more reflective that transformative change would not happen instantaneously and was instead a process that would ebb and flow and take years rather than months to play out. In both the footballing and the broader context facing Saudi leaders, the breakneck speed and ambition of flagship developments began to be tempered by greater pragmatism and realism in policy and political approaches.

This chapter builds on the analysis of the giga-projects in Chapter Three and of football in Chapter Five to examine the likelihood of vision becoming reality and assess what success may look like in practice. Saudi Arabia is by no means the first country to attempt to transform its football landscape, and the fate of previous startup leagues in the United States (twice), Japan, and China offers lessons for the Saudi model. While acknowledging that the Saudi Pro League is not a startup, and that Saudi Arabia has far greater depth as a football nation than the country examples above, tensions between short-term desires for immediate breakthroughs and organic and sustainable longer-term growth are readily apparent. A similar dynamic is evident in the wider array of Vision 2030-related initiatives, which are likely to become more pronounced as 2030 draws closer, and how the leadership resolves these points of tension will be critical.

Historical and comparative parallels

Parallels with football breakthroughs elsewhere are inexact in the Saudi case because organized football in Saudi Arabia has existed for many decades, as noted in Chapter One, and there is less of a blank slate as there was, to varying extents, in North America in the 1960s, Japan in the 1990s, and China in the 2000s. Even in those three cases, the formation of professional leagues (the North American Soccer League, NASL, in 1968, the J-League in 1993, and the Chinese Super League, CSL, in 2004), built upon existing structures, with the Chinese Super League perhaps the closest approximation to the SPL in being primarily an exercise in rebranding and top-down demands for change (and which turned out to be transient).[1] To the extent that comparisons are useful, it is analyzing the balance between objectives and outcomes and the ease (or otherwise) of translating visions of change into practical reality, especially as the North American, Japanese, and Chinese leagues provide time horizons not yet available for study of the SPL.

The North American Soccer League, which lasted from 1968 to 1984, and the Chinese Super League, which was rebranded as such in 2004, are cautionary tales in the perils of star-driven approaches that sought instant success and which became overextended and ultimately unsustainable. By contrast, the J-League, which formed in 1993, and Major League Soccer (MLS), which launched in 1996, had greater durability, in part because they focused on organic growth, although in each case survival was far from assured and both leagues made mistakes in their early years which left them close to collapse. All four examples

WILL VISION BECOME REALITY?

are relevant to aspects of the Saudi Pro League and the broader Saudi investment into football, and the MLS experience in the U.S. (and Canada) indicates how some of the challenges may be overcome.

Football in the U.S. became popularized using the Victorian slang term of "soccer" as shorthand for association football to distinguish the game from the already-entrenched American version of football.[2] A lack of a central soccer authority and the sheer size of the United States meant that multiple leagues often coexisted alongside one another, peaking in the 1960s with no fewer than six separate league systems in the U.S. and Canada, mostly regional or semi-professional in nature.[3] NBC televised the 1966 World Cup final between England and West Germany, which drew very favorable ratings, and this boost to soccer led to the emergence in 1967 of two rival competitions, the National Professional Soccer League (NPSL) and the North American Soccer League, before they agreed to merge in 1968 under the NASL label.[4] However, only five of the initial 17 clubs continued into a second season, and the league struggled to survive with fewer than ten teams and crowds of less than 5000 up until 1974, with all the franchises losing money and relying on the munificence of their owners, such as Lamar Hunt, to keep them going.[5]

An era of rapid growth began in 1974, when NASL expanded to the west coast, tapping into a regional hotbed of enthusiasm for soccer, and accelerated in 1975 with the signing of the first foreign superstars. These included Portuguese legend Eusebio, who signed for the Boston Minutemen from Benfica, and, more importantly, Pele, whose arrival at the New York Cosmos, a team barely four years old and bottom of the league (just as Inter Miami were when Lionel Messi joined in 2023), caused a sensation. Pele's first game for Santos, in a crumbling stadium built by the New Deal-era Works Progress Administration, took place on a pitch which had been spray-painted green for the television cameras.[6] His arrival nevertheless transformed the NASL, and the fortunes of the New York Cosmos, who won the title in 1977, Pele's final season, by which time the team was regularly attracting more than 70,000 spectators to Giants Stadium.

Two fundamental flaws ultimately doomed the North American Soccer League. The first was that the "star-driven approach" proved to be overly reliant on Pele and unable to replace him after he retired.

In a sport which was still a niche for most Americans in the late-1970s, Pele alone possessed the name recognition and drawing power to break into the mainstream for viewers and advertisers. None of Johan Cruyff, Franz Beckenbauer, or George Best, the three "heirs" to Pele in the NASL, were able to fill his figurative boots, with Best appreciating the relative anonymity of Los Angeles that "took me out of the goldfish bowl at home."[7] When Bobby Moore, England's World Cup-winning captain in 1966, joined the San Antonio Thunder on loan from Fulham in 1976, one observer of the local soccer scene noted that "The acquisition of such ageing international talent may have improved the quality of play, but it had little impact at the gate, as the Thunder quickly discovered. Few Texans had heard of Bobby Moore, and if they had it was bound to be the one who played wide receiver for the Minnesota Vikings."[8] For Alan Rothenberg, the Chairman of the United States Soccer Federation whose roles including delivering the 1994 men's World Cup, 1999 women's World Cup, and creating MLS in 1996, a problem with NASL was that "It sold short-term curiosity. The novelty of seeing world-renowned imported stars soon wore off."[9]

The second flaw with the NASL model, interconnected with the star-driven approach, was that Pele's success at the Cosmos, both on and off the field, led other clubs (including the Cosmos) to sign more stars from Europe and South America in an attempt to replicate the approach. However, this "strategy became an arms race that was economic folly" as "it took just a few inflated contracts in an era where good attendances were in the 18,000 range and the local and national television contracts were yielding scant revenue for the league to bankrupt most clubs."[10] As a comparative study of the NASL and the MLS put it, "NASL's failure was not due to foreign player recruitment *per se* but to the fact that teams overspent to attract those players when the economics did not justify it."[11] A vicious cycle developed whereby declining interest in the league led sponsors and broadcasters to walk away, with ABC's decision in 1982 to end a lucrative television deal (agreed in 1979) hitting NASL finances especially hard. Seven clubs folded in 1982, and just nine teams competed in the final season in 1984, from a peak of 24 between 1978 and 1980.[12]

Organized football in China began in 1956 (one year before the launch of the King's Cup in Saudi Arabia) with the creation of a league with two divisions, but the disruptive impact of the Cultural Revolution held back further development, which only began with Deng Xiaoping's economic opening-up after 1978.[13] China also withdrew from FIFA (as well as the International Olympic Committee) in 1958, in protest at the recognition of Taiwan through the "Two Chinas" policy, and did not rejoin until 1979.[14] In the 1980s, state-owned enterprises were required to support Chinese teams, a move which had some parallels with the PIF (and PIF-associated companies') move on select Saudi clubs forty years later.[15] A first attempt to rebrand the league, in 1992, failed to make significant progress, as allegations of corrupt activity, including match fixing, plagued Chinese football until a further rebranding into the CSL in 2004.[16] During this period, paradoxically, China's national teams enjoyed their greatest success, with the women's team reaching the final of the Olympic tournament in 1996 and the World Cup in 1999, and the men's team qualifying for the 2002 World Cup for the first (and, so far, the only) time, but failing to win a game or score a goal.

Several of the underlying challenges in Chinese football continued into the CSL era, illustrating a degree of continuity that linked the pre- and post-2004 periods together. A process of professionalization began in 1999, when clubs were required to become independent companies, and income from sponsorship replaced state funding, albeit that many of the sponsoring companies had their own links to the state.[17] It took further government intervention, in 2009, to address ongoing issues of corruption, and the rise of Xi Jinping to political leadership in 2012, to kickstart the era of breakneck growth that put Chinese football temporarily on the global map.[18] Private investment from Chinese corporations, such as Wanda, Fosun, and Evergrande, was facilitated in 2011, as the private sector "demonstrated willingness to contribute to the state's football project" and "accrued financial, political, and symbolic capital through its participation."[19] President Xi announced his "three dreams" for China to participate in, host, and win the World Cup by 2050, in time for the centenary of the proclamation of the People's Republic in 1949, and unveiled a three-stage development plan to transform China into an Asian football superpower by 2030.[20]

The resulting boom and later bursting of the Chinese football bubble echoed the NASL era in some respects and foreshadowed the

Saudi approach in others. Heavy investment from leading Chinese corporations financed a spending spree in the mid-2010s that shook up transfer markets just as the SPL did in 2023. In 2015, Chinese clubs spent more on foreign player transactions than every other country in the Asian Football Confederation combined, a sum which more than doubled in 2016 and continued into the winter transfer window in January 2017.[21] That month, Argentinian striker Carlos Tevez became the highest-paid player in the world when he joined Shanghai Shenhua, but he only played 16 games before he returned to Boca Juniors, and later stated that "I was on vacation for seven months."[22] Following the signals sent by the government, Chinese corporations spent more than two billion euros on acquiring stakes and (in some cases) ownership of football clubs abroad, especially in Europe, including giants such as AC Milan and Inter Milan, and a share in the City Football Group. The CEO of Espanyol, which received Chinese investment in 2015, observed that "In China, when the Government moves something, everybody follows it; some because they see clearly and others because they want to be part of the trend."[23]

Those same signals from the authorities in China changed abruptly in 2017 and brought the era of big spending and foreign ownership to an abrupt halt. A backlash against the amounts of money reportedly being lavished on the imported stars, combined with frustration at the continuing poor performances of the national team, prompted a reassessment of strategy.[24] The number of foreign players allowed per team was reduced, and a 100 percent tax was imposed on overseas signings, with the revenues allocated to domestic football development, in a bid to curb "irrational acquisitions" and change course. Such reverse signals hit the corporations that had acquired clubs overseas as a wave of divestment occurred.[25] Two years later, the Covid-19 pandemic, which originated in China in late-2019 and prompted a three-year lockdown that was one of the strictest in the world, landed further blows on the clubs and the corporations, and led the government to hand back the hosting rights to the 2023 AFC Asian Championship, which took place in Qatar instead.[26] The difficulties at Suning and Evergrande hit Chinese football particularly hard, and led *The Athletic* to caution that "the reality" of the CSL was that "it was built on investment from big corporations and billionaires, who danced to the president's tune. And it was always a question of what would happen once that tune changed or the music stopped altogether."[27]

Both the CSL and the NASL illustrate the pitfalls of an approach that relied heavily on the import of star talent and proved to be unsustainable once the interest (and the financial resources) faded away. This is not to say that there was no connection with the domestic game, as a less heralded but ultimately significant legacy of the NASL was the interest it inspired in grassroots and women's football in the U.S.[28] For the CSL, Covid-19 was an unforeseen event, but the brakes had already been applied to the football project in the two years prior to the pandemic, and the status of the National Football Plan unveiled in 2016, with three phases (2016–20, 2021–30, and 2031–50) is unclear.[29] The challenges that befell the NASL after Pele's retirement in 1977 raises the question of how the Saudi Pro League will manage the transition into the eventual post-Ronaldo era, given that Ronaldo turned 38 shortly after he joined Al-Nassr in 2023. While it is certainly the case that there is far wider and deeper interest in football in Saudi Arabia in the 2020s than in the U.S. in the 1970s and early 1980s, the replacement of the first superstar, who has done so much to talk up the Saudi project, will be an indication of the nature of that project going forward.[30]

The J-League in Japan played its first season in 1993 and, like MLS in the United States, its launch was connected with a successful campaign to host the FIFA men's World Cup. Japan was seeking the 2002 tournament and forming a professional league to supplant the existing Japan Soccer League, whose teams represented corporations such as Mazda, Nissan, Mitsubishi, and Hitachi, was a key element of the bid.[31] Similar to Saudi Arabia a generation later when the bid for the 2034 World Cup came together (in 2023), Japan in the late-1980s (when thoughts of hosting a World Cup first began) only had three stadia that met FIFA standards of a venue able to hold 40,000 spectators, and only one football-specific stadium. Japanese officials also used the allocation of J-League teams, as well as World Cup stadia, "as a major tool of urban redevelopment and relocation away from the capital" and to promote strong regional networks.[32]

Initially, the new J-League also targeted aging foreign stars who were coming toward the end of their careers in Europe and South

America. The inaugural season kicked off with Gary Lineker, the top scorer in the 1986 World Cup, playing for Nagoya Grampus Eight (formerly Toyota), eschewing the chance to play in the newly-created Premier League in England as a result, and, more memorably, the Brazilian legend Zico, who came out of retirement to join Kashima Antlers (formerly Sumitomo) in 1991, and who scored a hat-trick against Grampus Eight in the opening game of the J-League two years later.[33] Jubilo Iwata (formerly Yamaha) signed Dunga a year after he captained Brazil to World Cup glory in 1994. Other arrivals in the opening years of the J-League included Pierre Littbarski, the attacking midfielder who played for West Germany in the 1982 and 1990 World Cup finals, Salvatore Schillaci, the charismatic Italian striker who shot from obscurity to win the Golden Boot at the 1990 World Cup, and Dragan Stojkovic, the Yugoslavian captain who achieved great success at Grampus Eight, where his managers included Arsene Wenger, whose departure for Arsenal in 1996 provoked a British newspaper to ask "Arsene who?"[34]

Financial pressures in the late-1990s put severe stress on the still-young J-League, with more than half its members experiencing significant losses, and the league as a whole struggling to break through a sporting landscape dominated by baseball, golf, and sumo wrestling.[35] The league benefited from government support from the Ministry of International Trade and Industry (as it then was called) and from a centralized system of control over marketing, sponsorships, and club licensing, which helped to restrain the free-for-all that had marked the NASL and which was later emulated, to an extent, by the MLS.[36] The award, in 1996, of the 2002 World Cup to co-hosts Japan and South Korea, and the success of the tournament itself, assisted in the process of commercializing interest in football in hitherto largely-untapped markets.[37] In addition, the J-League survived the retirement of its first star, Zico, who remained in Japan as technical director (and later manager) of Kashima Antlers before becoming national team coach in 2002.[38] Zico's decades-long affiliation with Japanese football (he returned to Kashima Antlers as technical director in 2018, where he remains) suggests a potential post-retirement path for Cristiano Ronaldo in Saudi Arabia.

Although only twelve years separated the demise of the NASL in 1984 from the launch of Major League Soccer in 1996, the latter was not an attempt to pick up where the former left off. The creation of a new professional league was part of the commitment made by the United States Soccer Federation to FIFA in connection with the successful bid to host the 1994 men's World Cup. Organizing the World Cup, which set records for the highest average attendance which remain unmatched, meant that MLS did not begin until 1996, rather than have the league up and running before the tournament, as originally envisaged.[39] MLS thus missed an opportunity to capitalize on the post-World Cup soccer buzz in the U.S. and to make inroads into a crowded sports landscape during the long Major League Baseball strike in 1994–95.[40]

While there was some continuity between the NASL and the MLS, both in individuals in leadership positions and in franchise owners, there was also a concerted effort to absorb lessons learned from the NASL era and to do things differently. This did not prevent the MLS from nearly folding in its opening decade when two oil tycoons, Philip Anschutz and Lamar Hunt, at one point held stakes in nine of the twelve clubs and averted the league's collapse.[41] A scion of the Hunt Oil Company, which developed the oil sector in Yemen in the 1980s, Lamar Hunt had owned the Dallas Tornado in the NASL and went on to own the Kansas City Wizards, Columbus Crew, and FC Dallas in the MLS.[42] Alan Rothenberg, too, had been part of an investor group that had owned the Los Angeles Aztecs in the NASL, which made him advocate for a strongly centralized system in the MLS to prevent "independent team owners flaunting their wealth." Don Garber, the long-serving Commissioner of MLS who oversaw the policy of gradual and sustainable expansion after his appointment in 1999, also noted pointedly that "We have been forced to create a system that would allow us to make long-term decisions and fight all of the pressures to do things for today because it was the pressures to do things for today that forced the NASL out of business."[43]

Despite the cautionary approach, MLS came close to collapse in 2001, just five years into existence. Clubs did not have their own soccer-specific stadiums and found it difficult to generate passion when games were played in cavernous NFL arenas in front of tens of thousands of empty or roped-off seats. Every team was losing money and many of the original investors sold out, so that by the end of the

2000 season the league's survival was at stake.⁴⁴ Interest revived after the U.S. unexpectedly reached the quarter-finals of the 2002 men's World Cup, and the MLS began a period of expansion in the mid-2000s which saw the number of franchises increase from 10 in the 2004 season to 29 in 2024, and a thirtieth team in 2025.⁴⁵ The unique single-entity ownership structure was modified by the introduction of designated player exemptions, which permitted the Los Angeles Galaxy to make headlines worldwide in 2007 by signing former England captain David Beckham from Real Madrid.⁴⁶ While Beckham's time in MLS was not acclaimed by all, he nevertheless provided the league with credibility as it embarked on a period of growth accompanied by a sustained rise in revenues, including from broadcasting, that ensured its survival. In fact, the rate of growth only increased after Beckham left MLS as a player in 2012, as seen in the soaring value of expansion fees for new franchises, which included Beckham's part ownership of Inter Miami.⁴⁷

Beckham thus remained closely involved with the MLS, just as Zico had done with the J-League in Japan, and the fact that Inter Miami was able to put together a package of incentives that outmatched Al-Hilal in the pursuit of Lionel Messi in 2023 signaled that the MLS was at least on par with the Saudi Pro League. On other metrics, the average attendance at MLS games rose above 22,000 for the first time in 2023, roughly the same as Al-Nassr's average (and below that of Al-Hilal), but nearly three times higher than the SPL-wide average of 8,300.⁴⁸

The fact that SPL attendances fell by nearly ten percent, even after all the summer signings, was a source of some embarrassment for Saudi football authorities, but the experience both of MLS and the J-League in Japan indicated that processes of change are not instantaneous and can take many years to come to fruition. Carlos Nohra, the SPL's Chief Operating Officer, acknowledged that stadiums were "a major contributing factor" for the low crowds, and injected a note of realism into the Saudi football project as he added that "nothing is going to change overnight, especially with the kind of facilities we have at the moment."⁴⁹ Nohra stated also that clubs would have to become more sustainable financially and that there would not be a repeat of the 2023 transfer frenzy, as "it is imperative to the clubs to try to act, they will have to offload players to free up some budget to be able to buy new ones."⁵⁰

WILL VISION BECOME REALITY?

Rhetoric and reality

The comments by Nohra, at a Bloomberg forum in Jeddah in March 2024, demonstrated that, for all the "experiential" components of the SPL and its emphasis on "digital entertainment," which he had laid out to visiting journalists at the season's start in August 2023, rhetoric and reality had diverged.[51] SPL attendances continued to fall in 2024–25, as they dropped under 8,000 in the opening four months of the season, considerably below the nearly 10,000 average in League One in England's third tier.[52] Nohra's remarks nevertheless chimed with signals that several of the broader "giga-projects" might be scaled back and that some of the more ambitious targets could be reassessed. Reports emerged in April 2024 which indicated that just 2.4 kilometers of The Line would open by 2030 (or even 2034, as further media reports in 2025 suggested), as against initial expectations that the city would stretch over 170 kilometers, a drawing back that paradoxically is likely to make the project more achievable in practice, given the budgetary and logistical challenges of The Line as originally conceived.[53] A separate target to double Riyadh's population to 15 million by 2030 also appeared to be under review, with a more realistic aim of reaching ten million residents by the end of the decade.[54] Mohammed Al Jadaan, the Minister of Finance, acknowledged that while 87 percent of 1064 initiatives launched under Vision 2030 were on track, "there are challenges obviously" and "We will change, we will adjust [or] extend some of the projects. We will downscale some of the projects [and] accelerate other[s]."[55] The arrest, in January 2024, of the CEO of the Royal Commission for Al Ula, over allegations of money laundering and abuse of authority, cast a shadow over one of the most ambitious cultural development and heritage projects in Saudi Arabia.[56]

Greater pragmatism about what is achievable, both in financial feasibility as well as timescale, is a shift in tone from the pronouncements made as the giga-projects were announced to fanfare in (and after) 2017, when 2030 was more than a decade away. Initial suggestions had been that the Qiddiya entertainment complex outside of Riyadh would be operational, at least in part, by 2023, while early indications that Neom would have a transnational focus on Egypt and

Jordan appear to have been pared back.[57] Tempering utopian visions and anchoring projects in realism has been a feature of realizing grandiose experiments elsewhere, such as Masdar City in Abu Dhabi, where plans for a zero-carbon new city were downsized and delayed, but did lead to tangible if less far-reaching progress.[58] An academic study of the Masdar plans, first unveiled in 2006, captured a sense of exasperation from a "public stakeholder" who told the author that "In the Gulf, they don't start small-scale, but huge—with megaprojects! This is a big mistake; because where is the added value for the country; the UAE in our case? Almost non-existent!"[59]

Other mega-developments in the region, such as Silk City in Kuwait, which were less nimble in adapting plans to changing circumstances, struggled to get off the drawing board, suggesting that the ability to rethink aspects of the giga-projects will in fact boost their chances of eventual delivery. The Saudi projects have been notable for their gargantuan scale which has raised doubts as to their practicality, even among would-be developers, in addition to a skeptical public, especially outside the Kingdom.[60] In May 2023, one of the architects working on The Line went off-script when asked by Neom's chief urban planning officer if the project was going to "make it or not" as he responded that "it's an interesting possibility. You know I think [they'll] get a bit of it done" but went on to criticize the proposed height of the linear city, as he added that "I'm going to speak honestly now, as long as you don't cut me off—I think higher than 500m [in height] is a bit stupid and unreasonable and all our engineer friends will tell you this."[61] Any course corrections will be discretely messaged, without the glitz of the original project announcements, to avoid loss of face, as seen in the above-noted comments by Carlos Nohra in the football context as well.

Aside from resetting expectations and realigning project developments, a practical challenge for moving ahead with all the initiatives will be prioritizing the many commitments made by the Saudi leadership and ensuring that hard external deadlines are met. This is especially pertinent in the sports and entertainment sector, given the emphasis placed on attracting mega-events as part of the tourism drive and to populate the giga-projects. Thus, Saudi Arabia is set to host the 2027 AFC Asian Cup in football and the 2029 Asian Winter

WILL VISION BECOME REALITY?

Games at the as-yet-unbuilt Trojena resort in Neom, while Riyadh will organize the World Expo in 2030 after the Kingdom campaigned hard to land a major event to cap the year on which Mohammed bin Salman has placed so much emphasis.[62] The Saudi Ambassador to the European Union, Haifa Al Jedea, told *Politico* in 2023 that "The Saudi today is not the Saudi of five years ago and Saudi in 2030 will not look like what we have today," and hosting the expo in that symbolic year may offset any disappointment felt at missing out on the centenary FIFA men's World Cup.[63] 2034, of course, will see the Saudis organize the men's World Cup, in addition to the Asian Games, the second-largest international sporting event after the Olympic Games.

An element of double-dipping will mean that several of the mega-events will be able to use the same venues and expand sequentially in a process of phased development; stadiums being built or redeveloped for the AFC Asian Cup in 2027 will likely feature in the 2034 World Cup as well. Stadia and other facilities are likely also to be utilized twice in 2034, first for the World Cup, if it takes place in January and early February, and then for the Asian Games in November and December that year. It is the 2029 Asian Winter Games that may prove most problematic in terms of creating facilities from scratch and overcoming the practical challenges in devising an outdoor winter resort at scale in just six years.[64]

Officials in Riyadh may therefore find themselves in a position of having to allocate finite resources across the many competing projects and initiatives. These are not only financial, given the ongoing reliance on domestic financing, the contraction of oil revenues as oil prices retreated from 2022 highs and Saudi Arabia cut production in 2023, and the end of benign macroeconomic conditions as interest rates in the U.S. and other developed economies rose, but also logistical.[65] Bottlenecks and capacity constraints in construction equipment may impose limits on what can be developed and how fast. Hard choices may need to be made about which projects proceed, and the external deadlines associated with mega-events are likely to be less negotiable than those initiatives under the control of PIF or its many subsidiary entities. Speaking in June 2024, Ali Shihabi, a Saudi banker and member of Neom's advisory board, stated that the project "was meant to be over ambitious, with the clear understanding that only a part of it would be delivered on time," adding that "Projects where we have specific deadlines to meet will get prioritized."[66]

In September 2024, a country report on Saudi Arabia, published by the International Monetary Fund as part of its regular Article IV consultation with member states, laid bare the scale of the challenge facing the authorities in Riyadh in completing the "top five giga projects funded by the PIF." Using figures supplied by the *Middle East Economic Digest's* Saudi Gigaprojects 2024 Report, the IMF noted that the value of awarded contracts by December 2023 across the five giga-projects was US$42 billion, a mere 6.2 percent of the projects' combined total planned budget of US$634 billion. By far the greatest gap between planned budget and awarded contracts was at Neom, where the US$24 billion of contracts awarded by the end of 2023 was less than five percent of the (then) planned budget of US$500 billion. Other giga-projects, such as Red Sea Global and Qiddiya, showed significantly higher rates of progress, but the sheer amount of the budgetary shortfall at Neom likely accounted for the reported scaling back of its size and scope.[67]

That said, the new focus on 2034 for the World Cup creates a new time horizon that lessens the emphasis on 2030 as the defining endpoint for all the giga-projects. An additional four years carves out a "buffer zone" for project delivery and facilitates a narrative of phased openings and gradual expansion that gives the authorities greater flexibility and room for maneuver. This creates space for the Saudi leadership to manage and recalibrate expectations that may have been raised too high by the glitziness and rhetorical grandiosity of the projects as they were first unveiled. Particularly in a setting where critical discussion of evolving government priorities carries risks, the readjustment of policy positions is often communicated by careful signaling and strategic messaging to media outlets.[68]

There remains a possibility that Saudi Arabia will follow the Qatari approach inasmuch as the emphasis on attracting big name players into the rebranded Qatar Stars League in the early- and mid-2000s was gradually superseded by a focus on hosting mega-events—beginning with the Asian Games in 2006 and continuing through the 2010s to organizing the first FIFA World Cup in the Middle East in 2022.[69] This resulted in a wide array of events of regional but also global scale taking place in Qatar, including world championships in handball (2015), cycling (2016), gymnastics (2018), and athletics (2019), in addition to mega-events such as the aforementioned AFC Asian Cup in 2023 and the 2027 FIBA Basketball World Cup which ensured a pipeline of post-2022 events as well.[70] Qatar nevertheless experienced a post-World Cup slowdown in economic activity that was only partially offset by heavy investment in expanding the country's gas infrastructure.[71] The arrival of foreign stars, such as Xavi Hernandez, who played for Al Sadd from 2015 to 2019 and managed the team until his return to FC Barcelona in 2021, became more of a rarity, even as the national men's team scaled unprecedented heights by winning back-to-back AFC Asian Cups in 2019 and on home turf in February 2024 (the delayed 2023 tournament handed back by China).[72]

A multi-pronged approach may yield tangible results for Saudi Arabia, if Ronaldo and others (including Messi as a tourism ambassador, as well as the LIV golfers) generate sufficient interest in (and awareness of) the changing Saudi landscape, both at home and abroad.[73] There is higher global recognition that something different, even exciting, is underway in Saudi Arabia and many fewer people would likely have been aware of Vision 2030 and the process of change had it not been for sport. If investment in football and other sports does eventually contribute to the diversification of domestic economic sectors, such as tourism, entertainment, and hospitality, then it will be deemed to have worked, as Mohammed bin Salman noted in his interview with *Fox News* in September 2023.[74] It is the metrics and the timeframe over which "success" will be judged that are more uncertain and may only become clear in retrospect. A troubling indicator in the shorter-term is the weakening of oil revenues that gathered pace in 2024, despite persistent attempts by OPEC+ members, led by Saudi Arabia, to cut output to keep prices high.[75]

Football and politics

What, therefore, can be ascertained from the opening salvo of the Saudi moves into football? The final chapter in this book assesses the prospects for the 2034 FIFA men's World Cup, for which the Kingdom controversially emerged as the only bidder in October

2023. Before the focus moves onto what lies ahead, this chapter ends with a set of observations that look back at lessons learned to date from the proactive and visible engagement with football and sport since 2015. Separate from the questions of economic and practical feasibility analyzed above, a range of political and security challenges presented themselves, as did the ways in which the authorities chose to respond (and may do again in the future).

Football is a game that mobilizes and taps into passionate fanbases. The upsides of associating a project with football are manifest and are by no means unique to Saudi Arabia or even to national leaders. However, football is also intensely political, and this has been demonstrated time and again across much of the Middle East and North Africa in authoritarian settings in Egypt, Iran, and Libya under Qaddafi, as well as in Turkey and Jordan, as noted in Chapter One.[76] Thus far, the Saudi Arabia of Mohammed bin Salman has ruthlessly policed any form of dissent, arresting dozens of people in multiple round-ups and imposing lengthy prison sentences for seemingly innocuous activities. Those affected included Loujain Al Hathloul, imprisoned after advocating for women's rights and interacting with foreign diplomats and journalists,[77] Salma Al Shehab, a PhD student at the University of Leeds and a young mother, sentenced to 27 years' imprisonment for following Twitter accounts and liking Tweets which "cause public unrest and destabilize civil and national security,"[78] and Manahel Al Otaibi, a fitness instructor sentenced to 11 years in jail for calling for the end of the guardianship system and appearing in public without an abaya, in part because, as she told German broadcaster DW in 2019, she believed that "based on what the crown prince has said (…) I have the right to choose what I want to wear, as long as it is respectable."[79]

A determination to maintain control and keep politics out of football has been evident in Saudi Arabia, with several incidents since 2023 illustrative of the authorities' zero-sum approach toward any sign of political activity at or around football games. On 29 December 2023, the Turkish Super Cup between Galatasaray, the Super Lig champions, and Fenerbahce, winners of the Turkish Cup, was set to take place at the Al-Awwal Park in Riyadh, the (renamed) home of Al-Nassr. This was to be the first Turkish Super Cup to be played in

WILL VISION BECOME REALITY?

Saudi Arabia, earlier editions having taken place in Germany (2006 to 2008) and Qatar (2021), and it built upon the hosting of Italian and Spanish Super Cups in Riyadh and Jeddah since 2018.[80] However, the game was called off at the very last minute, with fans already in the stadium, after the organizers, the Riyadh Season, stated that "the two teams did not adhere to what had been agreed upon" in terms of "presenting the sport without any slogans outside its scope."[81] What had happened was that fans of both Galatasaray and Fenerbahce had planned to bring banners to the game that featured quotes from Mustafa Kemal Ataturk to mark the centenary of the creation of the Republic of Turkey in 1923. In addition, the players had wanted to wear T-shirts with Ataturk's image as they entered the pitch, an act that was reportedly blocked by the Saudi organizers, and sparked a nationalist backlash in Turkey.[82]

In the wake of the cancellation of the Turkish Super Cup, suggestions abounded that one of the Ataturk slogans, "peace at home, peace in the world" (which Fenerbahce fans had wanted to display) was "in solidarity with victims of Israel's war on the besieged Gaza Strip," and a Turkish sports journalist alleged that Saudi officials "did not want to appear to be taking sides in the Palestine issue."[83] There was no clear link between the banner and developments in Gaza, but the claims and counterclaims highlighted the sensitivity of any slogan that appeared to draw attention to regional political events. Two weeks after the 7 October 2023 attack by Hamas and other Palestinian militants that killed more than 1,200 people in Israel, Al-Hilal shared a post on X which showed one of their players wearing a Palestinian *keffiyeh*. As the Gulf correspondent for the *New York Times* later reported, "the post received an outpouring of positive responses—until it was suddenly deleted," and "Saudi sports journalists who had reposted it soon made a series of apologies for mixing politics with sports, and pro-government accounts attacked them."[84]

A First Division match between Al-Safa Club and Al-Bukiryah (from Qassim in central Saudi Arabia) attracted the notice of *Human Rights Watch* in March 2024 as the organization reported that twelve football fans were given prison sentences ranging from six to twelve months, after footage of them singing "a Shia religious song celebrating the birth of Imam Ali" at the game in January was posted on social media.⁸⁵ Opposition activists claimed that more than 150 people had been summoned for questioning, and that the Ministry of Sport had dissolved the management board of Al-Safa Club, a team based in the Eastern Province.⁸⁶ The charges, under the 2007 Anti-Cybercrime Law which has come in for criticism for broad and vague definitions, included "undermining public order through the spirit of sectarian intolerance by passing sectarian content in places of public gathering and social strife."⁸⁷ Legacies of political and economic marginalization by the state against Saudi Shia communities, and their record of participation in oppositional activity and organized dissent, likely heightened the sensitivities of any clash of teams from two regions considered to be bastions of Shia and Sunni communities, respectively.⁸⁸

While the reported conviction of the twelve fans illustrated how the authorities adopt a security-first approach to any activity that could develop into a political challenge, other recent incidents in the Saudis' foray into sport have raised additional issues. A curious and still-largely unexplained delay to a charter flight carrying wrestlers and other WWE personnel back from a Crown Jewel event in Riyadh in November 2019 sparked feverish speculation about a dispute between organizers and Saudi officials.⁸⁹ More seriously, the 2022 Dakar Rally, which has been held in Saudi Arabia since 2020 after previously taking place in South America for a decade, was marred by an explosion which left a French driver badly injured. The blast hit a support car belonging to the Sodicar team shortly after it left the hotel in Jeddah for the race route, and sources close to the French investigation believed it was caused by an improvised explosive device.⁹⁰ Two months later, the second staging of the Saudi Arabian Grand Prix in Jeddah took place against a backdrop of smoke billowing from a nearby fuel depot struck by Houthi rebels in Yemen.⁹¹ At least one ballistic missile and ten bomb-laden drones were fired at the Aramco-owned facility about 20 miles from the track as the second practice session went ahead amid drivers' concerns for their security.⁹²

The optics of Saudi Arabia under Houthi attack, beamed to a global audience of Formula One viewers, demonstrated the Kingdom's vulnerability to regional and geopolitical developments that could derail the plans to attract millions of new visitors and residents. Whereas sport could be used by the authorities in Riyadh to spread a message

WILL VISION BECOME REALITY?

of change to a global audience, the flipside was that the images from Jeddah fed into narratives which associate the region with conflict and insecurity. The fact that the Grand Prix took place on the seventh anniversary of the Saudi-led military intervention in Yemen explained the timing of the Houthi attack on Jeddah in 2022 and highlighted the Saudis' exposure to blowback from decisions taken in that cavalier early period in Mohammed bin Salman's rise to authority, as noted in Chapter Two. Between 2015 and 2022, the Houthis launched nearly 1000 rocket, missile, and drone attacks against targets in Saudi Arabia, reaching as far as King Khalid International Airport in Riyadh in November 2017.[93] The number of cross-border attacks decreased sharply in 2020 and largely ceased altogether in April 2022, shortly after the Jeddah strike, when a fragile ceasefire was reached in Yemen which has endured.[94]

Memories of the many strikes on civilian and infrastructure targets, as well as the separate missile and drone attack on Saudi oil infrastructure in September 2019 which evaded air defense systems and temporarily knocked out half the Kingdom's production capacity, remain fresh.[95] It is for this reason that officials are mindful of the damage to Saudi Arabia's image as a relatively safe place to live, work, and do business which will be critical if the giga-projects are to be successful when they eventually open. The fact that Neom (and The Line) as well as luxury tourism initiatives such as Sindalah and Amaala, are located on the Kingdom's hitherto mostly-untapped Red Sea coastline, means they may be susceptible to the optics of conflict if the attacks on shipping in the Red Sea launched by the Houthis in response to the Israel-Gaza war in 2023–2024 continue or intensify.[96] Here, the concern is not so much that the developments are within range of Houthi missiles and drones, but more that the Red Sea becomes indelibly linked to conflict, political risk, and regional instability in the eyes of the target audience of would-be investors or tourists.

A particular challenge for Saudi Arabia which pertains directly to the giga-projects is that there is stiff regional competition, especially from Dubai, which has had a 25-year head-start in developing similar economic sectors focused on travel, tourism, and entertainment.[97] Aside from first-mover advantage, Dubai has built up considerable aspirational and soft power reserves that has made the city-emirate very popular with foreign tourists but also for residents seeking a hub in the region. This will not be easy to dislodge, and the authorities in Dubai have responded to the new regional competition by further liberalizing, on issues such as the availability of alcohol and the cohabitation of unmarried couples, which cement the lifestyle components of their appeal, and which may be difficult for the Saudis to replicate.[98] Similarly, the fact that both Jordan Henderson, during his time at Al-Ettifaq, and his manager, Steven Gerrard, chose to live in Bahrain, across the King Fahd Causeway from Dammam, was revealing, as Bahrain has based much of its appeal to expatriates around its more relaxed, Western-friendly vibe.[99] There was a certain irony in this, given the Saudi authorities' attempts to use sport to portray the Kingdom as an attractive alternative to Dubai or Manama in Bahrain, long favored destinations for many expats and Saudis alike.

The Saudi approach to football thus draws upon some of the lessons from the historical and comparative examples of leagues elsewhere which sought rapid and transformational change. Like the NASL, the SPL has attracted aging stars, including era-defining players as they wound down their careers. Similar to the Chinese Super League, there has been heavy signaling from state (and state-linked) entities and an initial burst of transfer activity that put the league on the global landscape. The J-League and MLS examples suggest that leagues can overcome early headwinds and achieve levels of organic growth. An early test of the SPL's durability will be the transition into the post-Ronaldo era, although the challenge is very different from the one the NASL faced in replacing Pele, who alone had name recognition in 1970s America. For the Saudi Pro League, with its digital and experiential focus, it may be difficult to maintain the "buzz" if Ronaldo and the other stars who signed in 2023 leave the stage. Attention may begin to shift from the quick wins of 2023 onto the decadelong preparations for the FIFA World Cup in 2034, to which this book now turns.

8

THE ROAD TO 2034

On 4 October 2023, the FIFA Council took the football world by surprise when it announced that the 2030 men's World Cup would be hosted by Spain, Portugal, and Morocco, along with one game apiece in Argentina, Uruguay, and Paraguay in a nod to the centenary of the first World Cup in 1930. With the spread of the tournament across Europe, Africa, and South America, and with the 2026 edition in North America, the FIFA announcement all but guaranteed that the 2034 event would take place in Asia.[1] FIFA stated that it would accept bids from the Oceania Football Confederation as well as the Asian Football Confederation, but within minutes the Saudi Arabian Football Federation declared its interest in bidding. Prince Abdulaziz bin Turki Al Faisal, the Minister of Sport, said that hosting the tournament "would help us achieve our dream of becoming a leading nation in world sport" and that the World Cup "is a natural next step in our football journey."[2] Two months later, by which time FIFA had confirmed Saudi Arabia as the sole bidder for 2034, Prince Abdulaziz brushed off speculation that FIFA had engineered the bidding process to favor a Saudi bid by asserting that "we were ready to do it and maybe others weren't."[3]

This final chapter begins with the FIFA decision to bring forward the hosting race for 2034 and generate an outcome whereby Saudi Arabia emerged as the only bidding nation for the 25th men's World

Cup, all but guaranteeing a second World Cup in the Gulf, twelve years after Qatar hosted the 2022 tournament. Links between FIFA leaders and senior Saudi officials deepened from 2018, and signs that the Kingdom would seek to host a World Cup grew to the extent that it became more a question of when, not if it would happen. An opening section details the process by which FIFA and Saudi Arabia grew closer, before a second section examines how the decadelong preparation cycle may evolve, especially in view of regional geopolitical developments. The book ends by assessing whether 2034 will become the "new 2030" and may therefore relieve the pressure of 2030 as the defining endpoint for Mohammed bin Salman's vision and give additional time to demonstrate tangible results in the giga-projects.

FIFA and Saudi Arabia

The opening game of the 2018 men's World Cup in Russia saw the hosts thrash Saudi Arabia 5–0 in front of a watching Mohammed bin Salman, seated alongside Vladimir Putin and FIFA President Gianni Infantino at the Luzhniki Stadium in Moscow. Four years later, Mohammed bin Salman was also present at the opening ceremony for the 2022 men's World Cup in Doha, where he sat alongside Infantino and Qatar's Emir, Sheikh Tamim bin Hamad Al Thani, with the strain of the Saudi blockade of Qatar a thing of the past.[4] Between 2018 and 2022, signs of Saudi prominence in the FIFA orbit proliferated, with Chapter One noting the apparent links with a 2018 consortium which offered to invest US$25 billion to create new global tournaments, which included an expanded 24-team Club World Cup originally meant to launch in 2021 but which was delayed until 2025.[5]

In May 2021, the Saudi football federation proposed a feasibility study on moving the World Cup from a four-year cycle to every two years. Infantino responded that the suggestion was "eloquent and detailed," and the FIFA Congress voted by 166 to 22 to review the situation.[6] Arsene Wenger, the former long-serving manager of Arsenal and now the head of global football development at FIFA, led a consultation exercise on redesigning the international calendar, and branded critics of the scheme as "basically emotional."[7] By contrast, Pep Guardiola, the Manchester City manager, drew attention to the increasing demands on players and teams, as he said, only half in jest, "Maybe we should ask UEFA and FIFA to extend a year. Maybe we could have 400 days a year."[8] In December 2022, as the World Cup in Qatar was underway, Wenger acknowledged that the proposal for a World Cup every two years was dead but added that more winter World Cups would "democratize football" by increasing the range of countries able to host the tournament outside of the summer months.[9]

Qatar's World Cup took place amid a crescendo of criticism, primarily from British and northern European media, that began with the award of the tournament to Doha in 2010 and focused initially on allegations of irregularities in the bid process.[10] As the event drew closer, attention shifted to the condition of the migrant workforce which built the stadia and associated infrastructure, as well as concerns for the safety of LGBTQ+ communities.[11] A *Guardian* article in 2021 which asserted that 6,500 workers may have died in the ten years since 2010 entered mainstream coverage so thoroughly that the figure became one of the most cited "facts" associated with the tournament among European and North American fans.[12] The drumbeats of doom were so deafening that scholars identified a concept of "soft disempowerment" at work as hosting the tournament arguably did more harm than good to Qatar's international image.[13]

And yet, the 2022 World Cup proved a great success on the pitch. Playing during the European season caused disruption to national leagues but meant that the footballers were fresh and at the peak of their form, and many clubs used the winter break to head to the UAE for warm weather training camps in the Gulf.[14] Morocco's run to the semifinals galvanized the Middle East and North Africa as they defeated European powerhouses Belgium, Spain, and Portugal, and the ways the "Global South" engaged with the tournament were a sharp rebuke to the negativity from many quarters of northern Europe. Publics in Latin America, Asia, and Africa, as well as throughout the Arab world, responded favorably to an event that was seen to be more inclusive and accessible than many other sports mega-events.[15] Moreover, the sight of fans from across the Gulf States mingling in Doha provided an opportunity to repair and move beyond the fractured intra-regional political tensions that had marred much of the post-Arab Spring decade since 2011. The tournament culminated in a mesmerizing final as Argentina defeated France on penalties after a pulsating 3–3 draw and a personal duel for the ages between Lionel Messi and Kylian Mbappe.[16]

Early rumors about a Saudi bid for the men's World Cup began to circulate in the runup to the 2022 tournament. A sense of regional one-upmanship with Qatar was evident in a comment attributed to an anonymous source "familiar with the PIF's strategy," who told the *Financial Times* in 2023 that "After the World Cup there's definitely been a sense of bullishness to invest in global sports. It was driven by the fact that Qatar did it so well, and Saudi Arabia's performance in the World Cup. There's been a noticeable sea change in how they look at global sports."[17] However, it is also the case that reporting by the *New York Times* has indicated that, in September 2020, Infantino used a meeting with the Italian Prime Minister to pitch the idea that Italy might join Saudi Arabia and Egypt in a trilateral bid for the 2030 World Cup.[18]

An Italian-Saudi-Egyptian bid for 2030 did not materialize, and media attention moved to speculation that Greece might join with the Saudis and Egyptians in the three-confederation tie-up. Relations between Saudi Arabia and Greece strengthened considerably in the late-2010s, in part as a regional alignment to counter Turkey, and in July 2022 Mohammed bin Salman set foot on European Union soil for the first time since the Khashoggi killing in 2018 when he made a two-day visit to Athens before going on to France.[19] The visit saw the signing of 17 bilateral agreements between Greece and Saudi Arabia, and came just two weeks after President Joe Biden's trip to Jeddah symbolized the return of the Crown Prince to the fold following his post-Khashoggi isolation in Western diplomatic circles. Saudi officials reportedly offered to underwrite the costs incurred in co-hosting a World Cup by Egypt and Greece on condition that 75 percent of the tournament take place in the Kingdom. The ongoing economic crisis in Egypt and the memories in Greece of the financial legacy of the 2004 Athens Olympics meant that neither country was likely to be able to afford anything on the scale of a 48-team World Cup without significant external backing.[20]

A second men's World Cup in the Gulf in the space of eight years might have been a step too far, even for FIFA, although the example of countries sharing a border hosting World Cups in such a concentrated timeframe was not unprecedented, with France and Germany doing so in 1998 and 2006, and, further back, Italy and France organizing the second and third tournaments in 1934 and 1938. Such an outcome would have reinforced the shift in the geopolitical landscape of football to the Gulf, already seen in the AFC Asian Cup which will have three successive tournaments take place in the region, in the UAE (2019), Qatar (2024), and Saudi Arabia (2027), a run that extends to four in five if Qatar 2011 is included. What was noteworthy about the persistent rumors of apparent Saudi interest in a three-way bid was that the notion of a joint bid with the UAE did not appear to be a possibility, despite the logistical sense of organizing a tournament across a contiguous territory spanning the two nations. That such a bid did not materialize may have reflected a sense of growing competitive rivalry between Saudi Arabia and the UAE, which flared into disputes at OPEC+ meetings in 2020 and 2021 and the sudden imposition in mid-2021 of Saudi tariffs on goods made in free zones in the Gulf, which disproportionately targeted the UAE.[21]

Other challenges to organizing a World Cup in Saudi Arabia in 2030, even with games taking place in other nations, also presented themselves. As of 2023, only two stadia in the Kingdom—the King Fahd Sports City in Riyadh and the King Abdullah Sports City in Jeddah—met FIFA's 40,000 capacity requirement, with only the latter exceeding the 60,000-capacity threshold for a semifinal, and none reaching the 80,000 capacity required by FIFA to host a final, although work was underway in other stadia.[22] The decision to expand the men's World Cup, from the 32 teams in Qatar in 2022 to 48 beginning in 2026, has meant an increased requirement for stadia as well, with sixteen venues being used in the 2026 event across the U.S., Canada, and Mexico. Even if only twelve are needed for a standalone Saudi World Cup, constructing, or expanding ten new stadia in a seven-year span, with all the competing demands for materials and other resources from the existing giga-projects, would have been a challenge for 2030. Qatar had faced a similar difficulty in its own World Cup preparations for 2022, with the initial plan for twelve stadia being revised down to eight (seven of which were newbuilds) in 2013, nine years ahead of the tournament.[23]

KINGDOM OF FOOTBALL

While 2030 has become a pivotal year for Mohammed bin Salman, by virtue of being a timestamp for his vision for Saudi Arabia, the year is also one of great significance for FIFA, as it marks the centenary of the first men's World Cup, which took place in Uruguay in July 1930. For this reason, the bidding for 2030 was hotly contested, albeit in conditions of some uncertainty over the process after FIFA responded to the flaws in the 2018 and 2022 bid races (announced simultaneously in 2010) by changing the process for 2026 (to a vote of all member associations rather than the 24 members of the Executive Committee) and leaving open the procedure for 2030.[24] The bidding for 2030 was seen to be a race between a UEFA-backed bid of Spain and Portugal and a South American bid by Argentina, Chile, Paraguay, and Uruguay. Ultimately, after plans for Ukraine to join the Iberian bid proved impractical, Morocco was added to the Spain-Portugal bid, after having failed with five individual bids for World Cups between 1994 and 2026.[25]

The announcement by the FIFA Council on 4 October 2023 that only one bid for 2030—the six-nation Iberia-Morocco-South America tie-up—would go forward for approval by a FIFA Congress in 2024 was accompanied by a statement that the bidding process for 2034 would take place concurrently.[26] Part of the reason why the decision took many observers of FIFA by surprise was that the concept of concurrent bid cycles was believed to have been discredited after the many improprieties that marred the 2010 votes for the World Cups in 2018 and 2022, and which had a seismic impact on FIFA as well.[27] Despite the fact that 2034 was eleven years away, the FIFA Council declared that countries in the Asian and Oceanian confederations which wished to bid for the tournament had until 31 October 2023—just twenty-seven days—to submit a formal expression of interest.[28] Lise Klaveness, the President of the Norwegian Football Association criticized the alterations to the bid process made by the FIFA Council as she claimed that

> (…) it has not been transparent and it has not been done in an accountable way. There has to be competition, there has to be a discussion. Everything seems suffocated, so that discussions go away. It's not good governance. The council made decisions on the day of the announcement of the bid procedures, it locked [in] a lot of things.[29]

THE ROAD TO 2034

A sense that stars were being aligned in support of a bid from Saudi Arabia was reinforced by an apparent amendment to FIFA's overview of hosting requirements, by which would-be bidders only had to propose a minimum of four, rather than seven, existing stadia.[30] Saudi officials also announced their intent to bid within minutes of the statement from the FIFA Council, leading some to speculate that they were not as blindsided by the announcement as others across the football world had been. It was to counter this perception that the Saudi sports minister stated, somewhat cryptically, that "I don't think there was any lack of transparency from FIFA. It was only that we were ready to do it and maybe others weren't. That's not our fault," as noted in the introduction to this chapter.[31] Australia had also expressed interest in bidding for 2034, having just co-hosted, with New Zealand, a very successful women's World Cup in the summer of 2023. Notwithstanding the fact that Australia and Saudi Arabia both belonged to the Asian Football Confederation, the AFC President, Sheikh Salman bin Ibrahim Al Khalifa, a member of the ruling family of neighboring Bahrain and Senior Vice-President of the FIFA Council, picked a side, as he said that "The entire Asian football family will stand united in support of the Kingdom of Saudi Arabia's momentous initiative, and we are committed to working closely with the global football family to ensure its success."[32]

Chapter Six noted how bids for sports mega-events in countries and cities with more robust and multilayered systems of governance and accountability were becoming increasingly difficult to sustain, which part explains the plethora of events which have taken place in more authoritarian settings. Such a dynamic was observable in October 2023, as it proved impractical for Australia to align all the stakeholders at city, regional, and national levels in time to meet the end-of-month FIFA-imposed deadline.[33] Australian officials also faced pressure from their counterparts across the AFC, and from Infantino himself, as they urged the Asian confederation to unite around a single bid.[34] By contrast, the Saudi intent to bid did not face equivalent obstacles as it enjoyed the political support of the country's leadership, and on 31 October 2023 the Kingdom was duly declared the host-in-waiting for the 2034 World Cup. The fact that Infantino made the announcement on his *Instagram* page underlined just how surreal a process the bid had been, especially by comparison to the conventional bidding process for previous World Cups.[35]

Speaking to the *Financial Times*, a 'person familiar with FIFA's inner workings' acknowledged that "All the pieces fell into place to make it inevitable that a Saudi Arabian bid would win," while the head of CONCACAF, the confederation for North and Central America and the Caribbean, defended the concentration of decision-making authority in the much smaller FIFA Council by stating that "In the corporate world, shareholders don't get asked to vote on those decisions, it's the board."[36] Another observer with insight into the decision-making process at FIFA added that "A lot of things have been swept aside to make this happen very quickly."[37] An independent assessment of the human rights implications of the Saudi bid, prepared by the Saudi arm of a U.K.-based multinational law firm for the Saudi Arabian Football Federation and submitted to FIFA, raised eyebrows among many in the human rights space. The report was criticized by international human rights groups for its narrow remit and for an apparent over-reliance on desk research, interviews with government officials, and lack of broader consultation.[38]

An Extraordinary FIFA Congress met virtually on 11 December 2024 to approve the allocation of the hosting rights to the 2030 and 2034 World Cups. Rather than ask the 211 associations to vote on the two unopposed bids, the FIFA leadership invited representatives of each association to approve the hosting decision by acclamation, with Infantino encouraging officials to raise their hands to clap "near their heads" so that they would be visible on the giant screen displayed behind him at FIFA headquarters in Zurich.[39] FIFA also announced that Saudi Arabia had received a bid evaluation score of 4.2 out of 5, a figure that exceeded the 4 out of 5 that the USA-Canada-Mexico bid had received for the 2026 tournament, and was comfortably ahead of a score of 3.7 that three established European football nations, Belgium, Germany, and the Netherlands, received in their unsuccessful joint bid for the 2027 FIFA Women's World Cup.[40]

The significance of the FIFA decision to allocate the 2034 men's World Cup to Saudi Arabia was not lost on Saudi officials, who linked the success of the "bid" to the regeneration of Vision 2030. Ibrahim Alkassim, the general secretary of the Saudi Football Association, drew a direct link between the World Cup and the development projects, as he stated that "If we go back to 2016, when the country launched Vision 2030, seven years later you can see the huge progress that happened here in Saudi Arabia." Yasser Al Misehal, the president of the federation, added that "The 2034 FIFA World Cup is our invitation to the world to witness Saudi Arabia's development, experience its culture and become part of its history."[41]

When Saudi officials submitted their official bid book to FIFA in July 2024, they emphasized that the Kingdom would be the first sole host of a 48-team World Cup, after the three-nation North American tournament in 2026 and the six-way split in 2030.[42] The bid outlined plans to construct eleven new stadia and refurbish four others, for a total of fifteen venues spread among Riyadh, with eight, Jeddah, with four, and one apiece in Al Khobar in the Eastern Province, Abha near the southern border with Yemen, and Neom in the northwest.[43] Keen observers of the Saudi scene noted that "No estimate of the cost of hosting the 2034 tournament is provided in the Saudi bid book submitted to FIFA" and suggested that "Stadium construction and transportation infrastructure upgrades could cost at least $150 billion."[44] Once additional costs, such as on hotel accommodation in the five host cities and investments, are added, the cost of hosting the 2034 World Cup could approach or, with overruns, exceed the $200 billion+ spent by Qatar for 2022.[45]

By becoming the host-designate for the 2034 World Cup, Saudi Arabia stole a march on China and President Xi's aforementioned "three dreams" of participating in, hosting, and ultimately winning the (men's) tournament by 2050.[46] Large Chinese corporations, such as Wanda, became FIFA sponsors and were on prominent display at the 2018 tournament in Russia and the 2022 edition in Qatar, but early hopes that China might bid for the World Cups of 2030 or 2034 did not materialize.[47] In March 2024, FIFA ended the fifteen-year FIFA Partner deal with Wanda, which had been signed in 2016 at the height of the Chinese football bubble and was set to run until 2030, reportedly over missed payments.[48] Two months later, Saudi Aramco was announced as FIFA's Major Worldwide Partner, "exclusive in the energy category," in an agreement for the 2026 and 2027 men's and women's World Cups.[49] Aramco thus became one of FIFA's six preeminent partners, alongside Adidas, Coca-Cola, Hyundai Kia, Qatar Airways, and Visa. The Aramco-FIFA tie-up was first reported in 2023, before the withdrawal of Wanda, but their contrasting fortunes were symbolic of the rise of Saudi Arabia and decline of China in world football.[50]

Saudi involvement in women's football (and sport more broadly) may be a harbinger of the degree to which the Kingdom's greater enmeshment in global sport becomes normalized, as happened with initial protests at Newcastle's new ownership which quickly fell away, or a target for resistance. An attempt by FIFA in early 2023 to engage Visit Saudi as a sponsor of the Women's World Cup in Australia and New Zealand sparked an outcry among competing teams and players. Key figures in women's football, including Emma Hayes, the manager of Chelsea and (from 2024) the U.S. national team, as well as Alex Morgan, the celebrated American forward and two-time world champion, voiced concern, with Morgan labeling the proposed partnership "bizarre" and that "Pretty much everyone has spoken out against that because, morally, it just doesn't make sense."[51] For his part, Infantino dismissed the backlash as "a storm in a teacup," stated that "FIFA is an organization of 211 countries, for us they are all the same," and claimed that "This doesn't seem to be a problem. But between a global organization like FIFA and Visit Saudi there would have been an issue. There is a double standard here, which I really don't understand."[52]

A similar pushback was evident in women's tennis, where the announcement that the season-ending WTA Finals would take place in Riyadh over three years to 2026 provoked a sharp rebuke from Chris Evert and Martina Navratilova, two of the most successful female players with 18 Grand Slam titles each. Setting aside their fabled on-court rivalry of the 1970s and 1980s, Evert and Navratilova penned an op-ed for the *Washington Post* entitled "We did not help build women's tennis for it to be exploited by Saudi Arabia."[53] Their intervention, which included the assertion that staging the WTA Finals in the Kingdom "is entirely incompatible with the spirit and purpose of women's tennis," triggered an unusually blunt response from Princess Reema bint Bandar Al Saud, the aforementioned Saudi Ambassador to the U.S., who lamented as "beyond disappointing" the "outdated stereotypes and western-centric views of our culture."[54] In the event, the inaugural WTA Finals held in December 2024 was won by Coco Gauff, who expressed the view that "sport can have a way to open doors" and that "I really do feel like in order to ignite change, you have to start little by little. That's how I've been taught growing up Black in America, knowing our history."[55]

As the examples above indicate, international narratives over issues such as the opportunities open to women in sport in Saudi Arabia remain flashpoints and reflect the historically restricted role of women in a society where they were only legally permitted to drive in 2018. It remains to be seen how quickly Saudi investment in developing the domestic infrastructure for women's football, and other sports, translates into greater external recognition of the steps being taken to expand participation. At the top level, the pace of change has certainly accelerated, with the Saudi Women's Premier League entering its third season in 2024–25, having expanded from eight to ten teams, and with digital and broadcasting deals in place.[56] In addition, the 2022–23 season saw the formation of a First Division, 2023–24 the creation of a cup competition, and 2024–25 the launch of a Second Division, while the women's national team took shape under the stewardship of the veteran German coach and technical director, Monika Staab.[57] However, while the Kingdom launched a bid in 2022 to host the 2026 AFC Women's Asian Cup, a year ahead of the men's tournament which will take place in Saudi Arabia, they withdrew the bid in February 2024, weeks before the hosting decision, which left Australia the sole remaining country in the race.[58]

In early 2025, the sports division of Neom, in partnership with the Asian Football Confederation, released a report entitled *Pioneering Change: Women's Football in Saudi Arabia*. The 36-page report provided an overview of investments into grassroots women's football as well as initiatives to promote accessibility and social impact, and, perhaps unsurprisingly, painted an optimistic picture of a rosy future.[59] Drawing on interviews with domestic stakeholders, the report provided a snapshot of a game in rapid development across all age groups as well as the entire football ecosystem and, quoting Nelson Mandela that "Sport has the power to change the world," included a section on 'the power of storytelling.'[60] In addition to tracking the growth in coaches, referees, and training centers, as well as the formation of

Under-20 and Under-17 leagues, the number of girls playing football in schools rose from 0 in 2021 to 70,000 in 2023.[61] Neom's involvement in the report signified that women's football has top-down support from the Saudi leadership, and a forthcoming book by Norwegian academic Charlotte Lysa, drawing on years of fieldwork in the Kingdom that long predated the 2020s focus on football, will provide much new material of value.[62]

Regional and geopolitical dimensions

One of the characteristics of the long gap between the award of the World Cup to Qatar, in 2010 and the event itself, in 2022, was the sheer level of geopolitical intrusion of regional developments which began almost as soon as Blatter pulled Qatar's name out of an envelope in Zurich. Just fifteen days later, a Tunisian street vendor named Mohamed Bouazizi self-immolated in protest at police heavy-handedness and triggered a wave of uprisings across much of the Middle East and North Africa.[63] Divergent policy responses to the Arab Spring, in which Qatar was perceived to be sympathetic to political transitions while Saudi Arabia and the UAE supported an authoritarian *status quo*, generated deep regional rifts which pitted Qatar against several regional states first in 2013–14 and again in 2017.[64] Tensions only subsided in January 2021 with the lifting of the blockade of Qatar, less than two years before the World Cup began, and at several points in the three-and-a-half year rift it seemed that the tournament itself was a target.[65]

Saudi Arabia also faced an eruption of regional geopolitical developments, even faster than Qatar in 2010. Fewer than three days elapsed between the 4 October FIFA announcement, with its heavy hosting hints, and the attack on Israel by Hamas and other militants which killed more than 1,200 people and sparked the longest and deadliest round of Israeli-Palestinian fighting since 1948.[66] While the Israel-Hamas war was concentrated on Gaza, where the level of death and devastation led some observers to speak of acts of genocide, the possibility that the conflict would escalate into a regional conflagration was real. Violence by Israeli settlers in the occupied West Bank, skirmishes with Hezbollah in southern Lebanon, and Houthi attacks from Yemen on shipping in the Red Sea all presented escalatory risks. Tit-for-tat strikes by Israel and Iran in April and October 2024 brought the region closer than ever to a direct war between the two adversaries which would leave Saudi Arabia and the other Gulf States caught squarely in the middle.[67]

Even prior to the 7 October attacks and the war in Gaza, the mantra of "de-risking" the region featured prominently in analyses of the shifts in Saudi foreign policy away from the more confrontational aspects of the mid- and late-2010s, as noted in Chapter Two. This has been evident in Yemen, where a backchannel between Saudi and Houthi representatives, facilitated and hosted by Oman, has complemented the ceasefire in place since 2022 and ended the cross-border missile and drone attacks.[68] It also explains the Saudi rapprochement with Iran, which began in the aftermath of the September 2019 attacks on oil installations which temporarily knocked out half the Kingdom's production facilities and were widely attributed to Iran, when officials reached out indirectly through intermediaries in Iraq, and held multiple rounds of dialog between 2020 and 2022.[69] When tensions between Iran and the U.S. soared after the killing of Qassim Soleimani, the Iranian Revolutionary Guard Corps commander, in an American drone strike in January 2020, the Saudi Deputy Minister of Defense, Prince Khalid bin Salman, a younger brother of the Crown Prince, traveled to the U.S. to make the case in person for de-escalation.[70]

The March 2023 agreement by Saudi Arabia and Iran to restore diplomatic relations (which had been cut in 2016) took many in Western capitals, especially in Washington, DC, by surprise, as attention had been focused instead on the prospects of a historic normalization of ties between Saudi Arabia and Israel.[71] Announcing the deal in Beijing and securing Chinese participation in the trilateral statement illustrated the premium Saudi officials now placed on addressing and resolving a key source of regional vulnerability, while for Iranian officials the agreement undercut U.S.-led attempts to isolate Teheran in the international community.[72] Regular, high-level communication between Saudi and Iranian officials was a factor in ensuring that the Israel-Hamas war in Gaza did not regionalize, with Iran's then-president Ebrahim Raisi making the first visit to the

Kingdom by an Iranian head of state in more than a decade when he attended a regional summit in Riyadh in November 2023 to discuss the situation in Gaza and its regional impact.[73]

Regional stability is needed to enable officials in Riyadh to focus on domestic issues as 2030 draws closer. 2023 marked the symbolic halfway point in the timeline between 2016, when Mohammed bin Salman launched Vision 2030, and the year itself, a year that has become so synonymous with the projects associated with the Crown Prince.[74] The challenge for Saudi authorities is that the series of grandiose project launches have raised expectations so high that there is a risk that deliverables which fall short may underwhelm target audiences and be an "I told you so" moment for skeptics and critics alike. There is thus a need to demonstrate visible progress as the giga-projects move from the drawing board into the implementation and delivery phase. Vision 2030 is about far more than just the giga-projects, and many of the domestic initiatives have already generated demonstrable outcomes, but such has been the global attention on the giga-projects that they are the ones which will be watched most closely internationally.

Houthi attacks on shipping in the Red Sea demonstrate the delicate balancing act facing Saudi Arabia from the regional and international fallout from the war in Gaza. The attacks began in November 2023 in response to the scenes of carnage from Gaza, and they reflect the fact that the Houthis have, for years, used anti-Israel, anti-Jewish, and anti-American slogans as part of their mobilizational rallying-cry.[75] Rather than directing drones and missiles at targets in Saudi Arabia, as they did between 2015 and 2022, however, the Houthis concentrated their fire on ships at sea, on the pretext that they were targeting vessels linked to Israel and the U.S., despite mounting evidence that the attacks were indiscriminate.[76] The attacks on shipping caused significant disruption to global supply chains and forced tankers carrying oil and gas, as well as many other dry cargo ships, to re-route around the Cape of Good Hope, and triggered a campaign of U.S.- and U.K.-led airstrikes on Houthi targets in Yemen in response.[77] Moreover, the association of the Red Sea with renewed conflict and with missile and drone attacks may hinder Saudi attempts to market the giga-projects along the coast, even if they are not specific targets in themselves.

THE ROAD TO 2034

Economic competition between Saudi Arabia and the UAE is less likely to develop into a political rupture or a security risk, but could provide a bellwether for the prospects of several initiatives, especially in travel and tourism, linked with Vision 2030 projects and the Saudi moves into football. A foretaste of potential pressures came in 2021 when the Saudi government announced that foreign companies wishing to do business with government agencies had to locate their headquarters in the Kingdom by 2024. In preparation for the implementation of the Regional Headquarters Program (RHQ), more than 180 licenses were issued for companies establishing such a base in the Kingdom in 2023 alone.[78] There was slower progress among banks, law firms, and other professional services companies, many of which already had located their regional hubs in the UAE, and the *Financial Times* reported in 2024 that a "senior UAE-based lawyer said Saudi agencies had told them 'they're happy for it to be a nameplate type of thing, to comply with the spirit of regulation,'" comments that are unlikely to have been received warmly in Riyadh.[79]

Chapter Four described how the Public Investment Fund launched Riyadh Air in 2023 as part of the plan to rapidly upgrade Saudi Arabia's connectivity to international markets. The new airline, which is set to begin flying in 2025, made an immediate statement as it placed a massive order with Boeing for 39 787 Dreamliners along with an option for 33 more as part of its plans to serve 100 destinations worldwide by 2030.[80] Given the heavy use of sponsorship by other Gulf airlines to gain and develop recognition, it was unsurprising that one of Riyadh Air's first acts was to become the main sponsor of Atletico Madrid.[81] Two decades earlier, speaking in the context of Emirates Airline's pioneering tie-up with Arsenal for the naming rights of their new stadium in 2006, the airline's chairman, Sheikh Ahmed bin Saeed Al Maktoum, had noted the branding value of "Sport sponsorship [which] provides an international platform to connect with our customers. We believe sponsorship is one of the best ways of getting closer to our customers. It allows us to share and support their interests and to build a personal relationship with them."[82]

The fortune (and visibility) of Riyadh Air, especially as a logo on football shirts, may therefore be an indicator of the ability of Saudi entities to challenge the first-mover advantage enjoyed by the UAE in so many of the sectors earmarked as priorities for Vision 2030 and the giga-projects. Newcastle's task of catching up to Abu Dhabi-owned Manchester City is another parable in this regard, albeit that financial fair play regulations have become more stringent in the time between the acquisition of Manchester City by Sheikh Mansour bin Zayed Al Nahyan in 2008 and 2021 that parallels are inexact. The same goes for Team Jayco-Alula in professional cycling, as it competes with UAE Team Emirates and its four-time Tour de France winner, Tadej Pogacar, and seeks to popularize and spread awareness of Al Ula as a tourist destination. The challenge for Saudi entities effectively operating in a startup phase is that they are promoting an unbuilt future whereas their Emirati competitors are building on more than two decades of market penetration.[83] Any scaling back of the planned projects or shift to a sequential process of development that tempers grandiosity with greater pragmatism may also have a secondary impact on related initiatives such as Riyadh Air or the tourism objectives, and could result in their downsizing as well.

2034 the new 2030?

The hype given to Vision 2030 and the extraordinarily ambitious nature of the giga-projects as they were unveiled by Mohammed bin Salman, has raised expectations, both within and beyond Saudi Arabia, not only of the scale of change but also of 2030 as the defining date against which results will be measured. Put simply, the task of turning vision into reality is proving more challenging (and expensive) than imagined, and officials may have boxed themselves into a corner by putting so much emphasis on 2030. While officials have acknowledged that Vision 2030 is a roadmap and that not every target will be reached, the flipside of over-promising is under-delivering, and the subtle shift in messaging in 2024 is an indication that officials are adjusting expectations to avoid or at least minimize any sense of falling short. Moreover, using the World Cup to establish a new horizon based around 2034 creates a breathing space for the authorities by adding four years to timeframes for fully operationalizing the key initiatives and projects.

Trying to predict the future is a thankless (and sometimes pointless) task, and there are so many internal and external variables that could

THE ROAD TO 2034

impinge upon developments in Saudi Arabia and the broader region over the decade to 2034. Just as few outside an inner circle of Hamas operatives could have known what lay in store on 4 October 2023, so were officials and analysts taken mostly by surprise by the eruption of violence, with the U.S. National Security Advisor, Jake Sullivan, (in)famously saying in late-September 2023 that "The Middle East region is quieter today than it has been in two decades."[84] The assumption that a new regional compact, buttressed by the Abraham Accords signed in 2020 between Israel and the UAE, Bahrain, and Morocco, was taking shape, has been found wanting by the near-total destruction of Gaza and reminder that the Israeli-Palestinian conflict remains the unresolved fault-line in regional politics.[85]

Rather than seeking to anticipate future geopolitical twists and turns, *Kingdom of Football* ends by analyzing the trend-lines and changes on the ground that are more immediately visible as markers of progression in the years ahead. In the space of five years, Saudi Arabia has caught up with, and arguably surpassed, Qatar and the UAE as a host of major sporting events, and established its centrality in the Gulf's emergence as a destination of choice for FIFA and the Asian confederation. Whereas FIFA named Qatar as the host for five 48-team men's Under-17 World Cups between 2025 and 2029 (as the previously biennial tournament became an annual event), the Asian Football Confederation announced that Saudi Arabia would host the first five editions of a revamped "elite-final" stage of the AFC Champions League, also between 2025 and 2029, featuring single-game quarter-finals, semi-finals, and final.[86] Such decisions reinforce perceptions of the Gulf as critical nodes in the "new" geopolitics of football as part of the move beyond European (and Western) centricity which has caused so much angst in various quarters.[87]

As noted previously, an immediate challenge for the Saudi Pro League will be managing Ronaldo's eventual retirement or departure from Al-Nassr and avoiding a Pele-like situation which faced the North American Soccer League in the late-1970s. Football has a stronger base in Saudi Arabia than in the U.S., but it is likely a matter of some concern to the Saudi authorities that fans have not flocked to stadia in greater numbers, and whether they do as facilities improve and new grounds are built will be instructive. Top-flight attendances in England took several years to take off after the Premier League rebranding in 1992, and many matches in the first few seasons took place in front of banks of empty seats, including when England hosted Euro 96 when some of the stadia were only about half-full for the group games.[88] As new and redeveloped stadiums in Saudi Arabia open in the runup to the 2027 AFC Asian Cup, tracking the trend of attendances will be a litmus test of whether Saudis are buying into the football "revolution."

Assessing the influx of players in the next several transfer windows will be another test of the durability of the Saudi investment in football and an indicator of whether 2023 was a breakthrough or a one-off. Saad Al Lazeez, the Vice Chairman of the SPL, stated in May 2024 that the league would focus on signing players under the age of 21 in a further sign of a change of course from the at-times free-for-all in 2023.[89] This is roughly what transpired during the summer 2024 transfer window which was about as far removed from the frenetic pace and activity of a year earlier as the window of 2023 differed from that of 2022. Transfer spending by Saudi Pro League clubs fell by more than two-thirds, from 950 million Euros in 2023 to about 300 million Euros, with the rate of decline even more precipitous among the "PIF-4" which cut their expenditure on players from 823 million Euros to 212 million Euros.[90] Far fewer big names arrived in the SPL, with an unnamed official identifying a new "strategic focus on youth players [which] allows us to build long-term success, competitiveness, and sustainability for both the leagues and the clubs."[91] Although the number of foreign players permitted per club was raised from eight to ten, a new regulation stipulated that two must have been born in 2003 or after, while the foreign player cap in the First Division was reduced from seven to five, "to accommodate Saudi players being released by the top-tier sides."[92]

The high number of foreign imports on SPL teams meant that opportunities for Saudi players to break through became more limited in 2023 and 2024. This coincided with a dip in performance for the national team after their heroics at the 2022 World Cup in Qatar, as the Green Falcons exited the 2024 AFC Asian Cup at the Round of 16 and made a sluggish start to the qualifiers for the 2026 World Cup. Speaking after a disappointing 1–1 draw at home to Indonesia in

September 2024, Roberto Mancini expressed frustration that "I have 20 players sitting on the bench in local matches" and called for greater coordination between the football federation and the clubs to ensure Saudi players got more game time.[93] A month later, Mancini was ousted as manager after little more than a year in charge, and by the end of 2024, the team lay in fourth place in their six-team group with just one win from their opening six qualifying games.[94]

The interest shown in 2023 in ensuring that Mohammed Salah, the most famous Arab and Muslim footballer in the world, ends his career in the Kingdom means that the post-Liverpool destination of the Egyptian captain will be a further test of whether the SPL can rival MLS and other leagues in attracting stars outside the major European leagues, especially beyond the 2026 World Cup. MLS may prove to be a useful comparator for the SPL across multiple data-points, such as the market value of clubs and franchises, revenue streams from broadcasting and commercial activities, and investment in player development programs, albeit from a very different starting-point in terms of state links and support. Moreover, were Salah to move to the SPL after his Liverpool contract runs out, it would give the Saudi league a major boost that could entice further high-profile arrivals in 2026 when the three-year contracts of the initial arrivals in 2023 expire, as well as a transition into the post-Ronaldo era.

The progress of the four PIF-majority-owned Saudi clubs (Al-Hilal and Al-Nassr in Riyadh, Al-Ittihad and Al-Ahli in Jeddah) as well as the four lower-league teams taken over by state-linked companies, will be watched not merely for their performance on the pitch but also off it. Al-Qadsiah secured immediate promotion to the Saudi Pro League in their first season under Aramco ownership and after dispensing with Robbie Fowler's services early in the campaign, and immediately embarked on a spending spree that brought big-name foreign stars to the little-known club with a largely unremarkable pre-2023 record.[95] How quickly Al-Qadsiah and the other teams linked to Al Ula, Neom, and Diriyah become competitive and attract further keynote players will be indicative of the levels of resources being directed at the giga-projects and their associated marketing and branding as they move toward opening. For the "PIF 4," the acquisition of 75 percent of their shares in 2023 was presented as a move toward privatization, and in 2021 the PIF board envisaged a five-year timeframe to exit investments in domestic companies.[96]

PIF may be able to generate sufficient value from the clubs to attract bids from private sector entities, but alternatively a halfway house may become semi-permanent if private bids are not forthcoming and the teams remain indefinitely under PIF control. When the PIF acquisition of majority shares in the four leading teams was announced in June 2023, it was noted that this was just the opening move in a process by which all eighteen Saudi Pro League teams would eventually be transferred into private ownership. Thus, in July 2024, the Ministry of Sport announced a second phase of the sports clubs Investment and Privatization Project and put an additional six clubs on the market, with a further eight set to follow in a later phase.[97] How quickly the other clubs in the SPL secure investment (and whether that investment comes from genuinely private entities or alternatively from state-linked groups, such as SABIC, which has been linked with Al-Ettifaq) will test the privatization drive that has repeatedly been defined as one of the central pillars of Vision 2030 and has been such a perennial feature in Saudi football since the early 2010s.

Football has always functioned as a microcosm for wider processes of social and economic change and political developments, and this is as true for Saudi Arabia as it is elsewhere. The resources poured into the rebranding of the SPL in 2023 and the linking of football, and sport, to Vision 2030 and the giga-projects are testament to their centrality, as is the role of the Public Investment Fund. It is for this reason that further developments in Saudi football, both in relation to the evolution of the SPL and the 2034 FIFA World Cup and other forms of global engagement, will provide insight into the broader dynamics at play. The fact that Saudi Arabia is a largely closed political society places added importance on the observation and tracking of trends that are inherently political in their nature, inasmuch as they represent the outcome of decisions that reflect leadership priorities as well as recalibration if and where this is deemed prudent.

Responses and reactions by Saudi citizens and officials thus repay watching as the projects go forward and are either implemented or reassessed. Unrest among local inhabitants of areas of northwestern Saudi Arabia being displaced by the development made global headlines in 2020 after one man, Abdul Rahim Al Huwaiti, was shot dead by the security forces.[98] Saudi authorities acknowledge that more than 6,000 people have been relocated, but an in-depth investigation in May 2024 by the BBC found that three villages "have been wiped off the map" in areas earmarked for the giga-project.[99] A local backlash was also observable in dozens of neighborhoods of Jeddah slated for demolition in 2022 as work began on the Jeddah Central redevelopment which had been launched by the Crown Prince in December 2021.[100] A report by *Amnesty International* indicated that more than half a million people could be displaced by the project carried out by the Jeddah Central Development Company, a company wholly-owned by PIF.[101]

Cost overruns and supply bottlenecks may create additional pressures for the Saudi authorities and for all the projects and other ventures associated with the PIF, with the cost of the winter resort at Trojena said to have doubled in two years, according to documents seen by the *Wall Street Journal*.[102] The fact that Trojena has a "hard" external deadline by virtue of its hosting the Asian Winter Games in 2029 will make it a case study of the transformative ventures underway across Saudi Arabia and the ability of policymakers to transition from plan to practice and deliver 'real' outcomes on the ground. So, too, does the unlikely, even fanciful, nature of the project to develop a winter resort on the Arabian Peninsula in an era of rapid climate change when even established resorts in the Alps face uncertain futures.[103] Any scaling back of the giga-projects to make them more realistic and practicable may be no bad thing, but an advantage of the Kingdom's plans for football is that there is already an established interest and demand.

Thus, the 2027 AFC Asian Cup will be a staging-post in the journey toward the 2034 World Cup for the phased redevelopment of existing stadia and the construction of new venues. Further, the expiry in 2026 of many of the initial three-year contracts for players who joined the SPL in 2023 will be an early test of the league's ability to continue to attract talent. Finally, the fact that Saudi-based players generally performed well for their national teams at the European Champions in 2024 suggests that joining the SPL is not as career-damaging as some doomsayers predicted in 2023. The longer impact on player development, domestic as well as foreign, will only become apparent over time, as the Saudi "experiment" evolves, as will the trajectory of the trends identified in *Kingdom of Football* on the broader economy of Saudi Arabia as Vision 2030 moves inexorably toward its defining year of political reckoning.

NOTES

INTRODUCTION

1. Larry Rohter, 'Saudis Hook Rivelino, Eye Other Brazilian Stars,' *Washington Post*, 20 August 1978.
2. Ibid.
3. James Dorsey, 'Saudi Arabia Milks Ronaldo, For What It's Worth,' *jamesdorsey.net*, 7 January 2023; 'Cristiano Ronaldo Admits He's Happy to be Playing in South Africa at Al Nassr Unveiling in Saudi Arabia' *The Independent*, 4 January 2023.
4. John Krzyzaniak, 'The Soft Power Strategy of Soccer Sponsorships,' *Soccer & Society*, 19(4), 2018, p. 509.
5. Rory Miller, *Desert Kingdoms to Global Powers: The Rise of the Arab Gulf* (New Haven: Yale University Press, 2016), p. 8.
6. Karen Elliott House, 'Saudi Arabia is Changing Fast,' *Wall Street Journal*, 4 November 2019.
7. Jules Boykoff, 'Toward a Theory of Sportswashing: Mega-Events, Soft Power, and Political Conflict,' *Sociology of Sport Journal*, 39, 2022, p. 343.
8. 'Assessing the Saudi Government's Role in the Killing of Jamal Khashoggi,' *Office of the Director of National Intelligence*, 11 February 2021.
9. See especially Paul Michael Brannagan and Danyel Reiche, *Qatar and the 2022 FIFA World Cup: Politics, Controversy, Change* (Cham: Palgrave Macmillan, 2022), Abdullah Al-Arian (ed.), *Football in the Middle East: State, Society, and the Beautiful Game* (London: Hurst & Co, 2022), Thomas Ross Griffin, 'National Identity, Social Legacy, and Qatar 2022: The Cultural Ramifications of FIFA's First Arab World Cup,' *Soccer & Society*, 20(7–8), 2019, and a special issue of the *Journal of Arabian Studies* on 'Qatar's World Cup Goals,' 13(1), 2023.
10. An excellent volume with a strong collection of essays on the Arab world being Fan Hong and Lu Zhouxiang (eds), *The Routledge Handbook of Sport in Asia* (Abingdon: Routledge, 2020).
11. Simon Chadwick and Paul Widdop, 'Sports Washing and the Gulf Region: Myth or Reality?', in Simon Chadwick, Paul Widdop, and Michael Goldman (eds), *The*

Geopolitical Economy of Sport: Power, Politics, Money, and the State (Abingdon: Routledge, 2023), p. 153.
12. Simon Hart, 'How Saudi Arabia is Plotting a Multi-Million-Dollar Football Revolution,' *I News*, 13 June 2018; Jimmy Hill, *The Jimmy Hill Story* (London: Hodder & Stoughton, 1998), Kindle edition, location 3239 of 4938.
13. Yousef Teclab, 'The American Dream: Saudi Arabia's Momentous 1994 World Cup Campaign,' *These Football Times*, 5 April 2018.
14. Isaac Chotiner, 'A Middle Eastern-Studies Professor on His Conversations with Mohammed bin Salman,' *New Yorker*, 8 April 2019.
15. Alexis Montambault Trudelle, 'The Public Investment Fund and Salman's State: The Political Drivers of Sovereign Wealth Management in Saudi Arabia,' *Review of International Political Economy*, 2022 (online), p. 1.
16. Margherita Stancati and Ahmed Al Omran, 'Saudi Arabia Approves Economic Reform Program,' *Wall Street Journal*, 25 April 2016.

1. A BRIEF HISTORY OF FOOTBALL IN SAUDI ARABIA

1. Joe Bernstein, 'Don Revie and UAE: 'Nation Had a Vision for Football',' *The National*, 16 December 2010.
2. Michael Tombs, 'UAE: A Journey to the Unknown at Italia 90,' *These Football Times*, 30 May 2015.
3. Jim Krane, *Energy Kingdoms: Oil and Political Survival in the Persian Gulf* (New York: Columbia University Press, 2019), p. 49.
4. Steffen Hertog, *Princes, Brokers, and Bureaucrats: Oil and the State in Saudi Arabia* (Ithaca: Cornell University Press, 2010), pp. 84–85.
5. Toby Craig Jones, *Desert Kingdom: How Oil and Water Forged Modern Saudi Arabia* (Cambridge: Harvard University Press, 2010), p. 1.
6. 'Saudi Iceberg Plan: Will It Hold Water?', *New York Times*, 27 July 1977.
7. 'An Alaskan Iceberg Upstages a Saudi Prince at Conference in Iowa,' *New York Times*, 7 October 1977.
8. Houchang Chehabi, 'The Politics of Football in Iran,' *Soccer & Society*, 7(2–3), 2006, pp. 236–37; Ian Henry, Mahfoud Amara, and Mansour Al Tauqi, 'Sport, Arab Nationalism and the Pan-Arab Games,' *International Review for the Sociology of Sport*, 38(3), 2003, p. 301.
9. Murat Yildiz, 'Mapping the "Sports Awakening": Toward a Regional History of Sports in the Middle East,' in Tamir Sorek and Danyel Reiche (eds), *Sport, Politics and Society in the Middle East* (Oxford: Oxford University Press, 2019), p. 39.
10. Ardia Yunda Fauzul and Basuni Imamuddin, 'The Development Dynamics of Football and its Influence on Conservatism Culture in Saudi Arabia,' *International Review of Humanities Studies*, 8(2), 2023, p. 5.
11. Ulrike Freitag, *A History of Jeddah: The Gate to Mecca in the Nineteenth and Twentieth Centuries* (Cambridge: Cambridge University Press, 2020), pp. 214–15.
12. Ibrahim Ghazi Alkandi, 'A Resource-Based View of Al-Hilal Football Club: Using a Qualitative Approach,' *Academy of Entrepreneurship Journal*, 27(4), 2021, p. 2.

13. Freitag, *History of Jeddah*, pp. 78–79.
14. Madawi Al Rasheed, *A History of Saudi Arabia* (Cambridge: Cambridge University Press (Cambridge: Cambridge University Press, 2002), pp. 79–80.
15. Rosie Bsheer, *Archive Wars: The Politics of History in Saudi Arabia* (Stanford: Stanford University Press, 2020), pp. 40–44.
16. Sarah Yizraeli, *Politics and Society in Saudi Arabia: The Crucial Years of Development, 1960–1982* (London: Hurst & Co., 2012), p. 270.
17. Mahfoud Amara, 'The Importance of Culture: Sport and Development in the Arab World—Between Tradition and Modernity,' in Barrie Houlihan and Mick Green (eds), *Routledge Handbook of Sports Development* (Abingdon: Routledge, 2011), p. 118.
18. Christian Bromberger, 'Football and the Authoritarian Regime in Iran,' *Soccer & Society*, 21(6), 2020, p. 692.
19. Amara, *Importance of Culture*, p. 118.
20. Youssef Ibrahim, 'Atop High Horses, Neighbors Again Cross Swords,' *New York Times*, 26 February 1990.
21. Rory Jones, 'Gulf Aims to Get Back on Stream,' *Wall Street Journal*, 1 May 2013; 'Saudi Royals Compete for Prominence in Sports Management,' Vol. 47 Issue 1175, 31 August 2023, p. 17.
22. Simon Inglis, *League Football and the Men Who Made It: The Official Centenary History of the Football League, 1888–1988* (London: Collins Willow, 1988), pp. 220–224.
23. Jimmy Hill, *The Jimmy Hill Story* (London: Hodder & Stoughton, 1998), Kindle edition, location 3267 of 4938.
24. Ibid., location 3326 of 4938.
25. Ryan Dabbs, 'The Shortlist to Manage Saudi Arabia's National Team in 1977 Included Bob Paisley, Bobby Robson and Brian Clough,' *Four Four Two*, 21 December 2022.
26. Simon Hart, 'How Saudi Arabia is Plotting a Multi-Million-Dollar Football Revolution,' *The Independent*, 13 June 2018.
27. 'Rivelino Changed Saudi Football,' *World Today*, 11 February 2023.
28. Jyoti Mann, 'A Prince Sent His Private Boeing 747 Jumbo Jet to Paris to Pick Up Soccer Star Neymar and Fly Him to Saudi Arabia,' *Business Insider*, 20 August 2023.
29. John Duerden, 'How Roberto Rivelino Raised the Bar for Saudi Football,' *Arab News*, 20 October 2020.
30. Thomas Hegghammer and Stephane Lacroix, 'Rejectionist Islamism in Saudi Arabia: The Story of Juhayman Al-'utaybi Revisited,' *International Journal of Middle East Studies*, 39(1), 2007, p. 113; Toby Craig Jones, 'Rebellion on the Saudi Periphery: Modernity, Marginalization, and the Shi'a Uprising of 1979,' *International Journal of Middle East Studies*, 38(2), 2006, p. 213.
31. Talal Mohammad, *Iranian-Saudi Rivalry Since 1979: In the Words of Kings and Clerics* (London: I.B. Tauris, 2023), pp. 44–45; Madawi Al Rasheed, *Muted Modernists: The Struggle over Divine Politics in Saudi Arabia* (London: Hurst & Co., 2015), pp. 32–33.
32. Ibrahim Almuhanna, *Oil Leaders: An Insider's Account of Four Decades of Saudi Arabia*

and OPEC's Global Energy Policy (New York: Columbia University Press, 2021), p. 29; Robert McNally, *Crude Volatility: The History and the Future of Boom-Bust Oil Prices* (New York: Columbia University Press, 2017), pp. 150–52.

33. Hertog, *Princes, Brokers, and Bureaucrats*, p. 118.
34. Rayhan Uddin, 'Al Nassr: The Past and Present of Ronaldo's New Saudi Team,' *Middle East Eye*, 3 January 2023.
35. 'Saint & Greavsie Show,' 18 August 1989, https://www.youtube.com/watch?v=z0AUe6ufCS4&t=159s.
36. Gary Ralston, 'Ex-SFA Chief Still Raging 20 Years on From Day Scotland were Cheated in a World Cup Final,' *Daily Record*, 19 June 2009.
37. Christopher Clarey, 'A Regional Power Looks to the World Stage,' *New York Times*, 17 May 1994.
38. William Gildea, ''The Desert Pele' Scores with Fans,' *Washington Post*, 17 May 1994.
39. Christopher Clarey, 'Arrested After Shining in '94 World Cup, Owairan Battles Back: A Hopeful Return for Saudi Star,' *International Herald Tribune*, 4 May 1998.
40. Yousef Teclab, 'The American Dream: Saudi Arabia's Momentous 1994 World Cup Campaign,' *These Football Times*, 5 April 2018.
41. Billy Munday, 'The Confederations Cup: An Odd Tournament Now Consigned to History,' *These Football Times*, 12 November 2021.
42. Simon Burnton, ''Quarantine Our Sad, Sick Game': How Heysel Tragedy Changed English Football,' *The Guardian*, 2 June 2020.
43. Fraser Wilson, 'The Day Rangers Defeated Everton in Dubai Despite Having SIX Goals Disallowed to Become Unofficial Champions of Britain,' *Daily Record*, 20 March 2018.
44. Charlotte Lysa, 'Globalized, Yet Local: Football Fandom in Qatar,' *Soccer & Society*, 22(7), 2021, p. 749.
45. Rook Campbell, 'Staging Globalization for National Projects: Global Sport Markets and Elite Athletic Transnational Labour in Qatar,' *International Review for the Sociology of Sport*, 46(1), 2010, p. 50; James Montague, 'Explained: Why Does Saudi Arabia Want to Buy Newcastle United?', *The Athletic*, 6 October 2021.
46. Kristian Coates Ulrichsen, *Qatar and the Gulf Crisis* (London: Hurst & Co., 2020), p. 241.
47. Oliver Kay, 'Manchester City and Abu Dhabi: Triumphant Passion Project or Geopolitical Powerplay?', *The Athletic*, 8 June 2023; Xavier Ginesta and Jordi de San Eugenio, 'The Use of Football as a Country Branding Strategy. Case Study: Qatar and the Catalan Sports Press,' *Communication & Sport*, 2(3), 2014, p. 238.
48. David Conn, 'From Desert Skyscrapers to Manchester City's Sky Blue Land of Riches,' *The Guardian*, 18 September 2009.
49. John Krzyzaniak, 'The Soft Power Strategy of Soccer Sponsorships,' *Soccer & Society*, 19(4), 2018, p. 509.
50. David Wearing, *AngloArabia: Why Gulf Wealth Matters to Britain*, Cambridge: Polity Press, 2018, pp. 148–49.

51. Tom Taylor, Daniel Burdsey, and Nigel Jarvis, 'A Critical Review on Sport and the Arabian Peninsula—the Current State of Play and Future Directions,' *International Journal of Sport Policy and Politics*, 15(2), 2023, p. 368.
52. Natalie Koch, 'The Geopolitics of Gulf Sport Sponsorship,' *Sport, Ethics and Philosophy*, 14(3), 2020, p. 355.
53. Alan Nixon, 'Saudi Prince Backs Out of Maine Road,' *The Independent*, 9 September 1996.
54. 'Manchester United Agree Strategic Partnership with Saudi Arabia,' *ESPN*, 19 October 2017; Philip Proudfoot and Ali Reda, 'The Gulf and the British Regional Divide,' Middle East Research and Information Project, *MERIP 304*, Fall 2022.
55. Chris O'Brien, 'Al Hilal Beat United on Money-Making Trip to Saudi,' *The Football Network*, 27 January 2008.
56. Khaled Qadi, 'Brazilian Star Bebeto Joins Ittihad Club,' Arab News, 5 September 2002.
57. 'Saudi Bid for Keane Falls Through,' *BBC News*, 30 November 2005.
58. Naveed Raja, 'Figo Leaves Everyone Guessing on Al Ittihad Deal,' *Gulf News*, 6 January 2007.
59. Dana Moukhallati, 'Senior Saudi Figures Accused of Bribery and Extortion,' *The National*, 6 November 2017.
60. Naif Muhammed, 'Ittihad Club President Mansour Al-Balawi Resigns,' *Arab News*, 25 November 2007.
61. 'Kallon's Saudi Deal Collapses,' *BBC Sport*, 28 November 2007; Samir Al-Saadi, 'Plot Thickens: Kallon Wants Public Apology, Al-Balawi Says He Was Forced to Resign,' *Arab News*, 30 November 2007.
62. Alon Raab, 'Soccer in the Middle East: An Introduction,' *Soccer & Society*, 13(5–6), 2012, p. 624; Dag Tuastad, 'From Football Riot to Revolution. The Political Role of Football in the Arab World,' *Soccer & Society*, 15(3), 2014, p. 380; Bromberger, Football and the Authoritarian Regime in Iran, p. 696; James Dorsey, 'The Politics of Indonesian and Turkish Soccer: A Comparative Analysis,' *Soccer & Society*, 14(5), 2013, p. 620.
63. Malik Al Abdeh, 'Rise and Decline of a Syrian Tribe,' *Arab Digest*, 21 March 2024.
64. John Blasing, 'Hegemonic Discourses Clash in the Stadium: Sport, Nationalism, and Globalization in Turkey,' *International Journal of Middle East Studies*, 51(3), 2019, p. 475.
65. Shahrzad Mohammadi, 'State Control and the Online Contestation of Iranian Female Spectators and Activists,' *Communication & Sport*, 8(4–5), 2020, p. 653.
66. Shawki El-Zatmah, 'From Terso into Ultras: the 2011 Egyptian Revolution and the Radicalization of the Soccer's Ultra-Fans,' *Soccer & Society*, 13(5–6), 2012, pp. 807–08.
67. Daghan Irak, '"Shoot Some Pepper Gas at Me!" Football Fans vs. Erdogan: Organized Politicization or Reactive Politics?', *Soccer & Society*, 19(3), 2018, pp. 400–01.
68. James Dorsey, *The Turbulent World of Middle East Soccer* (London: Hurst & Co., 2016), pp. 131–32.

69. Ibid. pp. 15–16; Maher Mezahi, 'A Study of Football Chants as Political Expression in the Algerian Hirak,' in Abdullah Al-Arian (ed.), *Football in the Middle East: State, Society, and the Beautiful Game* (London: Hurst & Co., 2022), pp. 92–94.
70. 'Where the Popular Will Matters: Football in Saudi Arabia,' *The Economist*, 31 May 2014.
71. 'Saudi Football Election "Example to Gulf States"—FIFA President,' *Al Arabiya*, 8 January 2013; Ali Humayun, 'Saudi Arabia, Football, and Faith's Role in a Revolution,' *The Athletic*, 2 August 2023.
72. Dorsey, *Turbulent World of Middle East Soccer*, p. 21.
73. James Dorsey, 'Saudi Soccer: A Game of Geopolitics and Religion, Not Just Sports,' *jamesdorsey.net*, 5 August 2023.
74. Jones, *Gulf Aims to Get Back on Stream*.
75. Andy Sambidge, 'Saudi Prince Buys 50% of Sheffield United,' *Arabian Business*, 3 September 2013.
76. 'Saudi Council Recommends Privatisation of Clubs in Top Football League,' *Gulf News*, 15 November 2016.
77. 'Saudi Approves Privatisation of Professional Football Clubs,' *Gulf News*, 22 November 2016.
78. 'Saudi Arabia Strips Religious Police of Arresting Power,' *Al Jazeera*, 14 April 2016.
79. James Dorsey, *Soccer Versus Jihad: A Draw*,' *American Behavioral Science*, 60(9), 2016, p. 1072.
80. 'Saudi Hires Jadwa Investment to Advise on Selling Soccer Clubs—Sources,' *Al Arabiya*, 8 February 2017.
81. 'Saudi Hires Jadwa Investment to Advise on Privatisation of Football Clubs,' *Reuters*, 8 February 2017.
82. Steve Bainbridge and Ahmad Ayoub, 'Saudi Arabia's Privatisation Plans for Sports Clubs,' *Law in Sport*, 10 February 2017.
83. Tom Arnold, 'Saudi Arabia May Need Extra Time to Privatize Soccer Clubs,' *Reuters*, 3 January 2019.
84. Robert Mogielnicki, 'Expectation Gap Clouds Saudi Arabia's Investment Climate,' *Arab Gulf States Institute in Washington*, 28 October 2019.
85. Karen Young, 'Privatization in Saudi Arabia: Vision 2030 Ready to Sell,' *Arab Gulf States Institute in Washington*, 16 July 2018.
86. Steve Bainbridge and Andrew Moroney, 'The Privatisation of Saudi Arabia's Football Clubs: An Update,' *Law in Sport*, 15 June 2018.
87. Ibid.
88. Philip Buckingham, 'Saudi Pro League Clubs Ordered to Pay $16m to Aggrieved Players in Last Year,' *The Athletic*, 19 September 2023.
89. Rory O'Callaghan, 'Cristiano Ronaldo 'DIDN'T Reject' Al-Hilal Transfer as Saudi Club's President Reveals Why the Deal Collapsed,' *Sport Bible*, 28 September 2022; Josh Lawless, 'Cristiano Ronaldo's Al Nassr Have Been Banned from Registering New Players by FIFA,' *Sport Bible*, 12 July 2023.
90. Matt Monaghan, 'How the Saudi Professional League Became Essential Viewing,' *Sport 360*, 25 February 2019.

NOTES

91. Wael Jabir, 'Saudi Pro League to Increase to 16 Teams and First Division Winners to Land SR5 Million,' *Arab News*, 23 February 2018; Jacob Whitehead and Stuart James, 'Saudi Arabia, Football's Big Disruptors: The Story of the Money, the Motive and the Hidden Disputes,' *The Athletic*, 11 June 2023.
92. Monaghan, *Essential Viewing*.
93. Mahfoud Amara, 'Veiled Women Athletes in the 2008 Beijing Olympic Games: Media Accounts,' *The International Journal of the History of Sport*, 29(4), 2012, p. 643; Paulette Stevenson, 'Empowerment Discourses in Transnational Sporting Contexts: The Case of Sarah Attar, The First Female Saudi Olympian,' *Sociology of Sport Journal*, 35, 2018, p. 242.
94. Najah Al Osaimi, 'Women at the Olympics: Saudi Arabia's Image Paradox,' University of Southern California *Center on Public Diplomacy*, 8 August 2016.
95. Charlotte Lysa, 'Fighting for the Right to Play: Women's Football and Regime-Loyal Resistance in Saudi Arabia,' *Third World Quarterly* 41(5), 2020, p. 847.
96. Joanna Hartley, 'Saudi Women Take Part in Charity Football Game,' *Arabian Business*, 21 March 2009.
97. James Montague, 'Explained: Why Does Saudi Arabia Want to Buy Newcastle United?', *The Athletic*, 6 October 2021; Ali Humayun, 'Saudi Arabia, Football and Faith's Role in a Revolution,' *The Athletic*, 2 August 2023; Assile Toufaily, 'Saudi Women's Premier League: What You Need to Know,' *Forbes*, 12 October 2023.
98. Tariq Panja, 'The Brazen Bootlegging of a Multibillion-Dollar Sports Network,' *New York Times*, 9 May 2018.
99. Sam Carp, 'Walking the Plank: Why the BeIN-BeoutQ Piracy Saga Has Implications Beyond Qatar,' *SportsPro*, 14 December 2018.
100. Panja, *Brazen Bootlegging*; Tariq Panja, 'FIFA and Premier League Document Saudi Link in BeIN Piracy Fight,' *New York Times*, 16 September 2019.
101. World Trade Organization, 'Saudi Arabia—Measures Concerning the Protection of Intellectual Property Rights,' *Report of the Panel*, WT/DS567/R, 16 June 2020, para. 7.117, p. 79.
102. Ben Hubbard and David Kirkpatrick, 'Behind Prince Mohammed bin Salman's Rise, Two Loyal Enforcers,' *New York Times*, 14 November 2018; *Office of the Director of National Intelligence*, 'Assessing the Saudi Government's Role in the Killing of Jamal Khashoggi,' 11 February 2021, p. 3.
103. World Trade Organization, *Report of the Panel*, para. 8.1.b, p. 124.
104. Bradley Hope, Rory Jones, and Joshua Robinson, 'Saudi Sovereign-Wealth Fund in Talks to Buy U.K. Soccer Team Newcastle United,' *Wall Street Journal*, 25 January 2020.
105. Louise Taylor, 'Newcastle Takeover Nears as Saudi Director Named in Paperwork,' *The Guardian*, 28 April 2020.
106. Tariq Panja, 'Saudi Arabia Withdraws Bid to Buy Newcastle United.' *New York Times*, 30 July 2020.
107. Matt Slater, 'Newcastle Takeover: Why BeIN Digital Piracy Battle Was Always the Key,' *The Athletic*, 7 October 2021; 'Premier League Statement,' 7 October 2021, https://www.premierleague.com/news/2283712.

108. Alex Emmons, Aida Chavez, and Akela Lacy, 'Joe Biden, In Departure from Obama Policy, Says He Would Make Saudi Arabia a "Pariah",' *The Intercept*, 21 November 2019; Kristian Coates Ulrichsen, 'Saudi Fund's Newcastle United Purchase Puts Khashoggi Murder in Rearview,' *Responsible Statecraft*, 9 October 2021.
109. Graham Dunbarap, 'Saudi Minister Tweets Barb at UEFA Chief in TV Rights Row,' *Associated Press*, 21 June 2018.
110. MEE Staff, 'Saudi Sports Chief Lets Rip at UEFA Football Officials on Twitter,' *Middle East Eye*, 22 June 2018.
111. 'Joint Statement by FIFA, the AFC, UEFA, the Bundesliga, LaLiga, Lega Serie A, LFP and the Premier League on the Publication of an Investigative Report into the Operations of beoutQ,' 16 September 2019, https://www.uefa.com/insideuefa/about-uefa/news/0255-0f8e6f8509af-2354d5635b3c-1000--joint-statement-by-fifa-the-afc-uefa-the-bundesliga-laliga-l/.
112. Arash Massoudi and Murad Ahmed, 'SoftBank Teams Up with Investors for $25bn Fifa Shake-up Plan,' *Financial Times*, 11 April 2018.
113. Tariq Panja, 'FIFA's Boss Wants to Remake the Game. Europe Wants No Part of It,' *New York Times*, 22 January 2019.
114. Tom Arnold and Hardik Vyas, 'FIFA Should Expand 2022 World Cup to 48 Teams if Possible—Infantino,' *Reuters*, 2 January 2019.
115. Coates Ulrichsen, *Qatar and the Gulf Crisis*, pp. 244–45.

2. MOHAMMED BIN SALMAN, A PRINCE IN A HURRY

1. Special report, 'Politics, Succession and Risk in Saudi Arabia,' *Gulf States Newsletter*, 2010.
2. Ibid. p. 45.
3. 'Mohammed bin Salman Strengthened,' *Gulf States Newsletter*, Vol. 37 Issue 942, 7 March 2013, p. 1.
4. 'Abdelaziz bin Fahd Loses Cabinet Post,' *Gulf States Newsletter*, Vol. 38 Issue 969, 8 May 2014, p. 8.
5. The others being Saud (1953–64), Faisal (1964–75), Khalid (1975–82), Fahd (1982–2005), and Abdullah (2005–15).
6. Ginny Hill, *Yemen Endures: Civil War, Saudi Adventurism and the Future of Arabia* (London: Hurst & Co., 2017), p. 276.
7. David Rundell, *Vision or Mirage: Saudi Arabia at a Crossroads* (London: I.B. Tauris, 2020), p. 174.
8. Thomas Hegghammer, *Jihad in Saudi Arabia: Violence and Pan-Islamism Since 1979* (Cambridge: Cambridge University Press, 2010), pp. 100–101.
9. Madawi Al Rasheed, 'Circles of Power: Royals and Society in Saudi Arabia,' in Paul Aarts and Gerd Nonneman (eds)(eds), *Saudi Arabia in the Balance: Political Economy, Society, Foreign Affairs* (London: Hurst & Co., 2005), p. 200.
10. Karen Elliott House, 'Uneasy Lies the Head That Wears a Crown: The House of

Saud Confronts its Challenges,' Harvard Kennedy School, *Belfer Center Paper*, March 2016, p. 8.

11. Christopher Davidson, *From Sheikhs to Sultanism: Statecraft and Authority in Saudi Arabia and the UAE* (London: Hurst & Co., 2021), pp. 77–78.
12. Caryle Murphy, 'In with the Old in the New Saudi Arabia,' *Foreign Affairs*, 25 February 2015.
13. Joseph Kechichian, 'The Politics of Succession in Saudi Arabia: A Struggle for Primogeniture,' in Kristian Coates Ulrichsen (ed.), *The Changing Security Dynamics of the Persian Gulf* (London: Hurst & Co., 2017), p. 156.
14. Ibrahim Almuhanna, *Oil Leaders: An Insider's Account of Four Decades of Saudi Arabia and OPEC's Global Energy Policy* (New York: Columbia University Press, 2022), pp. 190–91.
15. David Roberts, *Security Politics in the Gulf Monarchies* (New York: Columbia University Press, 2023), p. 47.
16. Nora Doaiji, 'From Hasm to Hazm: Saudi Feminism beyond Patriarchal Bargaining,' in Madawi Al Rasheed (ed.), *Salman's Legacy: The Dilemmas of a New Era in Saudi Arabia* (London: Hurst & Co., 2018), pp. 130–31.
17. Haifa Alangari, *The Struggle for Power in Arabia: Ibn Saud, Hussein and Great Britain, 1914–1924* (Reading: Ithaca Press, 1998), p. 247.
18. Anthony Billingsley, *Political Succession in the Arab World: Constitutions, Family Loyalties and Islam* (Abingdon: Routledge, 2010), pp. 138–39; Joseph Kechichian, *Legal and Political Reforms in Sa'udi Arabia* (Abingdon: Routledge, 2013), pp. 231–36.
19. Christopher Boucek, 'Saudi Arabia's "Soft" Counterterrorism Strategy: Prevention, Rehabilitation, and Aftercare,' *Carnegie Papers No. 97*, September 2008, pp. 5–6.
20. Mark Mazzetti and Robert Worth, 'US Sees Complexity of Bombs as Link to Al Qaeda,' *New York Times*, 30 October 2010.
21. Youssef Ibrahim, 'Saudi King Issues Decrees to Revise Governing System,' *New York Times*, 2 March 1992.
22. Peter Salisbury, 'Risk Perception and Appetite in UAE Foreign and National Security Policy,' *Chatham House Research Paper*, 2020, p. 32.
23. Michael Knights, 'The U.A.E. Approach to Counterinsurgency in Yemen,' *War on the Rocks*, 23 May 2016.
24. 'Domestic Political Impact: Collateral Damage for MBS,' *Gulf States Newsletter*, Vol. 40 Issue 1025, 3 November 2016, p. 6; Mark Mazzetti and Ben Hubbard, 'Rise of Saudi Prince Shatters Decades of Royal Tradition,' *New York Times*, 15 October 2016.
25. Dave Mead and Porscha Stiger, 'The 2014 Plunge in Import Petroleum Prices: What Happened?', Bureau of Labor Statistics, *Beyond the Numbers*, Vol. 4 No. 9, May 2015, p. 3; Larry Elliott, 'Oil Price Falls to 11-Year Low with Global Glut Expected to Deepen in 2016,' *The Guardian*, 21 December 2015; 'US Oil Settles Down 96 Cents, or 3.26%, at $28.46 a Barrel,' *Reuters*, 19 January 2016.
26. Izabella Kaminska, 'Busting Currency Pegs, Saudi Arabia Edition,' *Financial Times*, 6 February 2015; 'Saudi Arabia Returns to the Bond Market,' *Oxford Business Group*,

17 August 2015; Simeon Kerr, 'Saudi Arabia Withdraws Overseas Funds,' *Financial Times*, 28 September 2015.
27. Marwa Rashad and Reem Shamseddine, 'Saudi State Claws Back Unspent Money as Finances Tighten,' *Reuters*, 12 October 2015; Rick Gladstone, 'Saudi Arabia, Squeezed by Low Oil Prices, Cuts Spending to Shrink Deficit,' *New York Times*, 28 December 2015.
28. Peter Waldman, 'The $2 Trillion Project to Get Saudi Arabia's Economy Off Oil,' *Bloomberg Businessweek*, 21 April 2016.
29. Ibid.
30. Thomas Friedman, 'Saudi Arabia's Arab Spring, at Last,' *New York Times*, 23 November 2017.
31. Ibid.
32. 'An Open Letter by Senior Middle East Scholars to the New York Times Regarding Thomas Friedman's Column, "Saudi Arabia's Arab Spring, at Last,"' *Middle East Report Online*, 30 November 2017.
33. Nafeesa Syeed and Kambiz Foroohar, 'Saudi Prince Ends Silicon Valley Tour at Facebook before UN Trip,' *Bloomberg*, 22 June 2016; 'Saudi Deputy Crown Prince, Trump Meeting a 'Turning Point,' Saudi Advisor Says,' *Reuters*, 14 March 2017.
34. Ben Hubbard, Mark Mazzetti, and Eric Schmitt, 'Saudi King's Son Plotted to Oust his Rival,' *New York Times*, 18 July 2017. Simon Henderson, 'Meet the Two Princes Reshaping the Middle East', *Politico*, 13 July 2017.
35. Author interview with a senior Obama administration official, Houston, March 2018.
36. Kristian Coates Ulrichsen, *Qatar and the Gulf Crisis* (London: Hurst & Co., 2020), p. 74.
37. Dexter Filkins, 'A Saudi Prince's Quest to Remake the Middle East,' *New Yorker*, 9 April 2018.
38. David Kirkpatrick, Ben Hubbard, Mark Landler, and Mark Mazzetti, 'The Wooing of Jared Kushner: How the Saudis Got a Friend in the White House,' *New York Times*, 8 December 2018.
39. Ben Hubbard, Mark Mazzetti, and Eric Schmitt, 'Saudi King's Son Plotted Effort to Oust His Rival,' *New York Times*, 18 July 2017; 'Addiction and Intrigue: Inside the Saudi Palace Coup,' *Reuters*, 19 July 2017.
40. 'Mohammed bin Salman Becomes Saudi Crown Prince with 31 Out of 34 Votes,' *Al Arabiya*, 21 June 2017.
41. 'Dead, Detained or Disappeared: A Who's Who of Mohammed bin Salman's Victims,' *Middle East Eye*, 12 March 2020.
42. 'Transcript: Interview with Muhammad bin Salman,' *The Economist*, 6 January 2016; Anjli Raval and Simeon Kerr, 'Saudi Arabia Considers Aramco Share Sale,' *Financial Times*, 7 January 2016.
43. 'A Very High-Profile List of Arrests and Violent Deaths,' *Gulf States Newsletter* special report, Vol. 41, 7 November 2017, p. 3.
44. 'Uncertainty Follows After Al-Salman Purge Establishes a New Model Saudi

Autocracy,' *Gulf States Newsletter*, Vol. 41, Issue 1048, 20 November 2017, p. 1; Dan De Luce, Ken Dilanian, and Robert Windrem, 'How a Saudi Royal Crushed His Rivals in a 'Shakedown' at the Ritz-Carlton,' *NBC News*, 3 November 2018.

45. Dominic Dudley, 'Saudi Arabia Suffers Shock Collapse in Inward Investment,' *Forbes*, 7 June 2018.
46. Simeon Kerr and Andrew England, 'Wealthy Saudis Sit on Cash as Purge Casts Shadow over Investment,' *Financial Times*, 23 July 2018; Martin Chulov, 'Night of the Beating: Details Emerge of Riyadh Ritz-Carlton Purge,' *The Guardian*, 19 November 2020.
47. Tom DiChristopher, 'Saudi Arabia Says it Raised $106 Billion From 'Anti-Corruption' Drive That Swept Up Royals,' *CNBC*, 30 January 2019; 'Saudi Prince Alwaleed Reached Secret Agreement with Government: BBG,' *Reuters*, 19 March 2018.
48. Robert Worth, 'Saudi Arabia Rejects U.N. Security Council Seat in Protest Move,' *New York Times*, 18 October 2013.
49. Kristian Coates Ulrichsen, 'Perceptions and Divisions in Security and Defense Structures in Arab Gulf States,' in Andreas Krieg (ed.), *Divided Gulf: The Anatomy of a Crisis* (Singapore: Springer, 2019), p. 22.
50. Alexandra Stark, *The Yemen Model: Why US Policy Has Failed in the Middle East* (New Haven: Yale University Press, 2024), p. 110.
51. Coates Ulrichsen, *Qatar and the Gulf Crisis*.
52. Samia Nakhoul, Laila Bassam, and Tom Perry, 'Exclusive: How Saudi Arabia Turned on Lebanon's Hariri,' *Reuters*, 12 November 2017.
53. Alissa Rubin, Anne Barnard, and Elian Peltier, 'Lebanese Prime Minister Meets Macron after Mysterious Saudi Stay,' *New York Times*, 18 November 2017.
54. Thomas Juneau, 'A Surprising Spat,' *International Journal*, 74(2), 2019, pp. 316–18.
55. Ashifa Kassam, 'Saudi Group Posts Photo of Plane About to Hit Toronto's CN Tower amid Canada Spat,' *The Guardian*, 8 August 2018.
56. Darren Major, 'Canada, Saudi Arabia Agree to Restore Relations 5 Years after Diplomatic Feud,' *CBC*, 24 May 2023.
57. 'German Spy Agency Condemns Saudi Policies,' *DW*, 2 December 2015.
58. Alison Smale, 'Germany Rebukes its Own Intelligence Agency for Criticizing Saudi Policy,' *New York Times*, 3 December 2015.
59. Hugh Miles, 'Saudi Royal Calls for Regime Change in Riyadh,' *The Guardian*, 28 September 2015.
60. Brian Whitaker, 'Editor Who Fought Saudi Religious Zealots Sacked,' *The Guardian*, 29 May 2003; 'Saudi Arabia: Editor Leaves Newspaper,' *Associated Press*, 17 May 2010.
61. Ben Flanagan, 'Prince Al Waleed and Bloomberg Plan Arab News Channel,' *The National*, 13 September 2011.
62. Ben Hubbard, 'Channel in Bahrain Goes Silent After Giving Opposition Airtime,' *New York Times*, 2 February 2015.

63. John Haltiwanger, 'Jamal Khashoggi Was Barred from Writing in Saudi Arabia After he Criticized Trump, Then Left his Native Country,' *Business Insider*, 20 November 2018.
64. Jon Allsop, 'Jamal Khashoggi on Press Freedom in Saudi Arabia,' *Columbia Journalism Review*, 8 October 2018.
65. Jamal Khashoggi, 'Saudi Arabia Wasn't Always this Repressive. Now it's Unbearable,' *Washington Post*, 18 September 2017.
66. Jamal Khashoggi, 'Saudi Arabia's Crown Prince is Acting Like Putin,' *Washington Post*, 5 November 2017.
67. Jamal Khashoggi, 'By Blaming 1979 for Saudi Arabia's Problems, the Crown Prince is Peddling Revisionist History,' *Washington Post*, 3 April 2018.
68. Ibid.
69. Sabrina Siddiqui, 'Saudi Prince Sells Image of Evolving Kingdom from DC to Hollywood,' *The Guardian*, 31 March 2018; David Pegg, Patrick Wintour, and Graeme Wearden, 'From Bezos to Bush: Saudi Crown Prince Met Array of VIPs on US Tour,' *The Guardian*, 22 January 2020.
70. Tweet by Lloyd Blankfein, 7:14PM—Mar 27, 2018, https://x.com/lloydblankfein/status/978787357146173447?s=20.
71. Speaking to this author before a panel discussion in Washington, D.C. in November 2017, Khashoggi stated that 'the Crown Prince is doing the right thing but in the wrong way' in pairing the economic reforms associated with Vision 2030 with the increase in repression.
72. 'Assessing the Saudi Government's Role in the Killing of Jamal Khashoggi,' *Office of the Director of National Intelligence*, 11 February 2021, p. 3.
73. Mark Landler and Edward Wong, 'Trump Says Saudi Account of Khashoggi Killing is 'Worst Cover-Up' in History,' *New York Times*, 23 October 2018; Madawi Al Rasheed, *The Son King: Reform and Repression in Saudi Arabia* (London: Hurst & Co., 2020), pp. 136–37.
74. Zahraa Alkhalisi, 'Saudi Investment Conference Opens in the Shadow of Khashoggi's Death,' *CNN*, 23 October 2018.
75. Tim Callen, 'Four Indicators to Track Saudi Reform Progress,' *Arab Gulf States Institute in Washington*, 31 January 2024.
76. Robert Mogielnicki, 'Expectation Gap Clouds Saudi Arabia's Investment Climate,' *Arab Gulf States Institute in Washington*, 28 October 2019.
77. 'Saudi Sovereign Wealth Fund: What the PIF Wants, the PIF Gets,' *Gulf States Newsletter*, Vol. 45 Issue 1131, 29 July 2021, p. 3.
78. Heba Kanso, 'Saudi Women Riled by Robot With no Hijab and More Rights than Them,' *Reuters*, 1 November 2017; Charles Phillips, 'With Major Tourism Projects, Saudi Arabia Pushes for Place on Global Tourism Map,' *Arab Gulf States Institute in Washington*, 9 May 2023.
79. Michael Ratner and Heather Greenley, 'Crude Oil Futures Prices Turn Negative,' *Congressional Research Service Insight*, 22 April 2020.
80. Almuhanna, *Oil Leaders*, pp. 228–30.

81. Tweet by Javier Blas, 11:54AM—Apr 4, 2020, https://x.com/JavierBlas/status/1246481361713668097?s=20; Timothy Gardner, Steve Holland, Dmitry Zhdannikov, and Rania El Gamal, 'Special Report: Trump Told Saudi: Cut Oil Supply or Lose US Military Support—Sources,' *Reuters*, 30 April 2020.
82. Javier Blas, 'Trump's Oil Deal: The Inside Story of How the Saudi-Russia Price War Ended,' *Bloomberg*, 14 April 2020.
83. Alex Emmons, Aida Chavez, and Akela Lacy, 'Joe Biden, in Departure from Obama Policy, says he Would Make Saudi Arabia a "Pariah",' *The Intercept*, 21 November 2019.
84. Emile Hokayem, 'Fraught Relations: Saudi Ambitions and American Anger,' *Survival*, 64(6), 2022, p. 9.
85. Zachary Basu, 'White House Announces End to US Support for Offensive Operations in Yemen,' *Axios*, 4 February 2021.
86. 'Aramco Announces Record Full-Year 2022 Results,' *Saudi Aramco News & Media*, 11 March 2023; 'Saudi Arabia Records Budget Surplus of $27.68bn; Revenue Up 31%,' *Arab News*, 9 March 2023.
87. Dominic Dudley, 'Surge in Spending Sends Saudi Budget Back into the Red,' *Forbes*, 25 May 2023.
88. John Irish, 'In Khashoggi's Shadow, Macron Holds Saudi Talks with Crown Prince,' *Reuters*, 4 December 2021.
89. Jon Gambrell, 'Saudi Arabia Puts 81 to Death in its Largest Mass Execution,' *Los Angeles Times*, 12 March 2022; 'UK PM Johnson Defends Saudi Visit after Mass Execution,' *Reuters*, 16 March 2022.
90. Stephen Kalin, Summer Said, and David Cloud, 'How US-Saudi Relations Reached the Breaking Point,' *Wall Street Journal*, 19 April 2022.
91. Steve Holland, Aziz El Yaakoubi, Jarrett Renshaw, and Maha El Dahan, 'Biden Fails to Secure Major Security, Oil Commitments at Arab Summit,' *Reuters*, 16 July 2022.
92. Barak Ravid, 'Biden Adviser: Saudi Arabia and UAE Have "More to Give" on Oil Production,' *Axios*, 27 July 2022.
93. Kristian Coates Ulrichsen, Mark Finley, and Jim Krane, 'The OPEC+ Phenomenon of Saudi-Russian Cooperation and Implications for US-Saudi Relations,' *Baker Institute*, 18 October 2022.
94. 'US President Biden Invites UAE President to Visit Washington,' *Al Arabiya*, 16 July 2022.
95. Kristian Coates Ulrichsen, 'Mohammed bin Salman's Regional Rebranding Campaign,' *Arab Center Washington*, 16 December 2021.
96. Sultan Alamer, 'The Saudi "Founding Day" and the Death of Wahhabism,' *Arab Gulf States Institute in Washington*, 23 February 2022.
97. 'Mohammed bin Salman on Iran, Israel, US and Future of Saudi Arabia: Full Transcript,' *Al Arabiya English*, 3 March 2022.

3. VISION 2030 AND THE PUBLIC INVESTMENT FUND

1. 'Full Transcript of Prince Mohammed bin Salman's Al Arabiya Interview,' *Al Arabiya News*, 25 April 2016.
2. Hala Aldosari, 'The Saudi National Transformation Program: What's in It for Women?', *Arab Gulf States Institute in Washington*, 1 February 2016.
3. Simeon Kerr, 'Saudi Arabia Redrafts Crown Prince's Transformation Plan,' *Financial Times*, 7 September 2016.
4. Katherine Zoepf, 'Sisters in Law,' *New Yorker*, 11 January 2016; Eman Alhussein and Tine Gade, 'Vision 2030 Has Transformed Saudi Arabia's Legal and Judicial Systems,' *Arab Gulf States Institute in Washington*, 20 November 2023.
5. Eman Alhussein, 'Saudi Arabia Walks the Line with Social Opening and Curbing Harassment,' *Arab Gulf States Institute in Washington*, 20 January 2022.
6. 'Crown Prince Says PIF Set to Invest SAR 1 Trln in Local Economy,' *Argaam*, 24 January 2021.
7. Rory Jones, 'Inside Saudi Arabia's Plan to Build a Skyscraper that Stretches for 75 Miles,' *Wall Street Journal*, 23 July 2022.
8. Martin Hvidt, 'The Emergence and Spread of the "Dubai Model" in the GCC Countries,' in Mehran Kamrava (ed.), *Routledge Handbook of Persian Gulf Politics* (Abingdon: Routledge, 2020), p. 210.
9. Marc Valeri, 'Oligarchy vs. Oligarchy: Business and Politics of Reform in Bahrain and Oman,' in Steffen Hertog, Giacomo Luciani, and Marc Valeri (eds)(eds), *Business Politics in the Middle East* (London: Hurst & Co., 2013), pp. 28–31.
10. Sophie Olver-Ellis, 'Building the New Kuwait: Vision 2035 and the Challenge of Diversification,' *LSE Middle East Centre Paper Series 30*, January 2020, p. 6.
11. 'What is the UAE Centennial 2071 Plan and Why is it Important?', *The National*, 31 December 2023; Adam Taylor, 'The UAE's Ambitious Plan to Build a New City—on Mars,' *Washington Post*, 16 February 2017.
12. Calvert Jones, 'All the King's Consultants,' *Foreign Affairs*, 98(3), 2019, p. 145.
13. Kristian Coates Ulrichsen, 'Economic Diversification Plans: Challenges and Prospects for Gulf Policymakers,' *Arab Gulf States Institute in Washington Policy Paper #2*, 2016, p. 6.
14. Farah Al Nakib, 'Kuwait's Modern Spectacle: Oil Wealth and the Making of a New Capital City, 1950–90,' *Comparative Studies of South Asia, Africa and the Middle East*, 33(1), 2013, p. 10; Reem Alissa, 'The Oil Town of Ahmadi since 1946: From Colonial Town to Nostalgic City,' *Comparative Studies of South Asia, Africa and the Middle East*, 33(1), 2013, pp. 43–47.
15. David Edens and William Snaveley, 'Planning for Economic Development in Saudi Arabia,' *Middle East Journal*, 24(1), 1970, pp. 22–25.
16. Sarah Yizraeli, *Politics and Society in Saudi Arabia: The Crucial Years of Development, 1960–1982* (London: Hurst, 2012), pp. 63, 124, & 142.
17. Ibrahim Almuhanna, *Oil Leaders: An Insider's Account of Four Decades of Saudi Arabia and OPEC's Global Energy Policy* (New York: Columbia University Press, 2022), p. 48.

NOTES

18. Tim Niblock, 'Saudi Arabia's Economic Development: Ambitious Visions, Difficult Dilemmas,' *Journal of Middle Eastern and Islamic Studies (in Asia)*, 2(2), 2008, pp. 20–22.
19. Tim Niblock with Monica Malik, *The Political Economy of Saudi Arabia* (Abingdon: Routledge, 2007), p. 184.
20. Jessie Moritz, 'Rentier Political Economy in the Oil Monarchies,' in Mehran Kamrava (ed.), *Routledge Handbook of Persian Gulf Politics*, pp. 170–71.
21. Steffen Hertog, *Princes, Brokers, and Bureaucrats: Oil and the State in Saudi Arabia* (Ithaca: Cornell University Press, 2010), pp. 179–80.
22. Fahd Al Rasheed, 'Learn from the Past, Build for the Future: Saudi Arabia's New City on the Red Sea,' *McKinsey & Company*, 29 August 2016.
23. Ahmed Al Omran, 'Saudi Arabia's Sleepy City Offers Prince a Cautionary Tale,' *Financial Times*, 27 May 2018.
24. Nader Habibi, 'Implementing Saudi Arabia's Vision 2030: An Interim Balance Sheet,' *Middle East Brief No. 127*, Brandeis University/Crown Center for Middle East Studies, 2019, p. 9.
25. 'Vision 2030,' *Kingdom of Saudi Arabia*, 2016, p. 50.
26. Ibid., p. 55.
27. Almuhanna, *Oil Leaders*, pp. 30–31 and 47–48.
28. 'The High Cost of Change: Repression Under Saudi Crown Prince Tarnishes Reforms,' *Human Rights Watch*, 4 November 2019.
29. Adel Abdel Ghaffar, 'Saudi Arabia's McKinsey Reshuffle,' *Brookings Doha Center*, 11 May 2016.
30. Gassan Al Kibsi, Lola Woetzel, Jan Mischke, Tom Isherwood, Jawad Khan, and Hassan Noura, 'Moving Saudi Arabia's Economy Beyond Oil,' *McKinsey Global Institute*, 1 December 2015.
31. Valeri, *Oligarchy vs. Oligarchy*, p. 26.
32. Anjli Raval and Neil Hume, 'Saudi Aramco Listing Presents Challenge for Investors,' *Financial Times*, 10 January 2016.
33. Nick Cleveland-Stout, 'The McKinsey Consulting Scandal You Might Not Have Heard About,' *Responsible Statecraft*, 3 February 2023.
34. Summer Said, Justin Scheck, and Bradley Hope, 'Former McKinsey Executive Imprisoned by Saudis,' *Wall Street Journal*, 28 December 2018.
35. Reem Shamseddine, 'Saudi Aramco Sets Financing Plans for Industrial Push,' *Reuters*, 27 April 2016.
36. Martin Hvidt, 'The Dubai Model: An Outline of Key Development-Process Elements in Dubai,' *International Journal of Middle East Studies*, 41(2), 2009, pp. 399–400.
37. 'Saudi Arabia Sets Itself Up for a Fall with Ambitious Economic Reform Plan,' *Gulf States Newsletter*, Vol. 40 Issue 1014, 5 May 2016, p. 4.
38. Kristin Smith Diwan, 'Max Weber in Arabia: Saudi's Character Enrichment Program,' *Arab Gulf States Institute in Washington*, 12 May 2020; Lauren Said-Moorhouse, 'Saudi Arabia Strips Religious Police of Arrest Powers,' *CNN*, 14 April

2016, Aseel Bashraheel, 'Rise and Fall of the Saudi Religious Police,' *Arab News*, 22 September 2019.
39. Julie Steinberg and Stephen Kalin, 'Hunt for Critical Minerals Draws World Powers to Saudi Arabia,' *Wall Street Journal*, 12 January 2024.
40. Ibid.
41. Harry Dempsey and Chloe Cornish, 'How Gulf States are Putting Their Money into Mining,' *Financial Times*, 31 March 2024.
42. David Roberts, *Security Politics in the Gulf Monarchies: Continuity amid Change* (New York: Columbia University Press, 2023), p. 127.
43. Karen Elliott House, 'Profile of a Prince: Promise and Peril in Mohammed bin Salman's Vision 2030,' Harvard Kennedy School, *Belfer Center Paper*, April 2019, p. 21.
44. Stephen Roll, "A Sovereign Wealth Fund for the Prince: Economic Reforms and Power Consolidation in Saudi Arabia," German Institute for International and Security Affairs, *SWP Research Paper* 8, July 2019, pp. 18–19.
45. Justin Scheck, Rory Jones, and Summer Said, 'A Prince's $500 Billion Desert Dream: Flying Cars, Robot Dinosaurs and a Giant Artificial Moon,' *Wall Street Journal*, 25 May 2019.
46. Rory Jones, Summer Said, and Stephen Kalin, 'Saudi Crown Prince's Vision for Neom, a Desert City-State, Tests His Builders,' *Wall Street Journal*, 1 May 2021; Rory Jones, 'Expatriate Executives Flee Saudi Arabia's Bad Bosses,' *Wall Street Journal*, 31 May 2022.
47. 'Saudi 'Giga-Projects' Press on Despite Austerity, as MBS Eyes Up Contractors,' *Gulf States Newsletter*, Vol. 45 Issue 1131, 29 July 2021, p. 1; 'Saudi Top Team Pushes on with Giga-Projects Supported by Web of Local Contractors,' *Gulf States Newsletter*, Vol. 45 Issue 1131, 29 July 2021, p. 10.
48. Yasser Elsheshtawy, 'Is Riyadh's Mukaab Compatible with Saudi Arabia's Climate Ambitions?', *Arab Gulf States Institute in Washington*, 17 May 2023; Eliot Brown and Rory Jones, 'What Went Wrong at Saudi Arabia's Futuristic Metropolis in the Desert,' *Wall Street Journal*, 9 March 2025.
49. 'Saudi Arabia Sets Itself Up for a Fall with Ambitious Economic Reform Plan,' *Gulf States Newsletter*, Vol. 40 Issue 1014, 5 May 2016, p. 4.
50. Rami Khrais, 'Saudis Refine Blueprint for Post-Oil Economy,' *Al-Monitor*, 26 April 2016.
51. Drew Johnson, 'Company Perspectives: Public Investment Fund of Saudi Arabia,' *International Directory of Company Histories*, Vol. 246, Gale/Cengage, 2022.
52. Jean-Francois Seznec, *The Financial Markets of the Arabian Gulf* (London: Croon Helm, 1987), pp. 112–13.
53. Khrais, *Saudis Refine Blueprint*; Sara Bazoobandi, *The Political Economy of the Gulf Sovereign Wealth Funds: A Case Study of Iran, Kuwait, Saudi Arabia and the United Arab Emirates* (Abingdon, Routledge, 2013), p. 70.
54. David Rundell, *Vision or Mirage: Saudi Arabia at a Crossroads* (London: I.B. Tauris, 2020), p. 215.

55. Niblock with Malik, *Political Economy of Saudi Arabia*, p. 112; Jean-Francois Seznec, 'The Gulf Sovereign Wealth Funds: Myth and Reality,' *Middle East Policy*, 15(2), 2008, p. 104.
56. Oliver McPherson-Smith, 'Diversification, Khashoggi, and Saudi Arabia's Public Investment Fund,' *Global Policy*, 12(2), 2021, pp. 193–94; Steffen Hertog, 'Petromin: The Slow Death of Statist Oil Development in Saudi Arabia,' *Business History*, 50(5), 2008, p. 651.
57. Alexis Montambault Trudelle, 'The Public Investment Fund and Salman's State: The Political Drivers of Sovereign Wealth Management in Saudi Arabia,' *Review of International Political Economy*, 2022 (online), p. 8.
58. Amanda Shakespeare, 'Managing Saudi Arabia's Wealth,' *Middle East Economic Digest*, 11 February 2014.
59. Khrais, *Saudis Refine Blueprint*.
60. Madawi Al Rasheed, *The Son King: Reform and Repression in Saudi Arabia*, pp. 126–28.
61. Jacob Whitehead, 'Yasir Al-Rumayyan: A Life of Power, Privilege and Risk for Golf's Most Powerful Man,' *The Athletic*, 28 March 2023.
62. 'The Public Investment Fund Program (2018–2020),' *Kingdom of Saudi Arabia*, 2017, p. 20.
63. Stephan Roll, 'A Sovereign Wealth Fund for the Prince: Economic Reforms and Power Consolidation in Saudi Arabia,' German Institute for International and Security Affairs, *SWP Research Paper 8*, July 2019, p. 10.
64. 'Falih's 'Empire' Scaled Down, Aramco IPO Accelerated in MBS's Latest Reshuffle,' *Gulf States Newsletter*, Vol. 43 Issue 1087, 5 September 2019, p. 10.
65. Kristin Smith Diwan, 'Saudi Ambition Confronts New Vulnerability,' *Arab Gulf States Institute in Washington*, 1 October 2019.
66. David Ottaway, *Mohammed bin Salman: The Icarus of Saudi Arabia?* (Colorado: Lynne Rienner Publishers, 2021), p. 104.
67. Robin Mills, 'Aramco, Ministry Reshuffle Highlight Role of Oil Giant in Saudi Economic Transformation,' *Arab Gulf States Institute in Washington*, 9 September 2019.
68. Robin Mills, 'Saudi Arabia Shelves SoftBank Solar Effort, Reflecting Challenges with Megaprojects,' *Arab Gulf States Institute in Washington*, 9 October 2019.
69. Summer Said, Rory Jones, and Georgi Kantchev, 'Mohammed bin Salman Meets Resistance—From His Own Bureaucrats,' *Wall Street Journal*, 4 February 2019.
70. Andrew England, Simeon Kerr, Ahmed Al Omran, and Anjli Raval, 'How Saudi Oil Minister Fell from Grace as MBS Pushes Aramco IPO,' *Financial Times*, 9 September 2019.
71. Anjli Raval, Andrew England, Arash Massoudi, and Simeon Kerr, 'The Aramco Reshuffle Shows the Rise of Saudi Wealth Fund,' *Financial Times*, 3 September 2019.
72. Robert Mogielnicki, 'Saudi Arabia's Economic Strategy: From Kitchen Sink to Virtuous Cycle?', *Arab Gulf States Institute in Washington*, 30 April 2021.

73. Tim Callen, 'Going Big: Assessing the Growth Ambitions of the Saudi Public Investment Fund,' *Arab Gulf States Institute in Washington*, 12 December 2023.
74. 'Crown Prince Announces Transfer of 8% of Aramco Shares to PIF-owned Firms,' *Arab News*, 8 March 2024.
75. Karen Kwok, 'Saudi Fund's Prudence Pivot Is Only Half Complete,' Reuters, 20 August 2024.
76. Gawdat Bahgat, 'Sovereign Wealth Funds in the Gulf—An Assessment,' in David Held and Kristian Coates Ulrichsen (eds), *The Transformation of the Gulf: Politics, Economics and the Global Order* (Abingdon: Routledge, 2012), pp. 218–19.
77. Marwa Rashad, 'Saudi Crown Prince Says PIF to Inject $40 Billion Annually in Economy in 2021, 2022,' *Arab News*, 13 November 2020.
78. 'Saudi Arabia's PIF Continues Shift to Home Market as Overseas Investments Fade in Importance,' *Gulf States Newsletter*, Issue 1191, published online 22 August 2024.
79. 'MBS Launches Potential New Military-Industrial Giant,' *Gulf States Newsletter*, Vol. 41 Issue 1037, 25 May 2017, p. 6.
80. Zoltan Barany, 'Indigenous Defense Industries in the Gulf,' *Center for Strategic and International Studies*, 24 April 2020.
81. 'Saudi Sovereign Wealth Fund: What the PIF Wants, the PIF Gets,' *Gulf States Newsletter*, Vol. 45 Issue 1131, 29 July 2021, p. 3.
82. Samer Al Atrush, 'Saudi Crown Prince Turns to 'State Capitalism' after Change in the Guard,' *Financial Times*, 27 May 2023.
83. Kateryna Kadabashy and Matthew Martin, 'Saudi Wealth Fund Invests $1.3 Billion in Construction Companies,' *Bloomberg*, 14 February 2023; Nicholas Parasie, 'Saudi Wealth Fund Aims to Buy Binladin Stake amid Building Boom,' *Bloomberg*, 22 February 2024.
84. 'Saudi Arabia's PIF Continues Shift to Home Market as Overseas Investments Fade in Importance,' *Gulf States Newsletter*, Issue 1191, published online 22 August 2024.
85. 'Riyadh Draws Line in the Sand as MBS Seeks to Reinvigorate Reform Programme,' *Gulf States Newsletter*, Vol. 43 Issue 1074, 7 February 2019, p. 3.
86. Josh Corder, 'Qiddiya Project Relaunched by Saudi Crown Prince Without Opening Date,' *Skift*, 8 December 2023.
87. Rory Jones, 'Inside Saudi Arabia's Plan to Build a Skyscraper That Stretches for 75 Miles'; Eliot Brown and Rory Jones, 'World's Biggest Construction Project Gets a Reality Check,' *Wall Street Journal*, 7 May 2024.
88. Andrew Hammond, 'Work Underway on Cube at Centre of New Murabba Giga-Project,' *Arabian Gulf Business Insight*, 20 March 2024; 'Saudi Authorities Try to Counter Criticism Over PIF's Jeddah Demolition and Redevelopment,' *Gulf States Newsletter*, Vol. 46 Issue 1141, 17 February 2022, p. 1.
89. Charles Phillips, 'With Major Tourism Projects, Saudi Arabia Pushes for Place on Global Tourism Map,' *Arab Gulf States Institute in Washington*, 9 May 2023; Shehzin Shaikh, 'NEOM: Here are 12 Ultra-Luxury Resorts, Which Will Redefine Sustainable Tourism in Saudi Arabia,' *Construction Week Online*, 14 July 2024.

4. REBRANDING SAUDI ARABIA AS A DESTINATION

1. Mariam Nihal, 'We Will Continue to Prove Neom Skeptics Wrong, Saudi Crown Prince Says,' *The National*, 26 June 2023.
2. Josh Corder, 'Saudi Arabia Says its 100 Million Visitor Goal is 'No Longer Sufficient',' *Skift*, 27 September 2023; Kristin Smith Diwan, 'Tourism Ambitions Transform Saudi Arabia,' *Arab Gulf States Institute in Washington*, 17 February 2022.
3. 'THE LINE: Saudi Arabia's City of the Future in NEOM,' Discovery UK, 26 June 2023, available at https://www.youtube.com/watch?v=oamD9QoTH9M (minute 22:40).
4. Tomas Mariano Guisado Litterio, 'The Olympic Truce: Tradition or International Law?,' *Blog of the European Journal of International Law*, 20 October 2022.
5. Adrian Harvey, ''An Epoch in the Annals of National Sport': Football in Sheffield and the Creation of Modern Soccer and Rugby,' *The International Journal of the History of Sport*, 18(4), 2001, pp. 53–87.
6. David Goldblatt, *The Ball is Round: A Global History of Football* (London: Penguin Books/Viking, 2006), p. 44.
7. Ulrike Freitag, *A History of Jeddah*, p. 214.
8. Jonathan Grix, 'Sport Politics and the Olympics,' *Political Studies Review* 11, 2013, p. 19.
9. cf. Richard Mandell, *The Nazi Olympics* (Urbana: University of Illinois Press, 1987).
10. Bill Smith, 'The Argentinian Junta and the Press in the Run-up to the 1978 World Cup,' *Soccer & Society*, 3(1), 2002, p. 69; Tamir Bar-On, 'Reflections on Soccer, Sovereignty and the State of Exception,' *Soccer & Society*, 19(4), 2018, pp. 545–46.
11. Jonathan Grix and Barrie Houlihan, 'Sports Mega-Events as Part of a Nation's Soft Power Strategy: The Cases of Germany (2006) and the UK (2012),' *The British Journal of Politics and International Relations*, 16, 2014, pp. 573 and 580.
12. David Black and Shona Bezanson, 'The Olympic Games, Human Rights and Democratisation: Lessons from Seoul and Implications for Beijing,' *Third World Quarterly*, 25(7), 2004, p. 1250; Tianwei Ren, 'A Special Salience: Media, Iconography, Nationalism: Modern Chinese Olympic Games and Heroes as Soft Power 'Projectiles',' in Tianwei Ren, Keiko Ikeda, and Chang Wan Woo (eds) (eds), *Media, Sport, Nationalism: East Asia: Soft Power Projection via the Modern Olympic Games* (Berlin: Logos Verlag, 2019), p. 61.
13. Billy Graeff and Jorge Knijnik, 'If Things Go South: The Renewed Policy of Sport Mega Events Allocation and its Implications for Future Research,' *International Review for the Sociology of Sport*, 56(8), 2021, p. 1247.
14. Jonathan Grix, Joonoh Brian Jeong, and Hyungmin Kim, 'Understanding South Korea's Use of Sports Mega-Events for Domestic, Regional, and International Soft Power,' *Societies* 11, 2021, p. 7.
15. Wolfram Manzenreiter, 'The Beijing Games in the Western Imagination of China: The Weak Power of Soft Power,' *Journal of Sport and Social Issues*, 34(1), 2010, pp. 32–33; Raymond Boyle and Richard Haynes, Power Play: Sport, the Media and Popular Culture (Edinburgh: Edinburgh University Press, 2009), pp. 148–49.

16. Donald McRae, *Winter Colours: Changing Seasons in World Rugby* (Edinburgh: Mainstream Publishing, 1998), pp. 61–64; Douglas Booth, *The Race Game: Sport and Politics in South Africa* (London: Frank Cass, 1998), pp. 206–7.
17. Lynette Steenveld and Larry Strelitz, 'The 1995 Rugby World Cup and the Politics of Nation-Building in South Africa,' *Media, Culture & Society*, 20(4), 1998, pp. 620–623.
18. Sayuri Guthrie-Shimizu, 'Japan's Sports Diplomacy in the Early Post-Second World War Years,' *International Area Studies Review*, 16(3), 2013, pp. 331–333.
19. Dennis Snelling, 'The Greatest Piece of Diplomacy Ever: The 1949 Tour of Lefty O'Doul and the San Francisco Seals,' *Society for American Baseball Research*, nd.
20. Pete Millwood, 'The Myths and Realities of Ping-Pong Diplomacy,' *History Today*, 29 October 2021.
21. Arthur Johnson, 'Government, Opposition and Sport: The Role of Domestic Sports Policy in Generating Political Support,' *Journal of Sport and Social Issues*, 6(2), 1982, p. 24; Thomas Stevenson, 'Football in Newly United Yemen: Rituals of Equity, Identity, and State Formation,' *Journal of Anthropological Research*, 56(4), 2000, pp. 463–64.
22. Andrew Strenk, 'Diplomats in Track Suits: The Role of Sports in the Foreign Policy of the German Democratic Republic,' paper presented at the *Annual Convention of the International Studies Association*, Washington, D.C., 24 February 1978, p. 36 and p. 39.
23. Katja Hoyer, *Beyond the Wall: A History of East Germany* (New York: Basic Books, 2023), pp. 235–36.
24. Grix and Houlihan, *Sports Mega-Events*, p. 578.
25. John Nauright, 'Global Games: Culture, Political Economy and Sport in the Globalised World of the 21st Century,' *Third World Quarterly*, 25(7), 2004, p. 1333.
26. Janis Van Der Westhuizen, 'Marketing Malaysia as a Model Modern Muslim State: The Significance of the 16th Commonwealth Games,' *Third World Quarterly*, 25(7), 2004, p. 1284.
27. Larry DeGaris, Mark Dodds, and James Reese, 'A Data-Driven Approach to Sponsorship Planning,' in Simon Chadwick, Nicolas Chanavat, and Michel Desbordes (eds), *Routledge Handbook of Sports Marketing* (Abingdon: Routledge, 2015), p. 80.
28. David Black and Janis Van Der Westhuizen, 'Editorial: The Neglected Allure of Global Games?', *Third World Quarterly*, 25(7), 2004, p. 1192; see also Paul Dimeo and Joyce Kay, 'Major Sports Events, Image Projection and the Problems of 'Semi-Periphery': A Case Study of the 1996 South Asia Cricket World Cup' in the same special issue, p. 1264.
29. Thomas Ross Griffin, 'National Identity, Social Legacy and Qatar 2022: The Cultural Ramifications of FIFA's First Arab World Cup,' *Soccer & Society*, 20(7–8), 2019, p. 1007.
30. Aaron Ettinger, 'Saudi Arabia, Sports Diplomacy and Authoritarian Capitalism in World Politics,' *International Journal of Sport Policy and Politics*, 15(3), 2023, p. 540.

31. Abdul Rahim Al Droushi, 'The Emergence and Development of the Islamic Solidarity Games,' in Fan Hong and Lu Zhouxiang (eds), *The Routledge Handbook of Sport in Asia* (Abingdon: Routledge, 2020), p. 448.
32. Mahfoud Amara, 'The Muslim World in the Global Sporting Arena,' *Brown Journal of World Affairs*, 14(2), 2008, p. 72.
33. Black and Van Der Westhuizen, *Neglected Allure of Global Games*, p. 1206.
34. Peter Beaumont, 'Saudi Arabia to Open Itself Up to Foreign Tourists for First Time,' *The Guardian*, 27 September 2019.
35. Rawan Rawan, 'Saudi Arabia Creates Ministries for Investment, Tourism and Sport,' *Arab News*, 26 February 2020. The new ministries replaced the Saudi Commission for Tourism and National Heritage, the General Sports Authority, and the Saudi Arabian General Investment Authority.
36. Charles Phillips, 'With Major Tourism Projects, Saudi Arabia Pushes for Place on Global Tourism Map,' *Arab Gulf States Institute in Washington*, 9 May 2023.
37. Ibid.
38. David Casey, 'Saudia Schedules London Route from Planned Mega-City,' *Aviation Week*, 16 November 2022.
39. 'MBS' Vision for Saudi Arabia Tests the Limits of the Art of Soft Power,' *Gulf States Newsletter*, Vol. 47 Issue 1170, 1 June 2023, pp. 9–11.
40. Sean Foley and Hatem Alzahrani, '"Listen to the Artist": US and Saudi Artists Develop Cultural Ties,' *Arab Gulf States Institute in Washington*, 21 February 2023; Reem Krimly, 'More than 700,000 People Attended Saudi Arabia's MDLBeast in 4 Day,' *Al Arabiya News*, 20 December 2021.
41. Adam Crafton, ''He Sold Himself to the Devil'—Messi, 2030 and a Very Uncomfortable Deal with Saudi Arabia,' *The Athletic*, 21 November 2022; Karim Zidan and Tariq Panja, 'Lionel Messi, Saudi Arabia and the Deal That Paid Off for Both Sides,' *New York Times*, 18 June 2023.
42. 'Cristiano Ronaldo Rejects $6m-a-Year Deal to Promote Saudi Arabian Tourism: Report,' *Middle East Eye*, 23 January 2021.
43. 'Saudi Tourism Launches Latest Brand Campaign Starring Lionel Messi,' *Arab News*, 27 January 2024.
44. Robert Mogielnicki, 'Saudi Regional Headquarters Program Deadline Looms,' *Arab Gulf States Institute in Washington*, 5 December 2023.
45. Eman Alhussein and Sara Almohamadi, 'Saudi Arabia Hikes its VAT, But for How Long?', *Arab Gulf States Institution in Washington*, 2 July 2020.
46. '$37bn Deal with Boeing as Riyadh Air Launched,' *Gulf States Newsletter*, Vol. 47 Issue 1166, 23 March 2023, p. 13.
47. Samer Al-Atrush, ''Super Aggressive' Riyadh Air to Focus Expansion on Saudi Market,' *Financial Times*, 27 August 2023.
48. Graham Dunn, 'Ambitions Shape Saudi Operators,' *Airline Business*, 39(2), June 2023, pp. 16–17.
49. David Held and Kristian Coates Ulrichsen, 'Editors' Introduction,' in David Held and Kristian Coates Ulrichsen (eds), *The Transformation of the Gulf: Politics, Economics and the Global*, p. 11.

NOTES

50. Jeremy Bogaisky, 'This 'Money Pit' Airline Says It's Finally Set Up to Profit for the Long Haul,' *Forbes*, 9 September 2022.
51. Hezha Barzani, 'How the Saudi Pro League Transformed from Being Unknown to Inescapable,' *Atlantic Council*, 14 June 2023.
52. Dunn, *Ambitions Shape Saudi Operators*.
53. 'Saudi Arabia's New Airline Signs its First Sports Sponsorship Deal with Leading Spanish Football Club,' *Riyadh Air*, 10 August 2023.
54. Stephen Kalin, Summer Said, and Andrew Tangel, 'Saudi Arabia Unveils a New Airline,' *Wall Street Journal*, 13 March 2023.
55. Dermot Corrigan, 'What a Clasico Supercopa in Jeddah Tells Us About the Relationship between Spain and Saudi Arabia,' *The Athletic*, 11 January 2025.
56. Ali Shihabi, 'A New Perspective on Saudi Arabia's Vision 2030,' *Arab News*, 12 March 2024.
57. 'Vision Realization Programs,' *Vision 2030*, https://www.vision2030.gov.sa/en/vision-2030/vrp/.
58. Yasser Elsheshtawy, 'Transforming Riyadh: A New Urban Paradigm?', *Arab Gulf States Institute in Washington*, 17 April 2019.
59. Jacob Whitehead and Stuart James, 'Saudi Arabia: Football's Big Disruptors: The Story of the Money, the Motive and the Hidden Disputes,' *The Athletic*, 11 June 2023.
60. Paul MacInnes, ''It's Not a Fad': The Truth Behind Saudi Arabia's Dizzying Investment in Sport,' *The Guardian*, 12 August 2023.
61. Joshua Robinson, 'The Saudi Power Broker of Spanish Soccer's Second Division,' *Wall Street Journal*, 27 July 2020; Mike Coppinger, 'Turki Alalshikh Tells ESPN He Has Plans to Fix 'Broken' Boxing,' ESPN, 6 May 2024.
62. Joseph Currier, 'Preview and Predictions for WWE's "Crown Jewel" in Saudi Arabia,' *Sports Illustrated*, 20 October 2021.
63. Ruth Michaelson, 'Saudi Arabia Has Spent at Least $1.5 Billion on 'Sportswashing,' Report Reveals,' *The Guardian*, March 28, 2021.
64. MacInnes, *It's Not a Fad*.
65. Ibid.
66. Ibid.
67. Dan Roan, 'Saudi Arabia World Cup 2034: Sports Minister Defends State's Right to Host,' *BBC Sport*, 8 December 2023.
68. Jim Chairusmi, 'Anthony Joshua, Andy Ruiz Defend Decision to Stage Rematch in Saudi Arabia,' *Wall Street Journal*, 6 September 2019.
69. Joshua Robinson, 'The Kingdom, the Heavyweights and the $60 Million Prize Fight in the Desert,' *Wall Street Journal*, 6 December 2019.
70. Philip Buckingham, 'Tommy Fury's Win over Jake Paul Crowned 72 Hours of Saudi 'Sportswashing,' *The Athletic*, 27 February 2023.
71. Mike Coppinger, 'Turki Alalshikh Tells ESPN He Has Plans to Fix 'Broken' Boxing,' ESPN, 6 May 2024.
72. Sussan Saikali, 'A New Virtual Reality: The Growth of Esports and Gaming in Saudi

Arabia,' *Arab Gulf States Institute in Washington*, 17 March 2022; Ian Oxborrow, 'Saudi Arabia's PIF Acquires $1bn Stake in Sweden's Embracer Gaming Group,' *The National*, 8 June 2022. Mohammed bin Salman is himself an avid gamer according to media reports.

73. Samer Al-Atrush and Tim Bradshaw, 'Saudi Arabia Spends Billions in Bid to Dominate Global Games Industry,' *Financial Times*, 13 June 2023.
74. Ibid.
75. Rawan Radwan, 'Mohammed bin Salman Announces New 5-Year Strategy for Saudi Arabia's Economy,' *Arab News*, 24 January 2021.
76. As outlined in the *Public Investment Fund Program 2021–2025*, 'Vision 2030 Direct Objectives of PIF Program,' p. 9.
77. Graham Dunbar, 'IOC and Saudi Arabia Agree on 12-Year Deal for Video Gaming Esports Olympics,' *Associated Press*, 12 July 2024; 'IOC Announces Olympic Esports Games to be Hosted in the Kingdom of Saudi Arabia,' *International Olympic Committee*, 12 July 2024.
78. 'McLaren Racing and Neom Announce Strategic Title Partnership,' *McLaren press release*, 27 June 2022.
79. Marco Ferrari, 'Saudi Government Orders Up to 100,000 Electric Vehicles from PIF-owned Lucid,' *Al Arabiya*, 27 April 2022.
80. MacInnes, *It's Not a Fad*.
81. Jack Bezants, 'Meet Yasir al-Rumayyan, the Golf Lover Set to Become Newcastle's New Chairman Who Plans to Increase Saudi Arabia's Unimaginable Wealth into the TRILLIONS…And He Has Colossal Ambitions for His New Football Club Too,' *Mail Online*, 24 April 2020.
82. Alan Blinder and Sarah Hurtes, 'Confidential Records Show a Saudi Golf Tour Built on Far-Fetched Assumptions,' *New York Times*, 11 December 2022.
83. Vivian Nereim and Ahmed Al Omran, 'Saudi Arabia Relishes a Triumph That Transcends Sports,' *New York Times*, 7 June 2023.
84. David Kirkpatrick and Kate Kelly, 'Before Giving Billions to Jared Kushner, Saudi Investment Fund Had Big Doubts,' *New York Times*, 10 April 2022.
85. Jason Lemon, 'LIV Golf Tournament at Trump Club Sees Thin Crowds, $1 Tickets: Reports,' *Newsweek*, 30 July 2022.
86. Zach Helfand, 'Will the Saudis and Donald Trump Save Golf—Or Wreck It?', *New Yorker*, 17 October 2022.
87. Alan Shipnuck, 'LIV and Let Die,' *The Firepit Collective*, 4 October 2023.
88. Tweet by Khalid Aljabri, MD., *X*, 24 January 2023, https://x.com/JabriMD/status/1618101111403208704.
89. Alan Shipnuck, LIV and Let Die: *The Inside Story of the War Between the PGA Tour and LIV Golf* (New York, Simon & Schuster, 2024), Kindle edition, p. 216 of 342.
90. Brendan Quinn, 'The PGA Tour, PIF and Understanding the Deal to Shape Golf's Future,' *The Athletic*, 7 July 2023.
91. Brendan Quinn, 'LIV Golf Is Not Going Away. Neither Are Questions About its Future,' *The Athletic*, 25 October 2023.

92. Dan Sheldon, 'Inside Saudi Arabia's Plan to Disrupt Global Football,' *The Athletic*, 1 July 2023.
93. 'International Cricket Council Announces Partnership with Aramco,' *Arab News*, 19 October 2022; Joey D'Urso, 'Saudi Arabia's Takeover of World Sport: Football, Golf, Boxing and Now Tennis?', *The Athletic*, 1 February 2024; Shrivathsa Sridhar, 'ATP Signs Multi-Year Strategic Partnership with Saudi Arabia's PIF,' *Reuters*, 28 February 2024; Matthew Futterman, 'Saudi Arabia Complete Deal to Host WTA Finals: The Backlash and the Money,' *The Athletic*, 4 April 2024.
94. Howard Fendrich, 'Women's Tennis Players Now are Eligible for Paid Maternity Leave Financed by Saudi Fund,' *Yahoo Sports*, 6 March 2025; Anon., 'NEOM, Tennis and Golf,' *Arab Digest*, 2 April 2025.
95. 'PGA Tour, DP World Tour and PIF Extend Merger Deadline,' *Sports Pro Media*, 2 January 2024; Gabby Herzig, 'PGA Tour, PIF Working Without Deadline for Agreement,' *The Athletic*, 28 August 2024.
96. Lukas Weese, 'Who is Involved in Strategic Sports Group, the New PGA Tour Investors?', *The Athletic*, 31 January 2024; 'Jon Rahm Jumps Ship to LIV Golf In a Stunning Blow to the PGA Tour,' *Al Jazeera*, 8 December 2023.
97. Philip Barker, 'How Packer's Revolution Changed Cricket,' *Inside the Games*, 26 February 2017.
98. Raymond Boyle and Richard Haynes, *Power Play: Sport, the Media and Popular Culture* (Edinburgh: Edinburgh University Press, 2009), pp. 50–51 and p. 72.
99. 'Aramco Announces Record Full-Year 2022 Results,' Aramco press release, 11 March 2023.
100. Samer Al-Atrush, 'Saudi Arabia Makes First Move in Mixed Martial Arts by Taking Stake in League,' *Financial Times*, 29 August 2023; Ivan Levingston and Samuel Agini, 'Sports Group Backed by Saudi Wealth Fund Seeks Stake in European Basketball,' *Financial Times*, 16 September 2024.

5. THE 2023 BREAKTHROUGH

1. Joseph Fronczak, 'Hobsbawm's Long Century,' *Jacobin*, 9 June 2017.
2. Rory Smith, 'Saudi Arabia Stuns Lionel Messi and Argentina for the World Cup's First Shock,' *New York Times*, 22 November 2022.
3. Dan Sheldon and Adam Crafton, 'Inside Jordan Henderson's Retreat from Saudi Arabia to Ajax,' *The Athletic*, 19 January 2024.
4. Andrew Cathorne, Angus McDowall, and Angus MacSwan, 'Saudis Enjoy Image Boost from Shock Win over Argentina,' *Reuters*, 23 November 2022.
5. Fabrizio Romano, 'Cristiano Ronaldo Completes Deal to Join Saudi Arabian Club Al Nassr,' *The Guardian*, 30 December 2022.
6. Andy Mitten, 'Ronaldo Interview: The Memories Should be Cherished but the Ending Certainly Won't,' *The Athletic*, 17 November 2022.
7. Dan Sheldon and Oliver Kay, 'Inside Cristiano Ronaldo's Move to Saudi Arabia's Al Nassr: Rejection, Revenge and Soft Power,' *The Athletic*, 10 January 2023.

8. Pablo Maurer, 'When Pele Made His NY Cosmos Debut—the Similarities and Differences to Messi in Miami,' *The Athletic*, 20 July 2023.
9. John Francis and Congcong Zheng, 'Learning Vicariously from Failure: The Case of Major League Soccer and the Collapse of the North American Soccer League,' *Group & Organization Management*, 35(5), 2010, p. 557.
10. Pablo Maurer, 'Pele in the United States: Stories of his Influence, Kindness and Humility From Those Who Knew Him,' *The Athletic*, 2 January 2023.
11. Oliver Kay, 'We Would Love to See Manchester United's Cristiano Ronaldo in the Saudi League—Yasser Almisehal,' *The Athletic*, 12 September 2022.
12. Sheldon and Kay, *Inside Cristiano Ronaldo's Move*.
13. Jacob Whitehead and Stuart James, 'Saudi Arabia, Football's Big Disruptors. The Story of the Money, the Motive and the Hidden Disputes,' *The Athletic*, 11 June 2023.
14. Richard Giulianotti, 'Supporters, Followers, Fans, and Flaneurs: A Taxonomy of Spectator Identities in Football,' *Journal of Sport & Social Issues*, 26(1), 2002, pp. 25–26; Jan Ludvigsen, 'The Premier League-Globalization Nexus: Notes on Current Trends, Pressing Issues and Inter-linked "-izatio" Processes,' *Managing Sport and Leisure*, 25(1–2), 2020, pp. 39–40.
15. Nicolas Scelles, Boris Helleu, Christophe Durand, Liliane Bonnal, and Stephen Morrow, 'Explaining the Number of Social Media Fans for North American and European Professional Sports Clubs with Determinants of Their Financial Value,' *International Journal of Financial Studies*, 5(25), 2017, pp. 2–3.
16. Leah Gillooly, Christos Anagnostopoulos, and Simon Chadwick, 'Social Media-based Sponsorship Activation: A Typology of Content,' *Sport, Business and Management: An International Journal*, 7(3), 2017, p. 294; Nicolas Chanavat and Michel Desbordes, 'Towards the Regulation and Restriction of Ambush Marketing?', in Simon Chadwick, Nicolas Chanavat, and Michel Desbordes (eds) (eds), *Routledge Handbook of Sports Marketing* (Abingdon: Routledge, 2018), p. 195.
17. Simon Hughes, 'Can You Really Support a Player Instead of a Club?', *The Athletic*, 13 August 2021.
18. 'Fan of the Future: Defining Modern Football Fandom,' *European Club Association*, August 2020, p. 14 and p. 31. The European Club Association was established in 2008 and currently represents the interests of 512 teams.
19. Sam McPhail, 'Football Fans' Loyalty No Longer Lies with Clubs, but Players,' *The Spectator*, 29 July 2023.
20. Dennis Deninger, *Live Sports Media: The What, How and Why of Sports Broadcasting* (Abingdon: Routledge, 2022), p. 86.
21. Josh Noble, 'What Will It Take to Get Gen Z Watching Sport?', *Financial Times*, 16 May 2024.
22. William Kunz, *The Political Economy of Sports Television* (Abingdon: Routledge, 2020), pp. 124–27.
23. 'The Influencer Olympics and the Future of Broadcast,' *FT Scoreboard* newsletter, 3 August 2024.

24. Raymond Boyle and Richard Haynes, 'How a Netflix Show Has Become a Key Driver Behind F1's Rising Popularity,' *The Conversation*, 1 March 2024.
25. Charlie Eccleshare and Jack Pitt-Brooke, 'All or Nothing: Filling in the Blanks in Amazon's Tottenham Series,' *The Athletic*, 14 September 2020.
26. Boyle and Haynes, *How a Netflix Show*.
27. Euan Ward, 'Under the Hollywood Spotlight, a Fading Welsh Town is Reborn,' *New York Times*, 29 April 2023. Although Wrexham is located in north Wales, the club has participated in the English football pyramid since 1890.
28. Sam Lee and Matt Slater, 'Special Report: City Football Group. Part Two—Does it Work?', *The Athletic*, 10 December 2020.
29. Paul MacInnes, 'Saudi Pro League: The Key Factors That Will Decide Project's Global Impact,' *The Guardian*, 15 August 2023.
30. Robbie Corey-Boulet, 'Humanizing Saudi Football: Netflix Show Paves Way for World Cup,' *AFP*, 10 December 2024.
31. Rory Smith, 'Selling Saudi Soccer, One Like at a Time,' *New York Times*, 15 September 2023.
32. Dan Sheldon, 'Inside Saudi Arabia's Plan to Disrupt Global Football,' *The Athletic*, 1 July 2023.
33. Oliver Kay, 'One Year of Cristiano Ronaldo in Saudi Arabia,' *The Athletic*, 29 December 2023.
34. Matt Slater, 'Is Football in Saudi Arabia Getting Any Better?', *The Athletic*, 14 December 2024.
35. Karim Zidan and Tariq Panja, 'Lionel Messi, Saudi Arabia and the Deal That Paid Off for Both Sides,' *New York Times*, 18 June 2023.
36. Amanda Davies and David Close, 'Lionel Messi Suspended by Paris Saint-Germain Following Unauthorized Trip to Saudi Arabia,' *CNN*, 3 May 2023.
37. Alex Silverman, 'Slice of the Apple: Messi and Miami,' *Sports Business Journal*, 21 July 2023.
38. Oliver Kay, 'Saudi Arabia's Transfer Window: Cold Calls, 'Eye-Watering' Wages but no Messi,' *The Athletic*, 7 September 2023.
39. Josh Noble, 'Saudi Arabia Passes Four Domestic Football Teams to Sovereign Fund,' *Financial Times*, 5 June 2023; Sean Yom, 'The Long Game: Saudi Arabia and Professional Golf,' *Foreign Policy Research Institute*, 21 June 2023.
40. Ahmed Walid, 'PIF to Take Control of Saudi Arabia's Four Biggest Clubs as Part of Major Shake-up in Pro League,' *The Athletic*, 5 June 2023.
41. John Duerden, 'Why Has Saudi Sovereign Fund Taken Over Kingdom's Football Clubs?', *Al Jazeera*, 8 June 2023.
42. Tariq Panja and Ahmed Al Omran, 'Saudi Soccer League Creates Huge Fund to Sign Global Stars,' *New York Times*, 6 June 2023.
43. Josh Sim, 'PIF Takes Ownership of Four Saudi Pro League Clubs as Aramco, Neom, Driyah Gate and Royal Commission for Al-Ula Also Buy In,' *Sports Pro Media*, 6 June 2023.
44. Adam Leventhal, 'Why Has Saudi Arabia Been So Quiet on Transfers This Summer? It's All Part of the Plan,' *The Athletic*, 19 July 2024.

NOTES

45. Wael Jabir, 'Three Things I Learned Watching 3rd Tier Football in Saudi Arabia,' *Medium*, 31 December 2024.
46. Larbi Sadiki and Layla Saleh, 'Playing Ball: Crowd and 'Contra-Crowd' in the Politics of Egyptian and Tunisian Football,' in Fan Hong and Lu Zhouxiang (eds), *The Routledge Handbook of Sports in Asia* (Abingdon: Routledge, 2020), pp. 474–76.
47. Gary King, Jennifer Pan, and Margaret Roberts, 'How Censorship in China Allows Government Criticism but Silences Collective Action,' *American Political Science Review*, 2012 (online), p. 14.
48. Mariwan Kanie, 'Civil Society, Language and the Authoritarian Context: The Case of Saudi Arabia,' *Orient*, 53(4), 2012, p. 43.
49. Steffen Hertog, 'National Cohesion and the Political Economy of Regions in Post-World War II Saudi Arabia,' in Bernard Haykel, Thomas Hegghammer, and Stephane Lacroix (eds)(eds), *Saudi Arabia in Transition: Insights on Social, Political, Economic and Religious Change* (Cambridge: Cambridge University Press, 2015), pp. 123–24.
50. Rory Smith, Tariq Panja, and Ahmed Al Omran, 'Inside the Saudi Gold Rush,' *New York Times*, 13 July 2023; Kay, *Saudi Arabia's Transfer Window*.
51. Jacob Whitehead, 'Ronaldo, Benzema, Messi and More? The Overhaul of Saudi Football—Explained,' *The Athletic*, 5 June 2023; Smith, Panja, and Al Omran, *Inside the Saudi Gold Rush*.
52. David Ornstein and Adam Crafton, 'Jordan Henderson: I Strongly Believe That Me Playing in Saudi Arabia Is a Positive Thing,' *The Athletic*, 5 September 2023.
53. Andrew Hankinson, 'Behind the Scenes of the Saudi Pro League: What Really Awaits Stars Like Neymar,' *The Athletic*, 18 August 2023.
54. Ibid.
55. Paul MacInnes, 'Saudi Pro League Insists It Will Soon be 'For Exceptional Players Only',' *The Guardian*, 12 August 2023.
56. 'Michael Emenalo, Former Chelsea Technical Director, Rejects Role at Newcastle United,' *Telegraph Online*, 4 December 2021.
57. Kay, *Saudi Arabia's Transfer Window*.
58. 'Saudi Pro League Interim CEO Reveals Kingdom's Transformative Football Strategy,' *Al Arabiya News*, 20 July 2023.
59. Matt Slater, 'Garry Cook to Leave Saudi Pro League Role to Become Birmingham City CEO,' *The Athletic*, 7 June 2023.
60. 'Saudi Pro League to Focus on Signing U21 Players,' 5 May 2024, https://www.spl.com.sa/en/news/497225/saad-al-lazeez-press-conference.
61. Cf. Ulrike Freitag, *A History of Jeddah: The Gate to Mecca in the Nineteenth and Twentieth Centuries* (Cambridge: Cambridge University Press, 2020).
62. James Dorsey, 'Saudi Soccer: A Game of Geopolitics and Religion, Not Just Sports,' *Substack*, 5 August 2023.
63. Hankinson, *Behind the Scenes of the Saudi Pro League*.
64. Kay, *Saudi Arabia's Transfer Window*.
65. Ibid.

66. Ibid.
67. 'Saudi Pro League Clubs Spend US$957 Million in Record-Breaking Football Transfer Window,' *Deloitte*, 9 September 2023.
68. Nick Miller, 'Turkey's Summer Spending Spree: 'They've Gone Crazy. I'm Not Sure Where They Found the Money,' *The Athletic*, 13 September 2023.
69. Zheng Lui, Ryan Chen, and Joshua Newman, 'The Football Dream of a Sleeping Dragon: Media Framing(s), East-West Geopolitics, and the Crisis of the Chinese Men's National Team,' *Communication & Sport*, 9(1), 2021, p. 74.
70. Emanuel Leite Junior and Carlos Rodriguez, 'The Chinese Plan for Football Development: A Perspective from Innovation Theory,' *Sport, Business and Management: An International Journal*, 9(1), 2019, p. 71.
71. Oliver Kay and Matt Slater, 'The Chinese Super League: From Unprecedented Salaries to Uncertain Restart Date, Unpaid Wages and Deepening Turmoil,' *The Athletic*, 27 November 2021.
72. Tom Bogert, 'With Messi in MLS and Ronaldo in Saudi Arabia, is a Battle for Star Players Emerging?', *The Athletic*, 18 July 2023.
73. Kay, *Saudi Arabia's Transfer Window*.
74. Dan Roan, 'Saudi Arabia World Cup 2034: Sports Minister Defends State's Right to Host,' *BBC Sport*, 8 December 2023.
75. 'Ronaldo Breaks Saudi League's Single-Season Scoring Record,' *ESPN*, 27 May 2024.
76. John Duerden, 'Saudi 'Clasico' Drama Shows Promise but Pro League Still Work in Progress,' *The Guardian*, 11 September 2023.
77. Joe Pacinella, 'Are Poor Attendances in the Saudi Pro League Becoming a Problem?', *Sportcal*, 7 November 2023; Wael Jabir, 'Saudi Pro League: Attendances Rising but Provincial Clubs Struggle to Attract New Fans,' *The National*, 14 February 2024.
78. Mariam Nihal, 'Neymar and Benzema Don Saudi Attire to Celebrate Kingdom's National Day,' *The National*, 23 September 2023.
79. Paul Williams, 'Al-Shabab's New Home Points the Way Forward for Saudi Football Stadiums,' *Arab News*, 31 October 2023.
80. Chris Byfield, 'Robbie Fowler Has Finally Broken His Silence on Being Dismissed as Manager of Al Qadsiah,' *Sport Bible*, 22 December 2023.
81. Steve Luckings, 'Robbie Fowler: Liverpool Great on Saudi Pro League, Mohamed Salah and his Coaching Journey,' *The National*, 22 December 2023.
82. Dan Sheldon and Adam Crafton, 'Inside Jordan Henderson's Retreat from Saudi Arabia to Ajax,' *The Athletic*, 19 January 2024.
83. Oliver Kay, 'The Speed of Jordan Henderson's Disillusionment Reflects How Great his Regret Must Be,' *The Athletic*, 7 January 2024.
84. James Pearce, 'Jordan Henderson, What Have You Done?', *The Athletic*, 17 January 2024.
85. Matt Slater and Guillermo Rai, 'Lyon Exploring Karim Benzema Transfer from Saudi Arabian Side Al Ittihad,' *The Athletic*, 22 January 2024; 'Benzema Returns to

'Furious' Saudi Club 17 Days Late,' *AFP*, 19 January 2024; Guillermo Rai, 'Karim Benzema's Rollercoaster Spell in Saudi Arabia: The Highs, the Lows, and Many Managers,' *The Athletic*, 10 January 2025.

86. Stephen Killen, 'Man City Hero Aymeric Laporte in U-Turn after Claiming Players are 'Unhappy' in Saudi Arabia,' *Manchester Evening News*, 20 January 2024.

6. THE SPORTSWASHING DEBATE

1. Simon Chadwick, 'The Business of Sports in the Gulf Cooperation Council Member States,' in Tamir Sorek and Danyel Reiche (eds), *Sport, Politics and Society in the Middle East* (London: Hurst & Co., 2019), p. 183.
2. Leite Junior and Rodrigues, *The Chinese Plan for Football Development*, p. 63.
3. Richard Giulianotti, Fred Coalter, Holly Collison, and Simon Darnell, 'Rethinking Sportland: A New Research Agenda for the Sport for Development and Peace Sector,' *Journal of Sport and Social Issues*, 43(6), 2019, p. 423; Felix Flemming, Marco Lunich, Frank Marcinkowski, and Christopher Starke, 'Coping with a Dilemma: How German Sport Media Users Respond to Sport Mega Events in Autocratic Countries,' *International Review for the Sociology of Sport*, 52(8), 2017, p. 1009.
4. Henry Bushnell, 'Saudi Arabia 2034: The Secretive End of FIFA World Cup Bidding as We Know It,' *Yahoo Sports*, 31 October 2023.
5. Craig LaMay, 'The World Cup and Freedom of Expression in Qatar,' in Tamir Sorek and Danyel Reiche (eds), *Sport, Politics and Society in the Middle East*, p. 114.
6. Jack Snape, 'Australia Chooses Common Sense on World Cup Bid That Was Doomed to Fail,' *The Guardian*, 31 October 2023; Jacob Whitehead, 'Why Australia Chose Not to Challenge Saudi Arabia for the 2034 World Cup,' *The Athletic*, 3 November 2023.
7. Jules Boykoff, 'Toward a Theory of Sportswashing: Mega-Events, Soft Power, and Political Conflict,' *Sociology of Sport Journal*, 39 (2022), pp. 342–43; Stephen Crossley and Adam Woolf, ''Fog on the Tyne'? The 'Common-Sense' Focus on 'Sportswashing' and the 2021 Takeover of Newcastle United,' *International Journal of Sport Policy and Politics*, 16(2), 2024, p. 308.
8. Emily Shelley, '2022: The Year of Sportswashing,' *Australian Institute of International Affairs*, 30 June 2022; Karim Zidan, 'Could 2022 Be Sportswashing's Biggest Year?,' *The Guardian*, 5 January 2022.
9. Benjamin Weiss, 'Senate Eyes Saudi 'Sportswashing' in Golfing Merger,' *Courthouse News*, 13 September 2023.
10. David Bond, 'Saudi Investor Takes Key Stake in Independent,' *Financial Times*, 29 July 2017.
11. Andrew Woodcock, 'Sale of Stake in Independent to Saudi Investor Has 'No Influence' on Editorial Coverage, Watchdog Rules,' *The Independent*, 16 September 2019.
12. Boykoff, *Toward a Theory of Sportswashing*. p. 342.

13. Ibid., p. 347; Mitt Romney, 'The Most Touching Moment Involved a Flag, a Choir, and an Anthem,' *Deseret News*, 7 September 2021.
14. Boykoff, *Toward a Theory of Sportswashing*. p. 345; Jonathan Grix and Nina Kramareva, 'The Sochi Winter Olympics and Russia's Unique Soft Power Strategy,' *Sport in Society*, 20(4), 2017, p. 464.
15. Mehran Haghirian and Paulino Robles-Gil, 'Soft Power and the 2022 World Cup in Qatar: Learning from Experiences of Past Mega-Sporting Event Hosts,' *Tajseer*, 3(2), 2021, p. 183; Andrew Higgins and Steven Erlanger, 'Gunmen Seize Government Buildings in Crimea,' New York Times, 27 February 2014.
16. 'Xi and Putin Show United Front amid Spiraling Tensions with West,' *Al Jazeera*, 4 February 2024; Yaroslav Trofimov, 'Russia Begins Military Operation in Ukraine,' *Wall Street Journal*, 24 February 2022.
17. Michael Skey, 'Sportswashing: Media Headline or Analytic Concept?', *International Review for the Sociology of Sport*, 58(5), 2023, p. 753 and p. 757.
18. Ibid., p. 760.
19. Ibid., p. 759.
20. David Black and Janis Van Der Westhuizen, 'Editorial: The Neglected Allure of Global Games?', *Third World Quarterly*, 25(7), 2004, p. 1192.
21. Crossley and Woolf, *Fog on the Tyne*, p. 310.
22. Ian Jones, Andrew Adams, and Joanne Mayoh, 'Fan Responses to Ownership Change in the English Premier League: Motivated Ignorance, Social Creativity and Social Competition at Newcastle United F.C.,' *International Review for the Sociology of Sport*, 2023 (online), p. 4.
23. Aaron Ettinger, 'Saudi Arabia, Sports Diplomacy and Authoritarian Capitalism in World Politics,' *International Journal of Sport Policy and Politics*, 15(3), 2023, pp. 534, 544.
24. Tom Taylor, Daniel Burdsey, and Nigel Jarvis, 'A Critical Review on Sport and the Arabian Peninsula—the Current State of Play and Future Directions,' *International Journal of Sport Policy and Politics*, 15(2), 2023, pp. 374–75.
25. Ali Khaled, 'From the Abyss to Hosting Mancini's Saudi Squad: How South Shields FC Turned Their Fortunes Around,' *Arab News*, 11 June 2024.
26. Natalie Koch, 'The Geopolitics of Gulf Sport Sponsorship,' *Sport, Ethics, and Philosophy*, 14(3), 2020, p. 370.
27. Jeremy Whittle, ''A Perfect Job': Pogacar and UAE Team Emirates Bask in Tour de France Glory,' *The Guardian*, 22 July 2024.
28. 'Prince Nasser: 'Bahrain Needed This Team',' *VeloNews*, 16 January 2017.
29. Ibid. See also Owen Bowcott, 'UK Police to be Asked to Investigate Torture Claims Against Bahraini Prince,' *The Guardian*, 7 October 2014.
30. Ali Rabea, 'Bahraini Uprising of 2011: The (No More) Hidden Political Role of Sports Journalism,' *International Review for the Sociology of Sport*, 57(7), 2022, p. 1046.
31. Joey D'Urso, 'Football and Cryptocurrency Sponsorship: Is the Free-for-all Over?', *The Athletic*, 18 January 2022.

32. Erin Griffith and David Yaffe-Bellany, 'How Tom Brady's Crypto Ambitions Collided with Reality,' *New York Times*, 6 July 2023;
33. Joey D'Urso, 'Why Cristiano Ronaldo is Being Sued in $1bn Lawsuit by People Who Bought His NFTs,' *The Athletic*, 30 November 2023.
34. Tristan Kennedy, 'The 'Sportswashing' Behind One of the World's Biggest Cycling Teams,' Vice News, *21 September* 2020.
35. Peter Aitken, 'Bret Baier Interviews Saudi Crown Prince: Israel Peace, 9/11 Ties, Iran Nuke Fears: 'Cannot See Another Hiroshima',' Fox News, 20 September 2023.
36. Charlotte Lysa, 'Fighting for the Right to Play: Women's Football and Regime-Loyalist Resistance in Saudi Arabia,' *Third World Quarterly*, 41(5), 2020, p. 844.
37. Abdulaziz Al Aquil, 'Field of Dreams: Turki Al-Sheikh's Year of Sporting Triumphs,' *Arab News*, 7 September 2018.
38. Roan, *Saudi Arabia World Cup 2034*.
39. Kristin Smith Diwan and Turki Buyabes, 'Saudi Arabia Sets Goals for Football On and Off the Pitch,' *Arab Gulf States Institute in Washington*, 18 July 2018.
40. Neil Partrick, 'Nationalism in the Gulf States,' in David Held and Kristian Coates Ulrichsen (eds), *The Transformation of the Gulf*, pp. 50–51; Miriam Cooke, *Tribal Modern: Branding New Nations in the Arab Gulf* (Berkeley: University of California Press, 2014), pp. 80–81.
41. Rosie Bsheer, *Archive Wars: The Politics of History in Saudi Arabia* (Stanford: Stanford University Press, 2020), p. 49.
42. Madawi Al Rasheed, *The Son King: Reform and Repression in Saudi Arabia*, p. 12.
43. Eman Alhussein, 'Football's Coming Home: Saudi League and Fan Base Get a Big Boost,' *Arab Gulf States Institute in Washington*, 22 June 2023.
44. Matt Slater, 'Might Saudi Arabia Actually Be a Good Choice for a Men's World Cup?', *The Athletic*, 11 December 2024.
45. Michael Silk, David Andrews, and C.L. Cole, 'Corporate Nationalism(s)? The Spatial Dimensions of Sporting Capital,' in Michael Silk, David Andrews, and C.L. Cole (eds), *Sport and Corporate Nationalism* (Oxford: Berg, 2005), p. 6.
46. Eric Hobsbawm, *Nations and Nationalism since 1870: Programme, Myth, Reality* (Cambridge: Cambridge University Press, 1990), p. 143.
47. Stephanie Kirchgaessner, 'Saudi Woman Given 34-Year Prison Sentence for Using Twitter,' *The Guardian*, 16 August 2022; Sondos Asem, 'Saudi Fitness Instructor Jailed for 11 Years over Clothing and Women's Rights Support,' *Middle East Eye*, 1 May 2024.
48. Jeff Eisenberg, 'It's Not About Sportswashing,' *Yahoo Sports*, 17 July 2023.
49. An exception is Stanis Elsborg at *Play the Game*.
50. Tariq Panja and Rory Smith, 'Saudi-led Group Completes Purchase of Newcastle United,' *New York Times*, 7 October 2021.
51. Tariq Panja, 'The Brazen Bootlegging of a Multibillion-Dollar Sports Network,' *New York Times*, 9 May 2018.
52. Murad Ahmed and Andrew England, 'How a Saudi-led Consortium Won Control of Newcastle United,' *Financial Times*, 8 October 2021.

53. James Robinson, 'Amanda Staveley: Flying Fixer of the Square Mile,' *The Guardian*, 25 January 2009.
54. Chris Waugh, 'Explained: Why Has Mike Ashley Failed to Sell Newcastle United?', *The Athletic*, 1 October 2019; Tariq Panja, 'England's Premier League Becomes Latest Proxy for Saudi-Qatar Dispute,' *New York Times*, 21 April 2020.
55. Bradley Hope, Rory Jones, and Joshua Robinson, 'Saudi Sovereign-Wealth Fund in Talks to Buy U.K. Soccer Team Newcastle United,' *Wall Street Journal*, 25 January 2020; George Caulkin, 'The Lockdown Takeover: What Newcastle's Proposed New Owners Plan to Do First,' *The Athletic*, 20 April 2020; George Caulkin, Chris Waugh, and Adam Crafton, ''The Gloves were Off' Then the Deal Was Off: Why Newcastle's Takeover Collapsed,' *The Athletic*, 30 July 2020.
56. David Dawkins, 'In a Blow to the Sale of Newcastle United, WTO Rules that Saudi Arabia Did Little to Prevent High-Profile Piracy,' *Forbes*, 16 June 2020.
57. Sean Ingle, 'New Legal Documents Raise Fresh Questions Over Newcastle Takeover Deal,' *The Guardian*, 11 May 2020; David Dawkins, 'Why the $380 Million Deal for Newcastle United No Longer Makes Sense for Anyone,' *Forbes*, 14 May 2020.
58. Louise Taylor, 'Newcastle Set Sights on Trophies after Saudi-backed Takeover Ends Ashley Era,' *The Guardian*, 7 October 2021; Jacob Whitehead, 'Are Newcastle United's PIF Owners Separate from Saudi Arabia—and Why Does it Matter?', *The Athletic*, 17 January 2024.
59. George Ramsay, 'For the First Time in 20 Years, Newcastle United Will Play in the Champions League,' CNN, 23 May 2023.
60. Chris Waugh, 'Newcastle Fans Made a Difference. That is a Rare Victory in Modern Football,' *The Athletic*, 20 August 2020; 'Newcastle United Takeover: Joyous Scenes as Fans Celebrate New Era,' BBC Sport, 8 October 2021.
61. Chris Waugh and Matt Slater, 'Explained: The Premier League's Letter About Newcastle's Failed Takeover,' *The Athletic*, 14 August 2020.
62. 'Newcastle MP Writes Once Again to Premier League as Petition is Presented to Parliament,' *The Mag*, 9 September 2020.
63. Patrick Wintour, 'Saudi Crown Prince Asked Boris Johnson to Intervene in Newcastle Bid,' *The Guardian*, 15 April 2021.
64. Adam Crafton, 'Newcastle's Saudi Takeover: The UK Government's Emails Revealed,' *The Athletic*, 6 April 2023.
65. Georgina Blakeley and Brendan Evans, *The Regeneration of East Manchester* (Manchester: Manchester University Press, 2013), pp. 33–34; Philip Proudfoot and Ali Reda, 'The Gulf and the British Regional Divide,' *Middle East Research and Information Project* (MERIP) issue 304, November 2022.
66. Crafton, *Newcastle's Saudi Takeover*.
67. Chris Waugh, 'Newcastle Release Third Kit in Same Colours as Saudi Arabia,' *The Athletic*, 28 June 2022.
68. Chris Waugh, 'We Need to Talk About Newcastle United and Saudi Arabia,' *The Athletic*, 28 June 2022; Louise Taylor, 'Newcastle Face Scrutiny After Signing £25m-a-year Saudi Sponsorship Deal,' *The Guardian*, 9 June 2023.

69. Amy Woodyatt, 'Court Filing Casts Doubt on 'Assurances Made' on Saudi State's Involvement with Newcastle United,' *CNN*, 2 March 2023.
70. Louise Radnofsky and Andrew Beaton, 'LIV Golf's Saudi Backers Ordered to Turn Over Information in PGA Tour Suit,' *Wall Street Journal*, 17 February 2023; Jacob Whitehead, 'Are Newcastle United's PIF Owners Separate from Saudi Arabia—And Why Does It Matter?', *The Athletic*, 17 January 2024.
71. Joel Beall, 'PGA Tour, LIV Golf Formally Drop Antitrust Lawsuits, Ending Year of Legal Battle,' *Golf Digest*, 16 June 2023.
72. Neil Murphy, 'Saudi Arabia's PIF Increases Newcastle Stake as Amanda Staveley Steps Down,' *The National*, 12 July 2024.
73. Lee Ryder, 'Amanda Staveley's Last Request to Newcastle United Board Revealed After Tearful Exit,' *Chronicle Live*, 19 July 2024.
74. George Caulkin, 'Amanda Staveley: Why She is Leaving Newcastle, Living With Huntingdon's—and What Comes Next,' *The Athletic*, 30 July 2024.
75. Oliver Kay, 'Newcastle's Moment of Triumph Felt so Wholesome. But We Still Need to Talk About Why It Wasn't Perfect,' *The Athletic*, 19 March 2025.
76. Dominic Scurr, 'Over 300,000 Newcastle United Supporters Given 'Spectacular Surprise' After £25m Partnership,' *The Shields Gazette*, 30 March 2025.

7. WILL VISION BECOME REALITY?

1. David Goldblatt, *The Age of Football: The Global Game in the Twenty-First Century* (London: Macmillan, 2019), pp. 431–32 and 529; Harald Dolles and Sten Soderman, 'Twenty Years of Development of the J-League: Analysing the Business Parameters of Professional Football in Japan,' *Soccer & Society*, 14(5), 2013, pp. 702–3.
2. Andrei Markovitz and Lars Rensmann, *Gaming the World: How Sports are Reshaping Global Politics and Culture* (Princeton, Princeton University Press, 2010), p. 15.
3. Phyllis Myers, 'The Formation of Organizations: A Case Study of the North American Soccer League,' PhD dissertation, Purdue University, 1984, p. 91.
4. Andrei Markovitz and Steven Hellerman, *Offside: Soccer and American Exceptionalism* (Princeton: Princeton University Press, 2001), p. 165; Arthur Hopcraft, *The Football Man* (London: Aurum Press, 2006 edition), p. 223.
5. Markovitz and Hellerman, *Offside*, p. 165.
6. Pablo Maurer, 'When Pele Made His NY Cosmos Debut—the Similarities and Differences to Messi in Miami,' *The Athletic*, 20 July 2023.
7. Fernando Delgado, 'Flawed Heroes and Great Talents: The Challenges Associated with Framing Soccer Legends in the NASL,' *Soccer & Society*, 15(5), 2014, pp. 782–83; Pablo Maurer, 'George Best in the US: A Reality More Unbelievable than the Myth,' *The Athletic*, 3 August 2020.
8. Delgado, *Flawed Heroes*, p. 786.
9. John Francis and Congcong Zheng, 'Learning Vicariously from Failure: The Case of Major League Soccer and the Collapse of the North American Soccer League,' *Group & Organization Management*, 35(5), 2010, p. 558.

10. Delgado, *Flawed Heroes*, p. 783.
11. Francis and Zheng, *Learning Vicariously from Failure*, p. 557.
12. Markovitz and Hellerman, *Offside*, p. 167.
13. Dong Jinxia and J.A. Mangan, 'Football in the New China: Political Statement, Entrepreneurial Enticement and Patriotic Passion,' *Soccer & Society*, 2(3), 2001, p. 82.
14. Ibid., p. 83.
15. Daniel Delgado and Francisco Villar, 'It Is Not a Game: Soccer and China's Search for World Hegemony,' *Soccer & Society*, 21(2), 2020, p. 230.
16. Yang Ma and Jinming Zheng, 'Governance of Chinese Professional Football during Xi's Authoritarian Era: What is Changing and What Remains Unchanged,' *Soccer & Society*, 23(2), 2022, p. 227.
17. Yiyong Liang, 'The Development Pattern and a Clubs' Perspective on Football Governance in China,' *Soccer & Society*, 15(3), 2014, pp. 431–32.
18. Goldblatt, *Age of Football*, pp. 433–34.
19. Jonathan Sullivan, Simon Chadwick, and Michael Gow, 'China's Football Dream: Sport, Citizenship, Symbolic Power, and Civic Spaces,' *Journal of Sport and Social Issues*, 43(6), 2019, pp. 499 and 504.
20. Emanuel Leite Junior and Carlos Rodrigues, 'The Chinese Plan for Football Development: a Perspective from Innovation Theory,' *Sport, Business and Management: An International Journal*, 9(1), 2019, pp. 65–66.
21. Ibid. p. 71.
22. 'Carlos Tevez: I Was on Holiday During Chinese Super League Spell,' BBC Sport, 16 January 2018.
23. Xavier Ginesta, Toni Sellas, and Mireia Canals, 'Chinese Investments in Spanish Football: A Case Study of RCD Espanyol New Management Trends after Rastar Purchase,' *Communication & Sport*, 7(6), 2019, pp. 757–59.
24. Zheng Liu, Ryan Chen, and Joshua Newman, 'The Football Dream of a Sleeping Dragon: Media Framing(s), East-West Geopolitics, and the Crisis of the Chinese Men's National Team, *Communication & Sport*, 9(1), 2021, pp. 74–76.
25. Sullivan, Chadwick, and Gow, *China's Football Dream*, p. 506.
26. Dominic Fifield, 'How China's 'Soft Power' World Cup Turned Into a Nightmare,' *The Athletic*, 17 December 2022.
27. James Horncastle and Matt Slater, 'Suning's Chinese Super League Collapse and What It Means for Inter Milan,' *The Athletic*, 3 March 2021; Oliver Kay and Matt Slater, 'The Chinese Super League: From Unprecedented Salaries to Uncertain Restart Date, Unpaid Wages and Deepening Turmoil,' *The Athletic*, 27 November 2021.
28. Ian Scott, 'From NASL to MLS: Transnational Culture, Exceptionalism and Britain's Part in American Soccer's Coming of Age,' *The Journal of Popular Culture*, 44(4), 2011, p. 844.
29. Sullivan, Chadwick, and Gow, *China's Football Dream*, p. 500.
30. Tim Spiers, 'Cristiano Ronaldo, What Are You Doing?', *The Athletic*, 9 April 2024.

31. Yoshio Takahashi, 'Why Zico is Called the 'God of Soccer' in Japan: The Legacy of Zico to Japanese Soccer,' *Soccer & Society*, 15(5), 2014, p. 795; Elise Edwards, 'Fields of Individuals and Neoliberal Logics: Japanese Soccer Ideals and the 1990s Economic Crisis,' *Journal of Sport and Social Issues*, 38(5), 2014, pp. 458–59.
32. John Horne, 'The Global Game of Football: The 2002 World Cup and Regional Development in Japan,' *Third World Quarterly*, 25(7), 2004, pp. 1238–39.
33. Takahashi, *God of Soccer*, p. 796.
34. Jamie Einchcomb, 'How 18 Months in Japan Set Arsene Wenger Up For Glory at the Top,' *These Football Times*, 17 May 2018; Kris Voakes, 'When "Arsene Who?" Changed the Face of English Football,' *The Sportsman*, 22 October 2021.
35. Edwards, *Fields of Individuals*, p. 460.
36. Takahashi, *God of Soccer*, p. 798; Dolles and Soderman, *Twenty Years of Development*, p. 711.
37. Edwards, *Fields of Individuals*, p. 436.
38. Takahashi, *God of Soccer*, p. 795.
39. Stephen Greyser and Kenneth Cortsen, 'MLS as a Sports Product—the Prominence of the World's Game in the US,' *Harvard Business School*, Working Paper 21–111, 2021, p. 14.
40. Markovitz and Hellerman, *Offside*, p. 183.
41. Nicholas Watanabe, 'The Economics of Major League Soccer from the NASL to the MLS: A Brief History of North American Professional Soccer,' in Paul Downard et al (eds), *The SAGE Handbook of Sports Economics* (Thousand Oaks: Sage Publishing, 2020), p. 3.
42. Bob Davis, 'Hunt Family Rushes in Where Big Oil Fears to Tread,' *Wall Street Journal*, 20 December 2007; Francis and Zheng, *Learning Vicariously from Failure*, p. 556.
43. Francis and Zheng, *Learning Vicariously from Failure*, p. 556.
44. Nick Firchau, 'Strike Force: The World Cup Heroes Who Helped MLS Survive and Thrive,' *MLS Soccer*, 25 May 2020.
45. John Charles Bradbury, 'Financial Returns in Major League Soccer,' *Journal of Sports Economics*, 22(8), 2021, p. 922.
46. Ibid, p. 927.
47. Ibid., p. 922.
48. Joe Pacinella, 'Are Poor Attendances in the Saudi Pro League Becoming a Problem?', *Sportcal*, 29 March 2024.
49. Matthew Cooper, 'Saudi Pro League Facing New Embarrassment as Average Attendances Paint Clear Picture,' *Daily Mirror*, 21 March 2024.
50. Fahad Abuljadayel, 'Saudi Football Clubs to Curb Spending in Next Transfer Window,' *Bloomberg*, 13 March 2024.
51. Paul MacInnes, 'Saudi Pro League: The Key Factors That Will Decide Project's Global Impact,' *The Guardian*, 15 August 2023.
52. Matt Slater, 'Is Football in Saudi Arabia Getting Any Better?', *The Athletic*, 14 December 2024.

53. Zainab Fattah and Matthew Martin, 'Saudis Scale Back Ambition for $1.5 Trillion Desert Project Neom,' *Bloomberg*, 5 April 2024; Jack Dutton, 'After Neom Cut, Saudi Arabia Expected to Scale Back More Vision 2030 Plans,' *Al-Monitor*, 10 April 2024; Eliot Brown and Rory Jones, 'What Went Wrong at Saudi Arabia's Futuristic Metropolis in the Desert,' *Wall Street Journal*, 9 March 2025.
54. Fahad Abuljadayel and Zainab Fattah, 'Saudi Capital to Cut Population Goal as City Reviews Strategy,' *Bloomberg*, 26 April 2024.
55. John Benny and Salim Essaid, 'Saudi Arabia May 'Scale Back Some Vision 2030 Projects and Speed Up Others,' *The National*, 28 April 2024.
56. 'CEO of Royal Commission for Al Ula Arrested for Corruption: Nazaha,' *Arab News*, 29 January 2024; Vincent Noce, 'Head of Saudi Arabia's Al Ula Cultural Development Arrested over Corruption Claims,' *The Art Newspaper*, 29 January 2024.
57. Stephen Kalin, 'Saudi Crown Prince Barrels Ahead with Big Projects to Boost Economy,' *Wall Street Journal*, 26 August 2020; Robert Mogielnicki, 'Neom is Becoming a Destination of Destinations,' *Arab Gulf States Institute in Washington*, 26 January 2024.
58. Dennis Kumetat, *Managing the Transition: Renewable Energy and Innovation Policies in the UAE and Algeria* (Abingdon: Routledge, 2015), pp. 143–46; Sussan Saikali, 'Smart and Sustainable: The Gulf Goes All In on Tech Cities,' *Arab Gulf States Institute in Washington*, 5 July 2023.
59. Kumetat, *Managing the Transition*, p. 137.
60. Rory Jones, Summer Said, and Stephen Kalin, 'Saudi Crown Prince's Vision for Neom, a Desert City-State, Tests His Builders,' *Wall Street Journal*, 1 May 2021.
61. Gino Spocchia, 'The Line Architect Peter Cook Questions Saudi Desert City's Buildability,' *Architects' Journal*, 26 May 2023.
62. Emma Bubola and Vivian Nereim, 'Saudi Arabia to Host World Expo 2030, in Victory for Crown Prince,' *New York Times*, 28 November 2023.
63. Giorgio Leali and Paul de Villepin, 'A Football Star, Caviar and a Water Show: Inside Saudi Arabia's Campaign to Host the 2030 Expo,' *Politico*, 27 November 2023.
64. Sameer Hashmi, 'Huge Saudi Construction Projects 'Might Get Scaled Down',' BBC News, 23 June 2024.
65. Aaron Timms, 'Beyond 2034: Can the Saudi Arabia Soccer Dream Truly be Sustainable?', *The Guardian*, 19 December 2024.
66. Ibid.
67. 'Saudi Arabia: 2024 Article IV Consultation—Press Release and Staff Report,' International Monetary Fund, *IMF Country Report No. 24/280*, September 2024, p. 5.
68. Donna Abdulaziz, 'A Saudi Rave Sparks Debate Over Kingdom's Cultural Transformation,' *Wall Street Journal*, 31 December 2022.
69. Malcolm Foley, David McGillivray, and Gayle McPherson, 'Policy Pragmatism: Qatar and the Global Events Circuit,' *International Journal of Event and Festival Management*, 3(1), 2012, pp. 110–12.

NOTES

70. Ahmed Al-Emadi, Abdel Latif Sellami, and Adam Mohamedali Fadlalla, 'The Perceived Impacts of Staging the 2022 FIFA World Cup in Qatar,' *Journal of Sport & Tourism*, 26(1), 2022, pp. 1–2.
71. Andrew England and Simeon Kerr, 'After the World Cup: What Next for Qatar?', *Financial Times*, 5 July 2023.
72. Chuck Booth, 'Qatar Win Back-to-Back AFC Asian Cup Championships Behind Three Penalties from Magic Man Akram Afif,' *CBS Sport*, 10 February 2024.
73. Karim Zidan, 'Lionel Messi Chose to Play in MLS. But He's Still Saudi Arabia's $25m Pitch Man,' *The Guardian*, 15 August 2023.
74. See Chapter Four.
75. John Kemp, 'Oil Bears Conclude OPEC + Has Run Out of Options,' daily email newsletter, 16 September 2024.
76. See also James Montague, *When Friday Comes: Football, War & Revolution in the Middle East* (Liverpool: deCoubertin Books, 2013), James Dorsey, *The Turbulent World of Middle East Soccer*; Sorek and Reiche (eds) *Sport, Politics and Society in the Middle East*, and Al-Arian (ed.), *Football in the Middle East: State, Society, and the Beautiful Game*.
77. Vivian Yee, 'Saudi Activist Who Fought for Women's Right to Drive is Sentenced to Prison,' *New York Times*, 28 December 2020.
78. Stephanie Kirchgaessner, 'Saudi Woman Given 34-Year Prison Sentence for Using Twitter,' *The Guardian*, 16 August 2022.
79. 'Manahel al-Otaibi: Saudi Women's Rights Activist Jailed for 11 Years,' BBC News, 1 May 2024.
80. Hamdullah Baycar, 'How a Football Spat Nearly Derailed Saudi-Turkey Rapprochement,' *Gulf International Forum*, 22 January 2024.
81. Ben Burrows, 'Galatasaray vs Fenerbahce Turkish Super Cup Final in Saudi Arabia Cancelled: Organizers Hit Back,' *The Athletic*, 29 December 2023.
82. Baycar, *Football Spat*.
83. Rayhan Uddin, 'Saudi Arabia 'Denied Turkish Teams Flying Banner Said to Be About Gaza',' *Middle East Eye*, 29 December 2023.
84. Vivian Nereim, Kate Kelly, and Ahmed Al Omran, 'As War Looms Over Mideast, Saudi Arabia Tries to Keep the Music Going,' *New York Times*, 26 October 2023.
85. 'Saudi Arabia: Football Fans Imprisoned for Chant,' *Human Rights Watch*, 28 March 2024.
86. 'Fans Arrested, Board Dissolved at Saudi Football Club after Chanting at Match,' *European Saudi Organization for Human Rights*, 8 February 2024.
87. Human Rights Watch, *Football Fans Imprisoned*; 'Saudi Arabia: Assault on Online Expression,' *Human Rights Watch*, 22 November 2014; James Shires, *The Politics of Cybersecurity in the Middle East* (London: Hurst & Co., 2021), pp. 164–66.
88. Toby Matthiesen, *The Other Saudis: Shiism, Dissent and Sectarianism* (Cambridge: Cambridge University Press, 2015), pp. 124–25 and 203; Toby Craig Jones, 'Rebellion on the Saudi Periphery: Modernity, Marginalization, and the Shi'a Uprising of 1979,' *International Journal of Middle East Studies*, 38(2), 2006, p. 213.
89. Ben Riley-Smith, 'WWE Blames 'Mechanical Issues' for Delayed Takeoff of Plane

Carrying Stars from Saudi Arabia after Claims of Row,' *The Daily Telegraph*, 5 November 2019.

90. Joseph Ataman, Anaelle Jonah, and Amy Woodyatt, 'France Begins Terrorism Probe into Saudi Arabia Blast Ahead of Dakar Rally,' CNN, 6 January 2022; 'French Probe Concludes IED Caused Dakar Rally Blast: Source,' *Agence France Press*, 11 February 2022.
91. Hassan Ammar, Jerome Pugmire, and Jon Gambrell, 'Yemen Rebels Strike Oil Depot in Saudi City Hosting F1 Race,' *Associated Press*, 25 March 2022.
92. Ben Church, 'F1 Organizers Insist Saudi Arabian Grand Prix Will Go Ahead Despite Houthi Attack on Nearby Oil Facility,' CNN, 26 March 2022.
93. 'Beyond Riyadh: Houthi Cross-Border Aerial Warfare 2015–2022,' *Armed Conflict Location and Event Data Project* (ACLED), 17 January 2023.
94. Ibid.
95. Ben Hubbard, Palko Karasz, and Stanley Reed, 'Two Major Saudi Oil Installations Hit by Drone Strike, and US Blames Iran,' *New York Times*, 14 September 2019.
96. Marcus Hand, '28 Houthi Drones Shot Down in Red Sea as Attacks Intensify,' *Seatrade Maritime*, 11 March 2024; Jim Krane, 'Houthi Red Sea Attacks Have Global Economic Repercussions,' *Arab Center Washington*, 5 April 2024.
97. Christopher Davidson, 'The Impact of Economic Reform on Dubai,' in Anoushiravan Ehteshami and Steven Wright (eds), *Reform in the Middle East Oil Monarchies* (Reading: Ithaca Press, 2008), pp. 163–66.
98. Simeon Kerr, 'UAE Introduces Secular-Leaning Reforms to Reassure Expats,' *Financial Times*, 8 November 2020; Natasha Turak, 'Dubai Nixes its 30% Alcohol Tax in a Bid to Attract More Tourism,' CNBC, 3 January 2023.
99. Oliver Kay, 'The Speed of Jordan Henderson's Disillusionment Reflects How Great his Regret Must Be,' *The Athletic*, 7 January 2024.

8. THE ROAD TO 2034

1. Tariq Panja, 'FIFA Will Host 2030 World Cup on Three Continents,' *New York Times*, 4 October 2023.
2. 'Saudi Arabia to Bid for 2034 World Cup,' *The Athletic*, 4 October 2023.
3. Dan Roan, 'Saudi Arabia World Cup 2034: Sports Minister Defends State's Right to Host,' *BBC Sport*, 8 December 2023.
4. Matthew Martin, 'Saudi Prince Pictured with FIFA Chief after Skipping Japan Trip,' *Bloomberg*, 20 November 2022.
5. Graham Dunbar, 'FIFA Wants to Charge Hosts of Planned 24-Team Club World Cup,' *Associated Press*, 13 April 2018.
6. John Duerden, 'Saudi Arabia's Proposal for FIFA World Cup Every Two Years Gaining Support in Asia,' *Arab News*, 4 September 2022.
7. 'Arsene Wenger Says Reluctance towards Biennial World Cups is an 'Emotional' Response,' *Sky Sports*, 9 November 2021.
8. 'Arsene Wenger Backs Plan for World Cup Every Two Years,' *The Athletic*, 5 July 2021.

NOTES

9. Ewan Roberts, 'Arsene Wenger Hints at More Winter World Cups but Backtracks on Biennial Suggestion,' *Metro*, 9 December 2022.
10. Heidi Blake and Jonathan Calvert, *The Ugly Game: The Corruption of FIFA and the Qatari Plot to Buy the World Cup* (New York: Scribner, 2015).
11. Jack Rathborn, 'Josh Cavallo "Very Scared" to Play at Qatar World Cup after Coming Out as Gay,' *The Independent*, 8 November 2021.
12. Pete Pattisson and Niamh McIntyre, 'Revealed: 6500 Migrant Workers Have Died in Qatar Since World Cup Awarded,' *The Guardian*, 23 February 2021.
13. Thomas Ross Griffin, 'National Identity, Social Legacy and Qatar 2022: The Cultural Ramifications of FIFA's First Arab World Cup,' *Soccer & Society*, 20(7–8), 2019, p. 1007; Paul Michael Brannagan and Danyel Reiche, *Qatar and the 2022 FIFA World Cup: Politics, Controversy, Change* (Cham: Palgrave Macmillan, 2022), p. 4.
14. Gregg Evans, 'Why Clubs are Going to the UAE While the World Cup Is On,' *The Athletic*, 3 December 2022.
15. Tony Karon and Daniel Levy, 'What Qatar's World Cup Tells Us About the World in 2022,' *The Nation*, 21 December 2022.
16. Kristian Coates Ulrichsen, 'Qatar's Successful World Cup Signals a New Era in the Gulf and Beyond,' *Arab Center Washington*, 5 January 2023.
17. Samer Al-Atrush and Samuel Agini, 'Saudi Arabia Set to Launch Multibillion-Dollar Sports Investment Group,' *Financial Times*, 5 July 2023.
18. Tariq Panja, 'Inside Man: How FIFA Guided the World Cup to Saudi Arabia,' *New York Times*, 15 November 2023.
19. Helena Smith, 'Greece Rolls Out Red Carpet for Crown Prince, as Khashoggi Killing Falls Off Agenda,' *The Guardian*, 27 July 2022.
20. Ali Walker, 'The Secret Saudi Plan to Buy the World Cup,' *Politico*, 7 February 2023.
21. Aziz El Yaakoubi, Marwa Rashad, and Davide Barbuscia, 'Saudi Arabia Amends Import Rules from Gulf in Challenge to UAE,' *Reuters*, 5 July 2021; David Gardner, 'Saudi-UAE Competition Threatens to Upend the GCC,' *Financial Times*, 7 July 2021.
22. Jack Snape, 'FIFA's Relaxed Stadium Rule Clears Path for Saudi Arabia to Host 2034 World Cup,' *The Guardian*, 9 October 2023.
23. Zainab Fattah, 'Qatar Is in Talks to Reduce World Cup Stadiums, BofA Says,' *Bloomberg*, 22 April 2013.
24. Matt Slater, 'Why 2030 World Cup is Split Across Six Continents—and all Roads Lead to Saudi Arabia 2034,' *The Athletic*, 4 October 2023.
25. Yousef Awad, 'Football in Arabic Literature in Diaspora: Global Influences and Local Manifestations,' *International Review for the Sociology of Sport*, 51(8), 2016, p. 1015.
26. 'FIFA Council Takes Key Decisions on FIFA World Cup Editions in 2030 and 2034,' *FIFA Media Release*, 4 October 2023.
27. David Conn, *The Fall of the House of FIFA: The Multimillion-Dollar Corruption at the Heart of Global Soccer* (New York: Nation Books, 2017), pp. 86–88.

28. 'Bidding Process 2034,' FIFA, n.d. available online at https://inside.fifa.com/about-fifa/bidding-processes/bidding-process-wc-2034.
29. Adam Crafton, 'Lise Klaveness: 'Promises Were Made about Qatar. If They Were Not Kept, We Want to Report It',' *The Athletic*, 16 November 2023.
30. Snape, *FIFA's Relaxed Stadium Rule*.
31. Roan, *Saudi Arabia World Cup 2034*.
32. Jack Snape, 'Australia Given 25-Day Deadline to Challenge Saudi Arabia's 2034 World Cup Bid,' *The Guardian*, 5 October 2023.
33. Jacob Whitehead, 'Why Australia Chose Not to Challenge Saudi Arabia for the 2034 World Cup,' *The Athletic*, 3 November 2023.
34. Jack Snape, 'Australia Opts Not to Bid for 2034 World Cup in Boost for Saudi Arabia Hopes,' *The Guardian*, 31 October 2023.
35. Gianni Infantino Instagram post, 31 October 2023, available online at https://www.instagram.com/p/CzErr6Uo1QJ/?utm_source=ig_embed&ig_rid=9e2f092d-c4c0-476e-9387-f375cccb3871.
36. Josh Noble, ''The Pieces Fell into Place': How Saudi Arabia Won Football's World Cup,' *Financial Times*, 3 November 2023.
37. Josh Noble, "How Saudi Arabia Won the World Cup," *Financial Times*, 13 December 2024.
38. Pete Pattisson, 'Saudi Arabia World Cup Bid Report Accused of 'Whitewashing' Rights Abuses,' *The Guardian*, 31 October 2024; Shanti Das, ''It's Created an Internal Shitstorm': Turmoil at UK Law Firm Accused of 'Whitewashing' Saudi World Cup Report,' *The Guardian*, 2 November 2024.
39. Josh Noble and Ahmed Al Omran, 'FIFA Confirms Saudi Arabia as Host of 2034 World Cup,' *Financial Times*, 11 December 2024.
40. Adam Crafton, 'FIFA Report: Saudi 2034 World Cup Bid Has 'Medium' Human Rights Risk, *The Athletic*, 30 November 2024.
41. Joshua Robinson, 'Saudi Arabia's Lavish Sports Push Earns it the 2034 World Cup,' *Wall Street Journal*, 31 October 2023.
42. Pramod Kumar, 'Saudi Arabia Formally Bids to Host FIFA World Cup in 2034,' *Arabian Gulf Business Insight*, 30 July 2024.
43. Ali Rampling, 'Saudi Arabia Unveils 2034 World Cup Plans: 11 New Stadiums, Five Cities,' *The Athletic*, 31 July 2024.
44. Tim Callen, Kristin Smith Diwan, and Robert Mogielnicki, 'Saudi Arabia on Global Stage for 2034 World Cup,' *Arab Gulf States Institute in Washington*, 10 December 2024.
45. Ibid.
46. Emanuel Leite Junior and Carlos Rodrigues, 'The Chinese Plan for Football Development: A Perspective from Innovation Theory,' *Sport, Business and Management: An International Journal*, 9(1), 2019, pp. 65–66.
47. Brook Larmer, 'China Won't Play in this World Cup. It Still Hopes to Profit,' *New York Times*, 30 May 2018; Dominic Fifield, 'How China's 'Soft Power' World Cup Turned Into a Nightmare,' *The Athletic*, 17 December 2022.

48. Ben Cronin and Martin Ross, 'Exclusive: FIFA Withdraws Wanda Sponsorship Rights over Missed Payments,' *Sport Business*, 5 March 2024.
49. 'Aramco and FIFA Announce Global Partnership,' *FIFA Press Release*, 25 April 2024.
50. Martyn Ziegler, 'Saudi State Oil Giant to Become FIFA's Biggest-Paying Sponsor,' *The Times*, 16 November 2023.
51. 'Alex Morgan Attacks 'Bizarre' Potential Saudi Women's World Cup Sponsorship,' *Associated Press*, 9 February 2023; Matt Slater, 'FIFA Set to Drop Visit Saudi Women's World Cup Sponsorship Plans after Player Backlash,' *The Athletic*, 14 March 2023.
52. Emma Smith, '2023 Women's World Cup: FIFA Drops Visit Saudi Sponsorship for Tournament,' *BBC Sport*, 16 March 2023.
53. Chris Evert and Martina Navratilova, 'We Did Not Help Build Women's Tennis for It to be Exploited by Saudi Arabia,' *Washington Post*, 24 January 2024.
54. Jon Turner, 'Saudi Ambassador Princess Reema: Evert and Navratilova Views Beyond Disappointing,' *The National*, 29 January 2024.
55. Charlie Eccleshare, 'Coco Gauff Looks for Saudi Arabia Progress at WTA Finals; 'Probably Wouldn't Come Back Without It,'' *The Athletic*, 1 November 2024.
56. Assile Toufaily, 'DAZN Acquire Saudi Women's Premier League's Global Broadcasting Rights,' *Forbes*, 13 October 2023.
57. John Duerden, 'Saudi Arabia Football Revolution Spreads to Women's Game,' *BBC Sport*, 12 October 2023.
58. Riccardo Bresaola, 'Australia Set to Host 2026 AFC Women's Asian Cup After Others Withdraw Bids,' *Sportcal*, 23 February 2024.
59. 'Pioneering Change: Women's Football in Saudi Arabia,' *Neom/AFC*, January 2025.
60. Ibid., pp. 30–34.
61. Ibid., pp. 10–11.
62. Charlotte Lysa, *Women, Football and Social Change in Saudi Arabia: Pioneer Players* (London: I.B. Tauris, 2025).
63. Marc Lynch, *The Arab Uprising: The Unfinished Revolutions of the New Middle East* (New York: Public Affairs, 2012), p. 7; Robert Worth, *A Rage for Order: The Middle East in Turmoil, from Tahrir Square to ISIS* (New York: Farrar, Straus, Giroux, 2016), pp. 11–12.
64. Kristian Coates Ulrichsen, *Qatar and the Gulf Crisis* (London: Hurst & Co., 2020).
65. David Roberts, *Security Politics in the Gulf Monarchies*, pp. 43–44.
66. Michael Horowitz, *Hope and Despair: Israel's Future in the New Middle East* (London: Hurst & Co., 2024), pp. 201–02; Imogen Foulkes, 'Gaza War: UN Rights Expert Accuses Israel of Acts of Genocide,' *BBC News*, 26 March 2024.
67. Raphael Cohen, 'The Iran-Israel War is Just Getting Started,' *Foreign Policy*, 22 April 2024.
68. Ahmed Nagi, 'Catching Up on the Back-Channel Peace Talks in Yemen,' International Crisis Group, 10 October 2023.
69. Farnaz Fassihi and Ben Hubbard, 'Saudi Arabia and Iran Make Quiet Openings to Head Off War,' *New York Times*, 4 October 2019; 'Intel Brief: Dialogue between Iran and Saudi Arabia Advances,' The Soufan Center, 5 May 2022.

70. Tamara Abueish, 'Saudi Arabia's Vice Defense Minister Discusses De-escalation with Esper,' *Al Arabiya News*, 7 January 2020.
71. Michael Crowley, Vivian Nereim, and Patrick Kingsley, 'Saudi Arabia Offers its Price to Normalize Relations with Israel,' *New York Times*, 11 March 2023; Shayndi Raice, 'Saudi Arabia-Iran Pact Marks Setback to Israel's Efforts to Counter Tehran,' *Wall Street Journal*, 12 March 2023.
72. Maria Fantappie and Vali Nasr, 'A New Order in the Middle East?', *Foreign Affairs*, 22 March 2023.
73. Kristian Coates Ulrichsen, 'Gulf Arab States Avoid Iran-Israel Tensions,' *Arab Center Washington*, 25 April 2024.
74. Kristian Coates Ulrichsen, 'Saudi Plans to 'De-Risk' Region Have Taken a Hit with Gaza Violence—but Hitting Pause on Normalization with Israel Will Buy Kingdom Time,' *The Conversation*, 18 October 2023.
75. Alexandra Stark, *The Yemen Model: Why US Policy Has Failed in the Middle East* (New Haven: Yale University Press, 2024), pp. 22–23; Ginny Hill, *Yemen Endures: Civil War, Saudi Adventurism and the Future of Arabia* (London: Hurst & Co., 2017), p. 180.
76. Maria Gloria Polimeno, 'Houthi Attacks on Shipping Are Not Just About the Israel-Hamas War,' *Manara Magazine*, 8 May 2024.
77. Jim Krane, 'Houthi Red Sea Attacks Have Global Economic Repercussions,' *Arab Center Washington*, 5 April 2024.
78. Robert Mogielnicki, 'Saudi Regional Headquarters Program Deadline Looms,' *Arab Gulf States Institute in Washington*, 5 December 2023.
79. Chloe Cornish and Andrew England, 'Big Companies Heed Saudi Arabia's Demand to Set Up Regional HQs,' *Financial Times*, 9 March 2024.
80. '$37bn Deal with Boeing as Riyadh Air Launched,' *Gulf States Newsletter*, Vol. 47 Issue 1166, 23 March 2023, p. 13; Deena Kamel, 'ATM 2024: Riyadh Air in Talks with Airbus and Boeing Over a New Order of Wide-Body Jets,' *The National*, 6 May 2024.
81. 'Riyadh Air Signs First Sports Sponsorship Deal with Atletico de Madrid,' *Arab News*, 10 August 2023.
82. Borja Garcia and Mahfoud Amara, 'Media Perceptions of Arab Investment in European Football Clubs: The Case of Malaga and Paris Saint-Germain,' *Sport & EU Review*, 5(1), 2013, p. 15.
83. Yasser Elsheshtawy, 'The Line: A Promising Vision for a Progressive Future?', *Arab Gulf States Institute in Washington*, 3 June 2021.
84. Gal Beckerman, ''The Middle East Region is Quieter Today Than It Has Been in Two Decades,' *The Atlantic*, 7 October 2023; Katie Rogers, 'Jake Sullivan's 'Quieter' Middle East Comments Did Not Age Well,' *New York Times*, 26 October 2023.
85. Lisa Strombom and Anders Persson, 'The Abraham Accords and Peace in the Middle East,' *Center for Advanced Middle Eastern Studies*, Lund University, 21 June 2023.
86. 'Saudi Arabia to Host AFC Champions League Elite-Final Stage,' *Asian Football Confederation press release*, 1 December 2023; 'FIFA Picks Qatar, Morocco to Host 5 Youth World Cups,' *Asharq Al-Awsat*, 14 March 2024.

NOTES

87. cf. Simon Chadwick, Paul Widdop, and Michael Goldman (eds), *The Geopolitical Economy of Sport: Power, Politics, Money, and the State* (Abingdon: Routledge, 2023); Miguel Delaney, *States of Play: How Sportswashing Took Over Football* (London: Orion Publishing, 2024).
88. Sean Ingle, 'England Winners at Nostalgia but we Should Not Believe the Euro 96 Hype,' *The Guardian*, 5 June 2016.
89. 'Saudi Pro League to Focus on Signing U21 Players,' 5 May 2024, https://www.spl.com.sa/en/news/497225/saad-al-lazeez-press-conference.
90. Samuel Agini, 'Premier League Clubs Slash Summer Transfer Spending,' *Financial Times*, 31 August 2024.
91. 'What Changes Are Being Made in Saudi Pro League for 2024/25 Season?', *The National*, 12 July 2024.
92. Adam Leventhal, 'Why Has Saudi Arabia Been so Quiet on Transfers This Summer? It's All Part of the Plan,' *The Athletic*, 19 July 2024; Simon Hughes, 'Who Moved to Saudi Arabia This Summer—And What It Reveals About the Pro League,' *The Athletic*, 5 September 2024.
93. 'Roberto Mancini Concerned by Lack of Saudi Pro League Minutes for National Team Players,' *The National*, 9 September 2024.
94. John Duerden, 'Roberto Mancini Departs Saudi Arabian Job Richer but With Team No Better Off,' *The Guardian*, 26 October 2024.
95. 'Al Qadsiah Returns to Saudi Pro League,' *Saudi Gazette*, 7 May 2024.
96. 'The PIF: Crowding Out Entrepreneurs,' *Gulf States Newsletter*, Vol. 45 Issue 1131, 29 July 2021, p. 4.
97. 'Saudi Arabia Announces Six Additional Sports Clubs for Privatization,' *Arab News*, 4 July 2024.
98. Frank Gardner, 'Saudi Tribe Challenges Crown Prince's Plans for Tech City,' *BBC News*, 22 April 2020.
99. Merlyn Thomas and Lara El Gibaly, 'Neom: Saudi Forces 'Told to Kill' to Clear Land for Eco-City,' *BBC News*, 8 May 2024.
100. 'Saudi Authorities Try to Counter Criticism over PIF's Jeddah Demolition and Redevelopment,' *Gulf States Newsletter*, Vol. 46 Issue 1141, 17 February 2022, pp. 1–3.
101. 'Saudi Arabia: Mass Demolitions and Forced Evictions Marred by Violations and Discrimination,' *Amnesty International*, 22 June 2022; Fatma Tanis, 'Demolition of Jeddah Neighbourhoods Sparks Rare Widespread Criticism in Saudi Arabia,' *National Public Radio* (NPR), 3 August 2022.
102. Eliot Brown and Rory Jones, 'World's Biggest Construction Project Gets a Reality Check,' *Wall Street Journal*, 7 May 2024.
103. Erika Solomon, 'Dwindling Snow Leaves Swiss Alpine Villages Staring at an Identity Crisis,' *New York Times*, 15 January 2023.

BIBLIOGRAPHY

Monographs

Alangari, Haifa, *The Struggle for Power in Arabia: Ibn Saud, Hussein and Great Britain, 1914–1924* (Reading: Ithaca Press, 1998).

Al-Arian, Abdullah (ed.), *Football in the Middle East: State, Society, and the Beautiful Game* (London: Hurst & Co., 2022).

Almuhanna, Ibrahim, *Oil Leaders: An Insider's Account of Four Decades of Saudi Arabia and OPEC's Global Energy Policy* (New York: Columbia University Press, 2021).

Al Rasheed, Madawi, *A History of Saudi Arabia* (Cambridge: Cambridge University Press, 2002).

———, *Muted Modernists: The Struggle over Divine Politics in Saudi Arabia* (London: Hurst & Co., 2015).

———, *The Son King: Reform and Repression in Saudi Arabia* (London: Hurst & Co., 2020).

Bazoobandi, Sara, *The Political Economy of the Gulf Sovereign Wealth Funds: A Case Study of Iran, Kuwait, Saudi Arabia and the United Arab Emirates* (Abingdon: Routledge, 2013).

Blake, Heidi and Jonathan Calvert, *The Ugly Game: The Corruption of FIFA and the Qatari Plot to Buy the World Cup* (New York: Scribner, 2015).

Billingsley, Anthony, *Political Succession in the Arab World: Constitutions, Family Loyalties and Islam* (Abingdon: Routledge, 2010).

Blakeley, Georgina and Brendan Evans, *The Regeneration of East Manchester* (Manchester: Manchester University Press, 2013).

Booth, Douglas, *The Race Game: Sport and Politics in South Africa* (London: Frank Cass, 1998).

Boyle, Raymond and Richard Haynes, *Power Play: Sport, the Media and Popular Culture* (Edinburgh: Edinburgh University Press, 2009).

BIBLIOGRAPHY

Brannagan, Paul Michael and Danyel Reiche, *Qatar and the 2022 FIFA World Cup: Politics, Controversy, Change* (Cham: Palgrave Macmillan, 2022).

Bsheer, Rosie, *Archive Wars: The Politics of History in Saudi Arabia* (Stanford: Stanford University Press, 2020).

Chadwick, Simon, Paul Widdop, and Michael Goldman (eds), *The Geopolitical Economy of Sport: Power, Politics, Money, and the State* (Abingdon: Routledge, 2023).

Coates Ulrichsen, Kristian, *Qatar and the Gulf Crisis* (London: Hurst & Co., 2023).

Conn, David, *The Fall of the House of FIFA: The Multimillion-Dollar Corruption at the Heart of Global Soccer* (New York: Nation Books, 2017).

Cooke, Miriam, *Tribal Modern: Branding New Nations in the Arab Gulf* (Berkeley: University of California Press, 2014).

Davidson, Christopher, *From Sheikhs to Sultanism: Statecraft and Authority in Saudi Arabia and the UAE* (London: Hurst & Co., 2021).

Delaney, Miguel, *States of Play: How Sportswashing Took Over Football* (London: Orion Publishing, 2024).

Deninger, Dennis, *Live Sports Media: The What, How and Why of Sports Broadcasting* (Abingdon: Routledge, 2022).

Dorsey, James, *The Turbulent World of Middle East Soccer* (London: Hurst & Co., 2016).

Freitag, Ulrike, *A History of Jeddah: The Gate to Mecca in the Nineteenth and Twentieth Centuries* (Cambridge: Cambridge University Press, 2020).

Goldblatt, David, *The Age of Football: The Global Game in the Twenty-First Century* (London: Macmillan, 2019).

———, *The Ball is Round: A Global History of Football* (London: Penguin Books/Viking, 2006).

Hegghammer, Thomas, *Jihad in Saudi Arabia: Violence and Pan-Islamism Since 1979* (Cambridge: Cambridge University Press, 2010).

Hertog, Steffen, *Princes, Brokers, and Bureaucrats: Oil and the State in Saudi Arabia* (Ithaca: Cornell University Press, 2010).

Hobsbawm, Eric, *Nations and Nationalism since 1870: Programme, Myth, Reality* (Cambridge: Cambridge University Press, 1990).

Hill, Ginny, *Yemen Endures: Civil War, Saudi Adventurism and the Future of Arabia* (London: Hurst & Co., 2017).

Hill, Jimmy, *The Jimmy Hill Story* (London: Hodder & Stoughton, 1988, Kindle edition).

Horowitz, Michael, *Hope and Despair: Israel's Future in the New Middle East* (London: Hurst & Co., 2024).

Hoyer, Katja, *Beyond the Wall: A History of East Germany* (New York: Basic Books, 2023).

BIBLIOGRAPHY

Inglis, Simon, *League Football and the Men Who Made It: The Official Centenary History of the Football League, 1888–1988* (London: Collins Willow, 1988).

Jones, Toby Craig, *Desert Kingdom: How Oil and Water Forged Modern Saudi Arabia* (Cambridge: Harvard University Press, 2010).

Kechichian, Joseph, *Legal and Political Reforms in Sa'udi Arabia* (Abingdon: Routledge, 2013).

Krane, Jim, *Energy Kingdoms: Oil and Political Survival in the Persian Gulf* (New York: Columbia University Press, 2019).

Kumetat, Dennis, *Managing the Transition: Renewable Energy and Innovation Policies in the UAE and Algeria* (Abingdon: Routledge, 2015).

Kunz, William, *The Political Economy of Sports Television* (Abingdon: Routledge, 2020).

Lynch, Marc, *The Arab Uprising: The Unfinished Revolutions of the New Middle East* (New York: Public Affairs, 2012).

Mandell, Richard, *The Nazi Olympics* (Urbana: University of Illinois Press, 1987).

Markovitz, Andrei and Lars Rensmann, *Gaming the World: How Sports are Reshaping Global Politics and Culture* (Princeton: Princeton University Press, 2010).

Matthiesen, Toby, *The Other Saudis: Shiism, Dissent and Sectarianism* (Cambridge: Cambridge University Press, 2015).

McNally, Robert, *Crude Volatility: The History and the Future of Boom-Bust Oil Prices* (New York: Columbia University Press, 2017).

McRae, Donald, *Winter Colours: Changing Seasons in World Rugby* (Edinburgh: Mainstream Publishing, 1998).

Miller, Rory, *Desert Kingdoms to Global Powers: The Rise of the Arab Gulf* (New Haven: Yale University Press, 2016).

Mohammad, Talal, *Iranian-Saudi Rivalry Since 1979: In the Words of Kings and Clerics* (London: I.B. Tauris, 2023).

Montague, James, *When Friday Comes: Football, War & Revolution in the Middle East* (Liverpool: deCoubertin Books, 2013).

Niblock Tim with Monica Malik, *The Political Economy of Saudi Arabia* (Abingdon: Routledge, 2007).

Ottaway, David, *Mohammed bin Salman: The Icarus of Saudi Arabia?* (Colorado: Lynne Rienner Publishers, 2021).

Roberts, David, *Security Politics in the Gulf Monarchies* (New York: Columbia University Press, 2023).

Rundell, David, *Vision or Mirage: Saudi Arabia at a Crossroads* (London: I.B. Tauris, 2020).

Seznec, Jean-Francois, *The Financial Markets of the Arabian Gulf* (London: Croon Helm, 1987).

BIBLIOGRAPHY

Shires, James, *The Politics of Cybersecurity in the Middle East* (London: Hurst & Co., 2021).

Stark Alexandra, *The Yemen Model: Why US Policy Has Failed in the Middle East* (New Haven: Yale University Press, 2024).

Wearing, David, *AngloArabia: Why Gulf Wealth Matters to Britain* (Cambridge: Polity Press, 2018).

Worth, Robert, *A Rage for Order: The Middle East in Turmoil, from Tahrir Square to ISIS* (New York: Farrar, Straus and Giroux, 2016).

Yizraeli, Sarah, *Politics and Society in Saudi Arabia: The Crucial Years of Development, 1960–1982* (London: Hurst & Co., 2012).

Book chapters

Al Droushi, 'The Emergence and Development of the Islamic Solidarity Games,' in Fan Hong and Lu Zhoxiang (eds), *The Routledge Handbook of Sport in Asia* (Abingdon: Routledge, 2020).

Al Rasheed, Madawi, 'Circles of Power: Royals and Society in Saudi Arabia,' in Paul Aarts and Gerd Nonneman (eds), *Saudi Arabia in the Balance: Political Economy, Society, Foreign Affairs* (London: Hurst & Co., 2005).

Amara, Mahfoud, 'The Importance of Culture: Sport and Development in the Arab World—Between Tradition and Modernity,' in Barrie Houlihan and Mick Green (eds), *Routledge Handbook of Sports Development* (Abingdon: Routledge, 2011).

Bahgat, Gawdat, 'Sovereign Wealth Funds in the Gulf—An Assessment,' in David Held and Kristian Coates Ulrichsen (eds), *The Transformation of the Gulf: Politics, Economics and the Global Order* (Abingdon: Routledge, 2012).

Chadwick, Simon, 'The Business of Sports in the Gulf Cooperation Council Member States,' in Tamir Sorek and Danyel Reiche (eds), *Sport, Politics and Society in the Middle East* (London: Hurst & Co., 2019).

Chadwick, Simon and Paul Widdop, 'Sports Washing and the Gulf Region: Myth or Reality?', in Simon Chadwick, Paul Widdop, and Michael Goldman (eds), *The Geopolitical Economy of Sport: Power, Politics, Money and the State* (Abingdon: Routledge, 2023).

Chanavat, Nicolas and Michel Desbordes, 'Towards the Regulation and Restriction of Ambush Marketing?', in Simon Chadwick, Nicolas Chanavat, and Michel Desbordes (eds), *Routledge Handbook of Sports Marketing* (Abingdon: Routledge, 2018).

Coates Ulrichsen, Kristian, 'Perceptions and Divisions in Security and Defense Structures in Arab Gulf States,' in Andreas Krieg (ed.), *Divided Gulf: The Anatomy of a Crisis* (Singapore: Springer, 2019).

BIBLIOGRAPHY

Davidson, Christopher, 'The Impact of Economic Reform on Dubai,' in Anoushiravan Ehteshami and Steven Wright (eds), *Reform in the Middle East Oil Monarchies* (Reading: Ithaca Press, 2008).

DeGaris, Larry, Mark Dodds and James Reese, 'A Data-Driven Approach to Sponsorship Planning,' in Simon Chadwick, Nicolas Chanavat, and Michel Desbordes (eds), *Routledge Handbook of Sports Marketing* (Abingdon: Routledge, 2015).

Doaiji, Nora, 'From Hasm to Hazm: Saudi Feminism beyond Patriarchal Bargaining,' in Madawi Al Rasheed (ed.), *Salman's Legacy: The Dilemmas of a New Era in Saudi Arabia* (London: Hurst & Co., 2018).

Held, David and Kristian Coates Ulrichsen, 'Editors' Introduction,' in David Held and Kristian Coates Ulrichsen (eds), *The Transformation of the Gulf: Politics, Economics and the Global Order* (Abingdon: Routledge, 2012).

Hvidt, Martin, 'The Emergence and Spread of the "Dubai Model" in the GCC Countries,' in Mehran Kamrava (ed.), *Routledge Handbook of Persian Gulf Politics* (Abingdon: Routledge, 2020).

Kechichian, Joseph, 'The Politics of Succession in Saudi Arabia: A Struggle for Primogeniture,' in Kristian Coates Ulrichsen (ed.), *The Changing Security Dynamics of the Persian Gulf* (London: Hurst & Co., 2017).

LaMay, Craig, 'The World Cup and Freedom of Expression in Qatar,' in Tamir Sorek and Danyel Reiche (eds), *Sport, Politics and Society in the Middle East* (London: Hurst & Co., 2019).

Mezahi, Maher, 'A Study of Football Chants as Political Expression in the Algerian Hirak,' in Abdullah Al-Arian (ed.), *Football in the Middle East: State, Society, and the Beautiful Game* (London: Hurst & Co., 2022).

Moritz, Jessie, 'Rentier Political Economy in the Gulf Oil Monarchies,' in Mehran Kamrava (ed.), *Routledge Handbook of Persian Gulf Politics* (Abingdon: Routledge, 2020).

Patrick, Neil, 'Nationalism in the Gulf States,' in David Held and Kristian Coates Ulrichsen (eds), *The Transformation of the Gulf: Politics, Economics and the Global Order* (Abingdon: Routledge, 2012).

Ren, Tianwei, 'A Special Salience: Media, Iconography, Nationalism: Modern Chinese Olympic Games and Heroes as Soft Power 'Projectiles',' in Tainwei Ren, Keiko Ikeda, and Chang Wan Woo (eds), *Media, Sport, Nationalism. East Asia: Soft Power Projection via the Modern Olympic Games* (Berlin: Logos Verlag, 2019).

Sadiki, Larbi and Layla Saleh, 'Playing Ball: Crowd and 'Contra-Crowd' in the Politics of Egyptian and Tunisian Football,' in Fan Hong and Lu Zhouxiang (eds), *The Routledge Handbook of Sports in Asia* (Abingdon: Routledge, 2020).

Silk, Michael, David Andrews, and C.L. Cole, 'Corporate Nationalism(s)?

BIBLIOGRAPHY

The Spatial Dimensions of Sporting Capital,' in Michael Silk, David Andrews, and C.L. Cole (eds), *Sport and Corporate Nationalism* (Oxford: Berg, 2005).

Valeri, Marc, 'Oligarchy vs. Oligarchy: Business and Politics of Reform in Bahrain and Oman,' in Steffen Hertog, Giacomo Luciani, and Marc Valeri (eds), *Business Politics in the Middle East* (London: Hurst & Co., 2013).

Watanabe, Nicholas, 'The Economics of Major League Soccer from the NASL to the MLS: A Brief History of North American Professional Soccer,' in Paul Downward et al (eds), *The SAGE Handbook of Sports Economics* (Thousand Oaks: Sage Publishing, 2020).

Yildiz, Murat, 'Mapping the "Sports Awakening": Toward a Regional History of Sports in the Middle East, in Tamir Sorek and Danyel Reiche (eds), *Sport, Politics and Society in the Middle East* (London: Hurst & Co., 2019).

Journal articles

Al-Emadi, Ahmed, Abdel Latif Sellami and Adam Mohamedali Fadlalla, 'The Perceived Impacts of Staging the 2022 FIFA World Cup in Qatar,' *Journal of Sport & Tourism*, 26(1), 2022.

Alissa, Reem, 'The Oil Town of Ahmadi since 1946: From Colonial Town to Nostalgic City,' *Comparative Studies of South Asia, Africa and the Middle East*, 33(1), 2013.

Alkadi, Ibrahim Ghazi, 'A Resource-Based View of Al-Hilal Football Club: Using a Qualitative Approach,' *Academy of Entrepreneurship Journal*, 27(4), 2021.

Al Nakib, 'Kuwait's Modern Spectacle: Oil Wealth and the Making of a New Capital City, 1950–90,' *Comparative Studies of South Asia, Africa and the Middle East*, 33(1), 2013.

Amara, Mahfoud, 'The Muslim World in the Global Sporting Arena,' *Brown Journal of World Affairs*, 14(2), 2008.

Amara, Mahfoud, 'Veiled Women Athletes in the 2008 Beijing Olympic Games: Media Accounts,' *The International Journal of the History of Sport*, 29(4), 2012.

Awad, Yousef, 'Football in Arabic Literature in Diaspora: Global Influences and Local Manifestations,' *International Review for the Sociology of Sport*, 51(8), 2016.

Bar-On, Tamir, 'Reflections on Soccer, Sovereignty and the State of Exception,' *Soccer & Society*, 19(4), 2018.

Black, David and Janis Van Der Westhuizen, 'Editorial: The Neglected Allure of Global Games?', *Third World Quarterly*, 25(7), 2004.

Black, David and Shona Bezanson, 'The Olympic Games, Human Rights and

BIBLIOGRAPHY

Democratisation: Lessons from Seoul and Implications for Beijing,' *Third World Quarterly*, 25(7), 2004.

Blasing, John, 'Hegemonic Discourses Clash in the Stadium: Sport, Nationalism, and Globalization in Turkey,' *International Journal of Middle East Studies*, 51(3), 2019.

Bradbury, John Charles, 'Financial Returns in Major League Soccer,' *Journal of Sports Economics*, 22(8), 2021.

Boykoff, Jules, 'Toward a Theory of Sportswashing: Mega-Events, Soft Power, and Political Conflict,' *Sociology of Sport Journal*, 39 (2022).

Bromberger, Christian, 'Football and the Authoritarian Regime in Iran,' *Soccer & Society*, 21(6), 2020.

Campbell, Rook, 'Staging Globalization for National Projects: Global Sports Markets and Elite Athletic Transnational Labour in Qatar,' *International Review for the Sociology of Sport*, 46(1), 2010. Chehabi, Houchang, 'The Politics of Football in Iran,' *Soccer & Society*, 7(2–3), 2006.

Crossley, Stephen and Adam Woolf, ''Fog on the Tyne'? The 'Common-Sense' Focus on 'Sportswashing and the 2021 Takeover of Newcastle United,' *International Journal of Sport Policy and Politics*, 16(2), 2024.

Delgado, Daniel and Francisco Villar, 'It Is Not a Game: Soccer and China's Search for World Hegemony,' *Soccer & Society*, 21(2), 2020.

Delgado, Fernando, 'Flawed Heroes and Great Talents: The Challenges Associated with Framing Soccer Legends in the NASL,' *Soccer & Society*, 15(5), 2014.

Dimeo, Paul and Joyce Kay, 'Major Sports Events, Image Projection and the Problems of 'Semi-Periphery': A Case Study of the 1996 South Asia Cricket World Cup,' *Third World Quarterly*, 25(7), 2004.

Dolles, Harald and Sten Soderman, 'Twenty Years of Development of the J-League: Analysing the Business Parameters of Professional Football in Japan,' *Soccer & Society*, 14(5), 2013.

Dorsey, James, 'The Politics of Indonesian and Turkish Soccer: A Comparative Analysis,' *Soccer & Society*, 14(5), 2013.

Dorsey, James, 'Soccer Versus Jihad: A Draw,' *American Behavioral Science*, 60(9), 2016.

Dunn, Graham, 'Ambitions Shape Saudi Operators,' *Airline Business*, 39(2), 2023.

Edens, David and William Snaveley, 'Planning for Economic Development in Saudi Arabia,' *Middle East Journal*, 24(1), 1970.

Edwards, Elise, 'Fields of Individuals and Neoliberal Logics: Japanese Soccer Ideals and the 1990s Economic Crisis,' *Journal of Sport and Social Issues*, 38(5), 2014.

BIBLIOGRAPHY

El-Zatmah, 'From Terso into Ultras: the 2011 Egyptian Revolution and the Radicalization of the Soccer's Ultra-Fans, *Soccer & Society*, 13(5–6), 2012.

Flemming, Felix, Marco Lunich, Frank Marcinkowski, and Christopher Starke, 'Coping with Dilemma: How German Sport Media Users Respond to Sport Mega Events in Autocratic Countries,' *International Review for the Sociology of Sport*, 52(8), 2017.

Foley, Malcolm, David McGillivray, and Gayle McPherson, 'Policy Pragmatism: Qatar and the Global Events Circuit,' *International Journal of Event and Festival Management*, 3(1), 2012.

Francis, John and Congcong Zheng, 'Learning Vicariously from Failure: The Case of Major League Soccer and the Collapse of the North American Soccer League,' *Group & Organization Management*, 35(5), 2010.

Garcia, Borja and Mahfoud Amara, 'Media Perceptions of Arab Investment in European Football Clubs: The Case of Malaga and Paris Saint-Germain,' *Sport & EU Review*, 5(1), 2013.

Gillooly, Leah, Christos Anagnastopoulos, and Simon Chadwick, 'Social Media-based Sponsorship Activation: A Typology of Content,' *Sport, Business and Management: An International Journal*, 7(3), 2017.

Ginesta, Xavier and Jordi de San Eugenio, 'The Use of Football as a Country Branding Strategy. Case Study: Qatar and the Catalan Sports Press,' *Communication & Sport*, 2(3), 2014.

Ginesta, Xavier, Toni Sellas, and Mireia Canals, 'Chinese Investments in Spanish Football: A Case Study of RCD Espanyol New Management Trends after Rastar Purchase,' *Communication & Sport*, 7(6), 2019.

Giulianotti, Richard, 'Supporters, Followers, Fans, and Flaneurs: A Taxonomy of Spectator Identities in Football,' *Journal of Sport & Social Issues*, 26(1), 2002.

Giulianotti, Richard, Fred Coalter, Holly Collison, and Simon Darnell, 'Rethinking Sportland: A New Research Agenda for the Sport and Development and Peace Sector,' *Journal of Sport and Social Issues*, 43(6), 2019.

Graeff, Billy and Jorge Knijnik, 'If Things Go South: The Renewed Policy of Sport Mega Events Allocation and its Implications for Future Research,' *International Review for the Sociology of Sport*, 56(8), 2021.

Griffin, Thomas Ross, 'National Identity, Social Legacy and Qatar 2022: The Cultural Ramifications of FIFA's First Arab World Cup,' *Soccer & Society*, 20(7–8), 2019.

Grix, Jonathan, 'Sport Politics and the Olympics,' *Political Studies Review* 11, 2013.

Grix, Jonathan and Barrie Houlihan, 'Sports Mega-Events as Part of a Nation's Soft Power Strategy: The Cases of Germany (2006) and the UK (2012), *The British Journal of Politics and International Relations*, 16 (2014).

BIBLIOGRAPHY

Grix, Jonathan and Nina Kramareva, 'The Sochi Winter Olympics and Russia's Unique Soft Power Strategy,' *Sport in Society*, 20(4), 2017.

Grix, Jonathan, Joonoh Brian Jeong, and Hyungmin Kim, 'Understanding South Korea's Use of Sports Mega-Events for Domestic, Regional, and International Soft Power,' *Societies* 11, 2021.

Guthrie-Shimizu, Sayuri, 'Japan's Sports Diplomacy in the Early Post-Second World War Years,' *International Area Studies Review*, 16(3), 2013.

Haghirian, Mehran and Paulino Robles-Gil, 'Soft Power and the 2022 World Cup in Qatar: Learning from Experiences of Past Mega-Sporting Event Hosts,' *Tajseer*, 3(2), 2021.

Harvey, Adam, ''An Epoch in the Annals of National Sport': Football in Sheffield and the Creation of Modern Soccer and Rugby,' *The International Journal of the History of Sport*, 18(4), 2001.

Hegghammer, Thomas and Stephane Lacroix, 'Rejectionist Islamism in Saudi Arabia: The Story of Juhayman Al-'utaybi Revisited,' *International Journal of Middle East Studies*, 39(1), 2007.

Henry, Ian, Mahfoud Amara, and Mansour Al Tauqi, 'Sport, Arab Nationalism and the Pan-Arab Games,' *International Review for the Sociology of Sport*, 38(3), 2003.

Hertog, Steffen, 'Petromin: The Slow Death of Statist Oil Development in Saudi Arabia,' *Business History*, 50(5), 2008.

Hokayem, Emile, 'Fraught Relations: Saudi Ambitions and American Anger,' *Survival*, 64(6), 2022.

Horne, John, 'The Global Game of Football: The 2002 World Cup and Regional Development in Japan,' *Third World Quarterly*, 25(7), 2004.

Hvidt, Martin, 'The Dubai Model: An Outline of Key Development-Process Elements in Dubai,' *International Journal of Middle East Studies*, 41(2), 2009.

Irak, Daghan, ''Shoot Some Pepper Gas at Me!' Football Fans vs. Erdogan: Organized Politicization or Reactive Politics?', *Soccer & Society*, 19(3), 2018.

Jinxia, Dong and J.A. Mangan, 'Football in the New China: Political Statement, Entrepreneurial Enticement and Patriotic Passion,' *Soccer & Society*, 2(3), 2001.

Johnson, Arthur, 'Government, Opposition and Sport: The Role of Domestic Sports Policy in Generating Political Support,' *Journal of Sport and Social Issues*, 6(2), 1982.

Johnson, Drew, 'Company Perspectives: Public Investment Fund of Saudi Arabia,' *International Directory of Company Histories*, Volume 246.

Jones, Calvert, 'All the King's Consultants,' *Foreign Affairs*, 98(3), 2019.

Jones, Ian, Andrew Adams, and Joanne Mayoh, 'Fan Responses to Ownership Change in the English Premier League: Motivated Ignorance,

BIBLIOGRAPHY

Social Creativity and Social Competition at Newcastle United F.C.,' *International Journal of Sport Policy and Politics*, 15(3), 2023.

Jones, Toby Craig, 'Rebellion on the Saudi Periphery: Modernity, Marginalization, and the Shi'a Uprising of 1979,' *International Journal of Middle East Studies* 38(2), 2006.

Juneau, Thomas, 'A Surprising Spat,' *International Journal*, 74(2), 2019.

Kanie, Mariwan, 'Civil Society, Language and the Authoritarian Context: The Case of Saudi Arabia,' *Orient*, 53(4), 2012.

King, Gary, Jennifer Pan, and Margaret Roberts, 'How Censorship in China Allows Government Criticism but Silences Collective Action,' *American Political Science Review*, 2012 (online).

Koch, Natalie, 'The Geopolitics of Gulf Sport Sponsorship,' *Sport, Ethics and Philosophy*, 14(3), 2020.

Krzyzaniak, John, 'The Soft Power Strategy of Soccer Sponsorships,' *Soccer & Society*, 19(4), 2018.

Leite Junior, Emanuel and Carlos Rodriguez, 'The Chinese Plan for Football Development: A Perspective from Innovation Theory,' *Sport, Business and Management: An International Journal*, 9(1), 2019.

Liang, Yiyong, 'The Development Pattern and a Clubs' Perspective on Football Governance in China,' *Soccer & Society*, 15(3), 2014.

Liu, Zheng, Ryan Chen, and Joshua Newman, 'The Football Dream of a Sleeping Dragon: Media Framing(s), East-West Geopolitics, and the Crisis of the Chinese Men's National Team, *Communication & Sport*, 9(1), 2021.

Lysa, Charlotte, 'Fighting for the Right to Play: Women's Football and Regime-Loyalist Resistance in Saudi Arabia,' *Third World Quarterly*, 41(5), 2020.

Lysa, Charlotte, 'Globalized, Yet Local: Football Fandom in Qatar,' *Soccer & Society*, 22(7), 2021.

Ma, Yang and Jinming Zheng, 'Governance of Chinese Professional Football during Xi's Authoritarian Era: What is Changing and What Remains Unchanged,' *Soccer & Society*, 23(2), 2022.

Manzenreiter, Wolfram, 'The Beijing Games in the Western Imagination of China: The Weak Power of Soft Power,' *Journal of Sport and Social Issues*, 34(1), 2010.

McPherson-Smith, Oliver, 'Diversification, Khashoggi, and Saudi Arabia's Public Investment Fund,' *Global Policy*, 12(2), 2021.

Mead, Dave and Porscha Stiger, 'The 2014 Plunge in Import Petroleum Prices: What Happened?', Bureau of Labor Statistics, *Beyond the Numbers*, 4(9), 2015.

Mohammadi, Shahrzad, 'State Control and the Online Contestation of

BIBLIOGRAPHY

Iranian Female Spectators and Activists,' *Communication & Sport*, 8(4–5), 2020.

Montambault Trudelle, Alexis, 'The Public Investment Fund and Salman's State: The Political Drivers of Sovereign Wealth Management in Saudi Arabia,' *Review of International Political Economy*, 2022 (online).

Nauright, John, 'Global Games: Culture, Political Economy and Sport in the Globalised World of the 21st Century,' *Third World Quarterly*, 25(7), 2004.

Niblock, Tim, 'Saudi Arabia's Economic Development: Ambitious Reforms, Difficult Dilemmas,' *Journal of Middle Eastern and Islamic Studies (in Asia)*, 2(2), 2008.

Raab, Alon, 'Soccer in the Middle East: An Introduction,' *Soccer & Society*, 13(5–6), 2012.

Rabea, Ali, 'Bahraini Uprising of 2011: The (No More) Hidden Political Role of Sports Journalism,' *International Review for the Sociology of Sport*, 57(7), 2022.

Seznec, Jean-Francois, 'The Gulf Sovereign Wealth Funds: Myth and Reality,' *Middle East Policy*, 15(2), 2008.

Scelles, Nicolas, Boris Helleu, Christophe Durand, Liliane Bonnal, and Stephen Morrow, 'Explaining the Number of Social Media Fans for North American and European Professional Sports Clubs with Determinants of Their Financial Value,' *International Journal of Financial Studies*, 5(25), 2017.

Scott, Ian, 'From NASL to MLS: Transnational Culture, Exceptionalism and Britain's Part in American Soccer's Coming of Age,' *The Journal of Popular Culture*, 44(4), 2011.

Skey, Michael, 'Sportswashing: Media Headline or Analytic Concept?', *International Review for the Sociology of Sport*, 58(5), 2023.

Smith, Bill, 'The Argentinian Junta and the Press in the Run-up to the 1978 World Cup,' *Soccer & Society*, 3(1), 2002.

Steenveld, Lynette and Larry Strelitz, 'The 1995 Rugby World Cup and the Politics of Nation-Building in South Africa,' *Media, Culture & Society*, 20(4), 1998.

Stevenson, Paulette, 'Empowerment Discourses in Transnational Sporting Contexts: The Case of Sarah Attar, The First Female Saudi Olympian,' *Sociology of Sport Journal*, 35, 2008.

Stevenson, Thomas, 'Football in Newly United Yemen: Rituals of Equity, Identity, and State Formation,' *Journal of Anthropological Research*, 56(4), 2000.

Sullivan, Jonathan, Simon Chadwick, and Michael Gow, 'China's Football Dream: Sport, Citizenship, Symbolic Power, and Civic Spaces,' *Journal of Sport and Social Issues*, 43(6), 2019.

BIBLIOGRAPHY

Takahashi, Yoshio, 'Why Zico is Called the 'God of Soccer' in Japan: The Legacy of Zico to Japanese Soccer,' *Soccer & Society*, 15(5), 2014.

Taylor, Tom, Daniel Burdsey, and Nigel Jarvis, 'A Critical Review on Sport and the Arabian Peninsula—the Current State of Play and Future Directions,' *International Journal of Sport Policy and Politics*, 15(2), 2023.

Tuastad, Dag, 'From Football Riot to Revolution: The Political Role of Football in the Arab World,' *Soccer & Society*, 21(6), 2020.

Van Der Westhuizen, Janis, 'Marketing Malaysia as a Model Modern Muslim State: The Significance of the 16th Commonwealth Games,' *Third World Quarterly*, 25(7), 2004.

Yunda Fauzul, Ardia and Basuni Imamuddin, 'The Development Dynamics of Football and its Influence on Conservatism Culture in Saudi Arabia,' *International Review of Humanities Studies*, 8(2), 2023.

Papers and briefs

Abdel Ghaffar, Adel, 'Saudi Arabia's McKinsey Reshuffle,' *Brookings Doha Center*, 11 May 2016.

Aldosari, Hala, 'The Saudi National Transformation Program: What's in It for Women?', *Arab Gulf States Institute in Washington*, 1 February 2016.

Alhussein, Eman and Sara Almohamadi, 'Saudi Arabia Hikes its VAT, But for How Long?', *Arab Gulf States Institute in Washington*, 2 July 2020.

Alhussein, Eman, 'Football's Coming Home: Saudi League and Fan Base Get a Big Boost,' *Arab Gulf States Institute in Washington*, 22 June 2023.

Alhussein, Eman and Tine Gade, 'Vision 2030 Has Transformed Saudi Arabia's Legal and Judicial Systems,' *Arab Gulf States Institute in Washington*, 20 November 2023.

Al Kibsi, Gassan, Lola Woetzel, Jan Mischke, Tom Isherwood, Jawad Khan, and Hassan Noura, 'Moving Saudi Arabia's Economy Beyond Oil,' *McKinsey Global Institute*, 1 December 2015.

Al Rasheed, Fahd, 'Learn from the Past, Build for the Future: Saudi Arabia's New City on the Red Sea,' *McKinsey & Company*, 29 August 2016.

Barany, Zoltan, 'Indigenous Defense Industries in the Gulf,' *Center for Strategic and International Studies*, 24 April 2020.

Barzani, Hezha, 'How the Saudi Pro League Transformed from Being Unknown to Inescapable,' *Atlantic Council*, 14 June 2023.

Baycar, Hamdullah, 'How a Football Spat Nearly Derailed Saudi-Turkey Rapprochement,' *Gulf International Forum*, 22 January 2024.

Boucek, Christopher, 'Saudi Arabia's "Soft" Counterterrorism Strategy: Prevention, Rehabilitation, and Aftercare,' *Carnegie Papers No. 97*, 2008.

Boyle, Raymond and Richard Haynes, 'How a Netflix Show Has Become a Key Driver Behind F1's Rising Popularity,' *The Conversation*, 1 March 2024.

BIBLIOGRAPHY

Callen, Tim, 'Going Big: Assessing the Growth Ambitions of the Saudi Public Investment Fund,' *Arab Gulf States Institute in Washington*, 12 December 2023.

———, 'Four Indicators to Track Saudi Reform Progress,' *Arab Gulf States Institute in Washington*, 31 January 2024.

Coates Ulrichsen, Kristian, 'Economic Diversification Plans: Challenges and Prospects for Gulf Policymakers,' Arab Gulf States Institute in Washington *Policy Paper #2*, 2016.

———, 'Mohammed bin Salman's Regional Rebranding Campaign,' *Arab Center Washington*, 16 December 2021.

Coates Ulrichsen, Kristian, Mark Finley, and Jim Krane, 'The OPEC+ Phenomenon of Saudi-Russian Cooperation and Implications for US-Saudi Relations,' *Baker Institute*, 18 October 2022.

Coates Ulrichsen, Kristian, 'Qatar's Successful World Cup Signals a New Era in the Gulf and Beyond,' *Arab Center Washington*, 5 January 2023.

———, 'Saudi Plans to 'De-Risk' Region Have Taken a Hit with Gaza Violence—but Hitting Pause on Normalization with Israel Will Buy Kingdom Time,' *The Conversation*, 18 October 2023.

Coates Ulrichsen, Kristian, 'Gulf Arab States Avoid Iran-Israel Tensions,' *Arab Center Washington*, 25 April 2024.

Dorsey, James, 'Saudi Soccer: A Game of Geopolitics and Religion, Not Just Sports,' *Substack*, 5 August 2023.

Elliott House, Karen, 'Uneasy Lies the Head That Wears a Crown: The House of Saud Confronts its Challenges,' Harvard Kennedy School, *Belfer Center Paper*, 2016.

———, 'Profile of a Prince: Promise and Peril in Mohammed bin Salman's Vision 2030,' Harvard Kennedy School, *Belfer Center Paper*, 2019.

Elsheshtawy, Yasser, 'Transforming Riyadh: A New Urban Paradigm?', *Arab Gulf States Institute in Washington*, 17 April 2019.

———, 'The Line: A Promising Vision for a Progressive Future?', *Arab Gulf States Institute in Washington*, 3 June 2021.

———, 'Is Riyadh's Mukaab Compatible with Saudi Arabia's Climate Ambitions?', *Arab Gulf States Institute in Washington*, 17 May 2023.

Foley, Sean and Hatem Alzahrani, '"Listen to the Artist": US and Saudi Artistst Develop Cultural Ties,' *Arab Gulf States Institute in Washington*, 21 February 2023.

Greyser, Stephen and Kenneth Cortsen, 'MLS as a Sports Product—the Prominence of the World's Game in the US,' *Harvard Business School*, Working Paper 21–111, 2021.

Habibi, Nader, 'Implementing Saudi Arabia's Vision 2030: An Interim Balance Sheet,' *Middle East Brief No. 127*, Brandeis University/Crown Center for Middle East Studies, 2019.

BIBLIOGRAPHY

Krane, Jim, 'Houthi Red Sea Attacks Have Global Economic Repercussions,' *Arab Center Washington*, 5 April 2024.

Mills, Robin, 'Aramco, Ministry Reshuffle Highlight Role of Oil Giant in Saudi Economic Transformation,' *Arab Gulf States Institute in Washington*, 9 October 2019.

Mogielnicki, Robert, 'Expectation Gap Clouds Saudi Arabia's Investment Climate,' *Arab Gulf States Institute in Washington*, 28 October 2019.

———, 'Saudi Arabia's Economic Strategy: From Kitchen Sink to Virtuous Cycle?', *Arab Gulf States Institute in Washington*, 30 April 2021.

———, 'Saudi Regional Headquarters Program Deadline Looms,' *Arab Gulf States Institute in Washington*, 5 December 2023.

———, 'Neom is Becoming a Destination of Destinations,' *Arab Gulf States Institute in Washington*, 26 January 2024.

Murphy, Caryle, 'In with the Old in the New Saudi Arabia,' *Foreign Affairs*, 25 February 2015.

Olver-Ellis, Sophie, 'Building the New Kuwait: Vision 2035 and the Challenge of Diversification,' *LSE Middle East Centre Paper Series 30*, 2020.

Phillips, Charles, 'With Major Tourism Projects, Saudi Arabia Pushes for Place on Global Tourism Map,' *Arab Gulf States Institute in Washington*, 9 May 2023.

Polimeno, Maria Gloria, 'Houthi Attacks on Shipping Are Not Just About the Israel-Hamas War,' *Manara Magazine*, 8 May 2024.

Proudfoot, Philip and Ali Reda, 'The Gulf and the British Regional Divide,' Middle East Research and Information Project, *MERIP 304*, 2022.

Ratner, Michael and Heather Greenley, 'Crude Oil Futures Prices Turn Negative,' *Congressional Research Service Insight*, 22 April 2020.

Roll, Stephen, 'A Sovereign Wealth Fund for the Prince: Economic Reforms and Power Consolidation in Saudi Arabia,' German Institute for International and Security Affairs, *SWP Research Paper 8*, 2019.

Saikali, Sussan, 'A New Virtual Reality: The Growth of Esports and Gaming in Saudi Arabia,' *Arab Gulf States Institute in Washington*, 17 March 2022.

Saikali, Sussan, 'Smart and Sustainable: The Gulf Goes All In on Tech Cities,' *Arab Gulf States Institute in Washington*, 5 July 2023.

Salisbury, Peter, 'Risk Perception and Appetite in UAE Foreign and National Security Policy,' *Chatham House Research Paper*, 2020.

Smith Diwan, Kristin and Turki Buyabes, 'Saudi Arabia Sets Goals for Football On and Off the Pitch,' *Arab Gulf States Institute in Washington*, 18 July 2018.

Smith Diwan, Kristin, 'Saudi Ambition Confronts New Vulnerability,' *Arab Gulf States Institute in Washington*, 1 October 2019.

———, 'Max Weber in Arabia: Saudi's Character Enrichment Program,' *Arab Gulf States Institute in Washington*, 12 May 2020.

BIBLIOGRAPHY

——, 'Tourism Ambitions Transform Saudi Arabia,' *Arab Gulf States Institute in Washington*, 17 February 2022.
Strenk, Andrew, 'Diplomats in Track Suits: The Role of Sports in the Foreign Policy of the German Democratic Republic,' paper presented at the *Annual Convention of the International Studies Association*, Washington, D.C., 24 February 1978.
Strombom, Lisa and Anders Persson, 'The Abraham Accords and Peace in the Middle East,' *Center for Advanced Middle Eastern Studies*, Lund University, 21 June 2023.
Yom, Sean, 'The Long Game: Saudi Arabia and Professional Golf,' *Foreign Policy Research Institute*, 21 June 2023.
Young, Karen, 'Privatization in Saudi Arabia: Vision 2030 Ready to Sell,' *Arab Gulf States Institute in Washington*, 16 July 2018.

Media and online resources

Agence France-Presse
Al Arabiya
Al Jazeera
Al-Monitor
Arab Digest
Arab News
Arabian Gulf Business Insight
Architects' Journal
Argaam
Armed Conflict Location and Event Data Project
Asharq Al Awsat
Associated Press
Aviation Week
Axios
BBC News
BBC Sport
Blog of the European Journal of International Law
Bloomberg
Bloomberg Businessweek
Business Insider
CBC
CBS Sport
Columbia Journalism Review
Courthouse News
CNBC
CNN
Daily Record
Daily Mirror

BIBLIOGRAPHY

Deloitte
Deseret News
DW
ESPN
European Club Association
European Saudi Organization for Human Rights
FIFA
Financial Times
Forbes
Four Four Two
Foreign Affairs
Foreign Policy
Fox News
Gulf News
Gulf States Newsletter
History Today
Human Rights Watch
I News
Inside the Games
Instagram
International Crisis Group
International Herald Tribune
International Monetary Fund
Jacobin
Law in Sport
Los Angeles Times
Mail Online
Manchester Evening News
Metro
Middle East Economic Digest
Middle East Eye
Middle East Report Online
MLS Soccer
National Public Radio (NPR)
NBC News
Newsweek
New York Times
New Yorker
Office of the Director of National Intelligence
Oxford Business Group
Politico
Reuters
Responsible Statecraft

BIBLIOGRAPHY

Saudi Aramco News & Media
Skift
Saudi Gazette
Saudi Professional League
Seatrade Maritime
Sky Sports
Society for American Baseball Research
Sport 360
Sport Bible
Sport Business
Sports Business Journal
Sportcal
Sports Illustrated
Sports Pro Media
Telegraph Online
The Art Newspaper
The Athletic
The Atlantic
The Daily Telegraph
The Economist
The Firepit Collective
The Guardian
The Independent
The Intercept
The Mag
The Nation
The National
The Shields Gazette
The Sportsman
The Soufan Center
The Spectator
The Times
These Football Times
UEFA
Vice News
Vision 2030
Wall Street Journal
War on the Rocks
Washington Post
World Today
World Trade Organization
Yahoo Sports
YouTube

INDEX

Abdullah, Majid, 17
Abdullah, Miteb bin, 40
Abha, 149
Abraham Accords, 157
Abu Dhabi, 2, 7, 19, 53, 75, 117, 132, 156
AC Milan, 126
Adidas, 150
AFC Asian Championship (2023), 126
AFC Asian Cup (2023), 135
AFC Asian Cup (2024), 158
AFC Asian Cup (2027), 8, 16, 21, 102, 132–3, 158, 161
AFC Asian Cup, 145
AFC Asian Cups (2019), 135
AFC Champions League, 23, 26
Afghanistan, 15
Africa, 105, 140, 143
Ajax, 87
Al Arab (media), 43
Al Arabiya (television), 51
Al Balawi, Mansour, 21–2
Al Baltan, Khalid, 94
Al Dakhil, Turki, 52
Al Faisal, Abdulaziz bin Turki, 12, 31, 79, 101, 111, 141
Al Falih, Khalid, 57, 63
Al Huwaiti, Abdul Rahim, 161

Al Jaber, Sami, 20–1
Al Jadaan, Mohammed, 131
Al Jedea, Haifa, 133
Al Khalifa, Nasser bin Hamad, 109
Al Khalifa, Salman bin Ibrahim, 147
Al Khobar, 95, 149
Al Lazeez, Saad, 98–9, 158
Al Maktoum, Ahmed bin Saeed, 155
Al Misehal, Yasser, 149
Al Mubarak, Khaldoun, 19
Al Mudaifer, Khalid, 58
Al Nahyan, Mansour bin Zayed, 19, 117 156
Al Nahyan, Mohammed bin Zayed, 38–9, 48
Al Omran, Ahmed, 3
Al Otaibi, Manahel, 136
Al Owairan, Saeed, 4, 17
Al Qaeda, 32, 72
Al Rumayyan, Yasir bin Othman, 28, 46, 61–3, 80–3, 115–18
Al Sadd, 135
Al Saud, Abdulaziz bin Abdulrahman, 2, 5, 9, 43, 101
Al Saud, Abdullah bin Abdulaziz, 3, 34, 35, 36, 39, 40, 41, 52, 55, 56, 145
Al Saud, Abdullah bin Mosaad, 23–4, 32, 36–41, 52, 61

INDEX

Al Saud, Faisal bin Salman, 24
Al Saud, Fahd bin Abdulaziz, 17, 32, 54, 72
Al Saud, Faisal bin Turki, 23
Al Saud Khalid bin Abdulaziz, 15
Al Saud, Khalid bin Bandar, 111
Al Saud, Khalid bin Salman, 153
Al Saud, Mohammed bin Faisal, 21–2
Al Saud, Mohammed bin Salman, 2, 4, 5, 8, 24–7, 31–2, 51–2
  FIFA and Saudi Arabia, 142–52
  Newcastle exception, 114–18
  Public Investment Fund, remaking, 60–6
  regional and geopolitical dimensions, 152–6
  Trump and Biden, 46–9
  Vision 2030, 4, 6, 8, 25, 26, 30, 36, 40, 45, 49, 51–6, 62, 65, 111, 122, 148, 154–6, 160
Al Saud, Nawaf bin Faisal, 23
Al Saud, Reema bint Bandar, 111, 150–1
Al Shehab, Salma, 136
Al Sheikh, Turki, 29
Al Tamimi & Co., 25
Al Thani, Tamim bin Hamad, 142
Al Ula, 49, 131, 159, 73–4
Al-Ahli, 11–12, 83, 93–4
Al-Awwal Park, 136
Al-Bukiryah, 137
Al-Diriyah Club, 95
Al-Ettifaq, 13, 87, 92, 97, 101–2, 140
Algeria, 23
Al-Hilal, 1, 13, 15, 20–1, 25–7, 54, 83, 93, 103
Alhussein, Eman, 112
Al-Ittihad, 5, 6–7, 11, 13, 26, 54, 69, 83, 93, 97, 99, 103
  challenges and breakthroughs, 14–18

Alkassim, Ibrahim, 148–9
All or Nothing (series), 91
Almuhanna, Ibrahim, 56
Al-Nassr, 1, 11, 13, 15, 21, 23, 26–7, 74, 83, 92–3, 136, 130
  PIF, rise of, 93–6
Al-Qadsiah, 16, 95, 102, 159
Al-Qahtani, Saud, 28
Al-Qassab, Ussama, 90
Al-Rasheed, Madawi, 32
Al-Safa Club, 137–8
Al-Shabab, 11, 15, 16, 94
Al-Sheikh, Mohammed, 37
Al-Suqoor, 95 Al-Tai, 13
Al-Ula FC, 95
Al-Watan (newspaper), 27, 43
Al-Wehda, 13
Al-Yamamah university, 27
Amaala, 139
Amazon Prime, 91
Anschutz, Philip, 129
Antarctica, 10
Anti-Cybercrime Law (2007), 137
Apple, 93
Arab News (newspaper), 15
Arabian American Oil Company (Aramco), 54, 61, 102
Arabian Gulf Cup, 13
Arabsat, 28
Archer, Portia, 83
Argentina, 6, 13, 17–18, 49, 65, 69, 74, 84, 87–8, 140, 144, 146
Arsenal, 19, 100
Ashley, Mike, 115–16
Asia, 26, 105, 143
Asian confederation, 146
Asian Football Confederation, 29, 126, 140, 147, 157
Asian Games (2006), 134
Asian Winter Games (2029), 77, 133
Asian Winter Games, 8

INDEX

Aspire Academy for Sport Excellence, 19
Al Assad, Hafez, 22
Ataturk, Mustafa Kemal, 137
Athens, 144
Athletic, The (newspaper), 92–3, 97, 100, 112, 116–19, 126–7
Atlantic, The (magazine), 49
Atletico Madrid, 76, 155
Australia, 147, 150–1
Australian Cricket Board (1979), 84
Azerbaijan, 106

Ba'ath Party, 22
Baghdad, 11, 14, 22
Bahrain, 27, 41, 53, 102, 109–10, 140
Bandar, Faisal bin, 111
Bankman-Fried, Sam, 110
Barcelona, 21, 91
Barclays Bank, 115
Bashar Al Assad regime, 41
Batistuta, Gabriel, 19
BBC, 14, 79, 101, 161
Bebeto, 21
Beckenbauer, Franz, 124
Beckham, David, 130
Bedminister, 82
Beijing Olympics, 89
Beijing Winter Olympics, 107
 Beijing, 106, 153
beIN Sports, 27–8, 114–15
Belgium, 4, 17, 46, 143, 148
Benfica, 123
Benzema, Karim, 97, 99, 101–3
BeoutQ, 27–8, 115
Bergkamp, Dennis, 101
Besiktas supporter group, 22–3
Best, George, 124
Bezos, Jeff, 45
Biden, Joe, 29, 144

Trump and, 46–9
"big five", 100
bin Laden, Osama, 32, 72
Binance, 110
Binladin Group, 64
Blackburn Olympic (1883), 68
Blair, Tony, 53
Blankfein, Lloyd, 45
Bloomberg, Mike, 45, 131
Blumenthal, Richard, 106
Borussia Dortmund, 95
Bosnia, 15
Boston Minutemen, 123
Boston, 105–6
Bouazizi, Mohamed, 152
Boykoff, Jules, 107
Brand Australia, 71
Brazil, 1, 72, 103, 128
Brexit, 71
BRICS group, 105
Brisbane, 105
Britain, 7, 29
British Marxist, 87
Budapest, 105–6
Bundesliga, 29
Burdsey, Daniel, 108
Bush, George H. W., 45, 107

Cairo, 11, 22
California, 38, 118
Callen, Tim, 63
Cameron, David, 71
Canada, 30, 42, 123, 145
Cape of Good Hope, 154
Capital Markets Authority, 61–2
Caribbean, 148
Causeway, King Fahd, 140
CBS News (Television broadcaster), 44
Ceferin, Aleksandar, 29–30
Celtic, 18
Cengiz, Hatice, 115

INDEX

Centennial Plan, 53
Central America, 148
Central Planning Organization, 54
Chadwick, Simon, 78–9
"Character Enrichment Program", 57
Chelsea, 20, 97, 100, 150
Chicago, 53
Chile, 146
China, 26, 38, 72, 96, 100, 105, 122–6, 149–50
Chinese Super League, 7–8, 16, 100, 122, 140
City Football Group, 91, 126
Clinton, Bill, 45
Clough, Brian, 14
CN Tower, 42
Coca-Cola, 150
Columbus Crew, 129
Commonwealth Games (2010), 105
Commonwealth Games, 71
CONCACAF, 148
Concorde, 15
Conte, Antonio, 100
Cook, Garry, 98–9
Corbyn, Jeremy, 116
Cordesman, Anthony, 64
Corinthians, 16
Cosmos, 89
Costa Rica, 117
Council of Economic and Development Affairs (CEDA), 24, 51
Coventry City, 4, 14
Covid-19 pandemic, 5, 30, 46, 48, 73, 126–7
Crossley, Stephen, 108
Crown Jewel, 137
Crushers, 83
Cruyff, Johan, 21, 124
Cruz, Ted, 47

CSL, 125–7
Cultural Revolution, 125

Dakar Rally, 137
Dallas Tornado, 129
Damascus, 11
Dammam, 11, 140
Davidson, Christopher, 113
de Klerk, F.W., 70
Delaney, Miguel, 106
Deloitte, 24, 100
Denmark, 17
Diriyah Gate Development Authority, 95
Diriyah, 78–9, 159
Discovery Channel (channel), 67
Dispute Resolution Chamber, 25
Doha, 30, 41, 75, 84, 87, 113, 142–3
Donadoni, Roberto, 21
Dorsey, James, 3
Douglas, Tony, 75
DP World Tour, 82
Drive to Survive (series), 91
Dubai Champions Cup, 18
Dubai, 2, 19, 21, 25, 73, 84, 139–40
Duerden, John, 3
Dunga, 128

East Germany, 70
East Manchester, 117
Eastern Europe, 47
Eastern Province, 11, 12, 13, 15, 95, 149
Economic Development Committee, 54
Economist, The (magazine), 23
Effenberg, Stefan, 19
Egypt, 12, 22–3, 27, 77, 131–2, 136, 144
Eighth five-year plan, 54

INDEX

Emenalo, Michael, 97–8
Emerick-Aubameyang, Pierre, 95
England, 7, 9, 17, 68, 100, 131, 157
Erdogan, Recep Tayyip, 22–3
ESPN (media company), 79, 90
Esports World Cup, 80
Esteghlal, 16
Etihad, 2, 19, 75
Ettinger, Aaron, 72, 108
Euro 2024, 95
Euro 96, 158
Europe, 6, 9, 124
European Club Association, 90
European Cup, 18
European leagues, 26
European Super League, 92
European Union (EU), 71, 133
Eusebio, 123
Evergrande, 125
Evert, Chris, 150

FA Cup, 68
Facebook, 23
Fahd, Faisal bin, 72
Fakeih, Adel, 57
FC Barcelona, 135
FC Dallas, 129
FC Women's Asian Cup, 151
Federal Intelligence Service (BND), 43
Fenerbahce, 23, 136, 137
Fernandez, Nacho, 95
FIBA Basketball World Cup (2027), 135
FIFA and Saudi Arabia, 142–52
rise of, 18–21
FIFA World Club Championship, 12, 16, 21, 30, 129 and Saudi Arabia, 142–52
FIFA World Cup (2022), 7, 134–5
FIFA World Cup (2034), 92, 160

Figo, Luis, 16, 21
Filkins, Dexter, 39
Financial Times (newspaper), 55, 63, 90, 144, 148, 155
Fireballs, 83
Fiscal Balance Program, 52
Flamengo, 1
Football Association (England), 9
Ford Foundation, 54
Foreign Investment Initiative (FII), 46
Formula One Bahrain Grand Prix, 110
Formula One World Championship, 81
Fosun, 125
Fowler, Robbie, 102
Fox News (media), 111, 135
France, 17, 67–8, 87–8, 100, 144–5
French Revolution, 87
Friedman, Thomas, 37–8
FTX, 110
Fulham, 100, 124
Fury, Tyson, 79

G-20 countries, 73
Galatasaray, 23, 136, 137
Gates, Bill, 45
Gauff, Coco, 151
Gaza, 112, 152–4, 137, 157
General Presidency for Youth Welfare, 23, 24
Geopolitical Economy of Sport, *The* (Simon Chadwick and Paul Widdop), 3
Germany, 4, 7, 17, 42–3, 69, 100, 137, 148
Gerrard, Steven, 92, 101–2, 140
Gezi Park protests (2013), 22
Ghouta, 41
Gigaprojects 2024 Report, 134

INDEX

"giga-projects", 46, 52, 66, 112, 131–2, 139, 142, 161
  Vision 2030, 56–60
Glasgow, 16
"Global South", 143
Golden Boot, 128
Goldman Sachs, 45
Grabban, Lewis, 25–6
Grand Mosque, 15
Grand Prix, 78
GREAT Britain, 71
Greece, 144
Green Falcons, 87, 109
Guardian (newspaper), 143
Guardiola, Pep, 19, 142–3
Gulf Air, 20
Gulf Cooperation Council, 49, 53
Gulf Cup (1972), 13
Gulf States Newsletter (newsletter), 31
Gullit, Ruud, 101

Hajj, 73
Hamas, 112, 157
Hamburg, 105–6
Hampden Park, 16
Al Harbi, Ahmed Eid, 23
Hariri, Saad, 42
Hayes, Emma, 150
Hearn, Eddie, 79
Henderson, Jordan, 6, 15, 87, 97, 102, 140
Henry, John, 84
Hernandez, Xavi, 135
Heysel tragedy, 18
Hezbollah, 152–3
Hierro, Fernando, 19
Hijaz region, 11, 12, 69
Hijazi Sports Club, 11, 69
Hill, Jimmy, 4, 14–15
Hillsborough stadium disaster, 18
Hitachi, 127

Hobsbawm, Eric, 87, 112
Hogan, James, 75
Honecker, Erick, 71
Houston, 45
Houthi attacks, 152–3
Houthi forces, 32, 112, 137, 153–4
Human Rights Watch, 137
Hunt Oil Company, 129
Hunt, Lamar, 129
Hussein, Saddam, 22
Hyundai Kia, 150

Icke, David, 14
Independent (newspaper), 106
India, 105
Indonesia, 11, 22, 158–9
INEOS, 110
Infantino, Gianni, 29, 106, 142, 144, 147–50
Instagram, 92–3
Inter Miami, 21, 93, 110, 126, 130
International Cricket Council, 83
International Monetary Fund (IMF), 54, 134
International Olympic Committee, 12
Iran, 2, 11, 12, 13, 72, 136, 153
Iranian Revolutionary Guard Corps, 153
Iraq, 12
Iron Heads, 83
Islam, 99
Islamic Solidarity Games, 72
Israel, 153, 157
Israel-Gaza war, 139
Israel-Hamas, 152
Istanbul, 3, 11, 22, 28, 45
Italian Super Cup, 137
Italy, 69, 100, 145
Ivory Coast, 17

Jadwa Investment, 24

INDEX

Jahra, Battle of, 13
Japan Soccer League, 127
Japan, 7, 16, 69, 70, 105, 122, 127–30
Jarvis, Nigel, 108
Jeddah, 5, 10–11, 12, 13, 21, 24, 48, 65, 93–6, 99, 101, 131, 137–8, 161
   FIFA and Saudi Arabia, 142–52
J-League, 122, 127–30, 140
Jinping, Xi, 125, 149
Johnson, Boris, 48
Joint Comprehensive Plan of Action, 41
Jordan, 22, 131–2, 136
Joshua, Anthony, 79
Jubilo Iwata, 128
Juventus, 18

Kallon, Mohammed, 22
Kansas City Wizards, 129
Kashima Antlers, 9, 128
Kay, Oliver, 93, 100
Keane, Roy, 21
Khashoggi, Jamal, 3, 28, 45, 47, 65–6, 72, 78, 115–18, 144
Khobar, 13
King Abdullah Economic City (KAEC), 55, 62–3
King Abdullah Financial District, 56
King Abdullah Sports City, 145
King Fahd Cup, 17–18
King Fahd Sports City, 145
King Khalid International Airport, 139
Klaveness, Lise, 146–7
Klinsmann, Jurgen, 101
Koch, Natalie, 109
Kuala Lumpur, 71
Kushner, Jared, 39, 82
Kuwait, 13, 32, 53, 132

La Liga, 29
Labour Party, 116
Laporte, Aymeric, 103
Latin America, 143
Lawrence of Arabia (film), 102
League One, 24, 131
Lebanon, 3, 12, 42, 152
Leeds United, 9
Leicester City, 26
LGBTQ+ communities, 97, 143
Liberty Media, 91
Libya, 23, 136
Lineker, Gary, 128
Littbarski, Pierre, 128
LIV Golf League, 7, 51, 81–4, 106, 116–18
LIV Invitational Series, 83, 84
Liverpool FC, 18, 84, 87, 97, 99–102, 159
London Heathrow, 73
London Olympics, 27
London, 20, 84, 89, 119
Long-Term Strategic Plan, 54–5
Los Angeles Aztecs, 129–30
Los Angeles Galaxy, 130
Los Angeles, 71, 105
Lucid Motors, 81
Luzhniki Stadium, 142
Lysa, Charlotte, 27, 152

MacArthur, Douglas, 70
MacInnes, Paul, 78
Macron, Emmanuel, 42, 48
Mahrez, Riyad, 99
Major League Soccer (MLS), 7, 100, 122–4, 128–30, 140, 159
Malay Peninsula, 11
Malaysia, 71
Manama, 140
Manchester City, 7, 19, 91–2, 97–8, 103, 117, 142–3, 156
Manchester United, 1, 20–1

231

INDEX

Mancini, Roberto, 109, 159
Mandela, Nelson, 70, 151–2
Mane, Sadio, 99, 101
Maradona, Diego, 17, 19
Masdar City, 132
Mass Participation Federation, 111
Mauritius, 103
Mazda, 127
Mbappe, Kylian, 97, 144
McGarry, Bill, 14
McKinsey Global Institute, 56
McKinsey, 55, 56–60
McLaren Group, 80–1
Mecca, 13, 15, 43, 72, 73, 99
Medina, 99
Menem, Carlos, 17
Messi, Lionel, 74, 90–1, 95, 130, 144
Mexico, 17, 30, 87, 145
Michel, 102
Middle East Economic Digest (Media company), 134
Middle East, 2, 11, 17, 96, 105, 143, 136, 152
UAE and Qatar, rise of, 18–21
Mitrovic, Aleksandar, 101
Mitsubishi, 127
Montague, James, 3
Montambault Trudelle, Alexis, 61
Moore, Bobby, 124
Morgan, Alex, 150
Morocco, 17, 140, 143, 146
Moscow, 142
Mrsool Park, 89
Munich, 106
Musa, Ahmed, 26

Nagoya Grampus Eight, 128
Najd, 11
National Football Plan, 127
National League North, 109
National Professional Soccer League (NPSL), 123

National Transformation Plan, 52
National, The (newspaper), 102
Nations and Nationalism since 1870 (Hobsbawm), 113
Navratilova, Martina, 150
Nazer, Hisham, 54
NBA, 90
NBC Olympics, 90–1, 123
NCUK Investment Ltd, 28
Neom Bay Airport, 73
Neom development, 8, 46, 55, 62–3, 77, 131–5, 139, 149, 151–2, 159
Neom Sports Club, 95
Netflix, 91, 92
Netherlands, 17, 148
New Jersey, 82
New York Cosmos, 123
New York Times (newspaper), 27, 37, 41, 49, 94, 137, 144
New York, 41, 45
New Yorker (magazine), 39, 82
New Zealand, 70, 147, 150
Newcastle United Supporters Trust, 116
Newcastle United, 7, 20, 28-9, 51, 81, 89, 108–9, 150
Newcastle exception, 114–18
Neymar, 6–7, 15, 102–3
NFL, 129–30
Niblock, Tim, 54
Nigeria, 70
9/11 terrorist attacks, 42, 67, 72, 107
Ninth Development Plan, 54
Nissan, 127
Nohra, Carlos, 92, 130, 131–2
North Africa, 115, 136, 143, 152
North America, 30, 105, 122, 140, 148
North American Soccer League (NASL), 7–8, 100, 123, 124–9, 140, 157

INDEX

Northern Europe, 7
Norway, 106
Norwegian Football Association, 146
Nottingham Forest, 25
Nye, Joseph, 81

Obama, Barack, 41
Oceania Football Confederation, 140
Oceanian confederation, 146
Olympia (film), 69
Olympic Council of Asia, 77
Oman, 12–13, 20, 53, 153
  see also Yemen
Omicron spasm, 30
Onwurah, Chi, 116
OPEC+ members, 135, 145
OPEC+ price agreement, 47
Organization of Islamic Cooperation, 72
Oslo, 106
Ottaway, David, 62

Packer, Kerry, 84
Paisley, Bob, 14
Paraguay, 140, 146
Paris Saint-Germain, 93, 97, 100
Paris, 10, 105
Paul, Jake, 79
PCP Capital Partners, 114–15
Pele, 1, 19, 89, 100, 123–7
Petromin, 61
PGA Tour, 82–4, 106, 118
PGA Tour-LIV Golf agreement, 106
PIF WTA Maternity Fund Program, 83
PIF. *See* Public Investment Fund (PIF)
Pioneering Change: Women's Football in Saudi Arabia (report), 151
Pirelli, 110

Player Acquisition Center of Excellence (PACE) program, 98–9
Pogacar, Tadej, 156
Poland, 87
Politico (newspaper), 133
Portugal, 98, 140, 143, 146
Premier League, 117, 19, 100, 114
"Project Wedge", 82
Public Investment Fund (PIF), 7, 25, 30, 51, 52, 61–5, 75, 79–83, 93, 114, 125, 144, 155, 159–60
  remaking, 60–6 rise of, 93–6
Puskas, Ferenc, 14
Putin, Vladimir, 29–30, 107, 142

Qaddafi regime (in Benghazi), 23
Qaddafi, Muammar, 136
Qamishli, 22
Qatar Airways, 75, 150
Qatar Sports Investment, 19
Qatar Stars League, 18–19, 21, 134–5
Qatar, 1, 2, 3, 7, 10, 16, 26–8, 42, 49, 53, 72–4, 78, 81, 87, 126, 142
Qiddiya, 59, 65, 77, 131–4

Raisi, Ebrahim, 153–4
Raja Casablanca, 16
RB Sports & Media, 114
Real Madrid, 16, 97, 130
Real Madrid-Barcelona rivalry, 94
Red Sea Global, 134
Red Sea, 10, 12, 59, 121, 139, 154
Regional Headquarters Program (RHQ), 155
Republic of Turkey, 137
Revie, Don, 9
Riefenstahl, Leni, 69
Rio de Janeiro, 27

INDEX

Ripper, 83
Ritz-Carlton affair, 40–6 Ritz-Carlton hotel, 40
Ritz-Carlton, 21, 57, 65
Rivelino, Roberto, 1, 15
Riyadh Air, 74–6, 155–6
Riyadh, 1, 11, 12, 13, 14, 17–18, 20–4, 27, 57, 65, 74, 131–2
    FIFA and Saudi Arabia, 142–52
    PIF, rise of, 93–6
    Vision 2030, 130–5 Roan, Dan, 101
Robson, Bobby, 14
Romario, 18
Ronaldo, Cristiano, 1–2, 6, 15, 18, 21, 25–6, 74, 79, 89–93, 101–2, 110, 127, 135, 140
    PIF, rise of, 93–6
Rothenberg, Alan, 129
Routledge, 3
Rubicon, 68–9
Rugby World Cup (1995), 70
Ruiz, Andy, 79
Rundell, David, 60
Russia, 4, 17, 27, 38, 105, 107
    FIFA and Saudi Arabia, 142–52
Russia-Ukraine border, 47

Saint & Greavsie (television show), 16
Salah, Mohammed, 97, 99, 159
Salt Lake City, 107
San Francisco Seals, 70
Sanabil Investments, 61
Sartori, Andrea, 78
Saudi Arabia, 1–3, 27
    challenges and breakthroughs, 14–18
    club, origins and early development, 10–13
    development planning in, 51–6
    FIFA and, 142–52

football and politics, 135–40
foreign players, 96–103
and giga-projects, 56–60
PIF, rise of, 93–6
Public Investment Fund, remaking, 60–6
sport and politics, 68–73
Vision 2030, 4, 6, 8, 25–6, 30, 36, 40, 45, 49, 62, 65, 111, 122, 130–5, 148, 154–6, 160
see also Salman, Mohammed bin
Saudi Arabian Football Federation, 4, 11, 24–5, 72, 140, 148
Saudi Arabian Grand Prix, 137–9
Saudi Arabian Military Industries (SAMI), 64
Saudi Arabian Mining Company, 58
Saudi Arabian Monetary Agency (SAMA), 60–1
Saudi Arabian National Guard, 40
Saudi Aramco, 84
Saudi Basic Industries Corporation (SABIC), 60–1
Saudi Consulate, 28, 45
Saudi First Division club, 95, 102
Saudi football federation, 12
    origins and early development, 10–13
Saudi Fransi Capital, 61–2
Saudi Premier League (1975), 13
Saudi Pro League (SPL), 6, 13, 18–19, 21, 23, 25–6, 77, 91–2, 100–3, 113, 122, 126–30, 131, 140, 158–9
    PIF, rise of, 93–6
Saudi Pro League: Kickoff (series), 92
Saudi Research and Marketing Group, 31
Saudi Shia communities, 137
Saudi Telecommunications Company, 25

INDEX

Saudi Third Division, 95
Saudi Women's Premier League, 27, 151
Saudi-Israeli relations, 48
Savvy Games Group, 79–80
Scandinavia, 7
Schillaci, Salvatore, 128
Scholz, Olaf, 48
Scotland, 16, 18
Scottish Football Association, 16–17
Seattle, 45
Sela, 117, 119
Serie A, 29
Sheffield United, 24
Shihabi, Ali, 4, 76, 133
Shilton, Peter, 16–17
Shipnuck, Alan, 82
Silk City, 132
Sindalah, 139
Singapore, 16, 57
Skey, Michael, 107–8
Smash, 83
Sochi, 107
Socialist Unity Party, 71
SoftBank, 29–30
Solari, Jorge, 17
Soleimani, Qassim, 153
Sophia (robot), 46
Soriano, Ferran, 91–2
South Africa, 70, 105
South Africa's World Cup (2010), 105
South America, 124, 127–8, 140
South Korea, 21, 105, 117, 128
South Shields FC, 109
Southampton, 99
Spain, 76, 94, 100, 102, 140, 143, 146
Spanish Super Cup, 137
Sports Boulevard project, 77
Sports Clubs Investment and Privatization Project, 94, 160

Sports mega events (SMEs), 69
Sportswashing, 3, 4, 7, 29, 66, 67, 72, 79
  new term, 106–10
  Newcastle exception, 114–19
  shadow of, 110–14
SRJ Sports Investments, 85
St James' Park, 29, 117
St. John, Ian, 16
Staab, Monika, 151
Stanford Research Institute (SRI), 54
States of Play: How Sportswashing Took Over Football (Delaney), 106–7
Staveley, Amanda, 115
Stoichkov, Hristo, 21
Stojkovic, Dragan, 128
Sudan, 77
Sullivan, Jake, 157
Summer Olympics (2000), 71
Summer Olympics (2008), 105
Summer Olympics (2016), 105
Summer Olympics (2024), 105, 106
Summer Olympics in Berlin (1936), 69
Super Lig champions, 136
Suwon Samsung Bluewings, 21
Sweden, 17
Sydney, 71
Syria, 12–13, 22, 41, 72

Tabuk, 95
Tahrir Square, 22
Taiwan, 125
Talal, Alwaleed bin, 15, 40–1
Taylor, Tom, 108
Team Bahrain Victorious, 109
Team Jayco-Alula, 156
Teheran, 41, 153
Tevez, Carlos, 126

INDEX

The Line, 59, 67–8, 131–2, 139
Thunder, San Antonio, 124
Tokyo Olympics (1964), 69–70
Toon Army, 118
Toronto, 42
Tour de France, 109, 156
Trafalgar Square, 119
Trojena, 8, 77, 133
Trump, Donald, 38–9, 41, 44–5, 64, 82
    and Biden, 46–9
Tunisia, 38
Turkey, 22, 100, 136, 144
Turkish Cup, 136
Turkish Super Cup, 136–7
Twitter, 29, 136

UAE Team Emirates, 109, 156
UEFA Champions League, 18, 29–30, 76, 99, 102, 116, 121, 143
Ukraine, 17, 146
    Russian invasion of, 30, 47, 49, 84, 107, 116
Umrah, 73
United Arab Emirates (UAE), 2, 9–10, 27, 41, 53
    FIFA and Saudi Arabia, 142–52
    regional and geopolitical dimensions, 152–6
    rise of, 18–21
United Kingdom (U.K.), 9, 28, 71, 118
United Nations Security Council, 41
United States (U.S.), 4, 7, 13, 17, 30, 45, 106–7, 123, 157
    PIF, rise of, 93–6
    Vision 2030, 130–5
United States Soccer Federation, 129
University of Leeds, 136
Uruguay, 140, 146

Valcke, Jerome, 106
VeloNews (Magazine), 109
Vialli, Gianluca, 101
Virginia, 44
Visa, 150
Vision 2020, 53
Vision 2035, 53
Vision 2040, 53
Visit Saudi, 2

Wall Street Journal (newspaper), 57, 59, 161
Wanda, 125, 149
Warner, 89
Washington Post (newspaper), 1, 44, 150
Washington, D.C., 44–5, 62–3, 153
Webb Ellis trophy, 70
Welcome to Wrexham (Documentary), 91
Wembley Stadium, 119
Wenger, Arsene, 100
West Bank, 152–3
West Germany, 69, 71, 72, 128
Wilder, Deontay, 79
Wimbledon tennis championship, 90
Winter Olympics (2002), 107
Winter Olympics (2014), 105, 107
Winter Olympics (2022), 106
Woodfield, David, 14
Woolf, Adam, 108
Works Progress Administration, 123
World Champions Brazil, 18
World Cup (1966), 123
World Cup (1970), 1
World Cup (1978), 12–13, 69
World Cup (1986), 128
World Cup (1990), 9, 128
World Cup (1994), 21

INDEX

World Cup (2006), 69
World Cup (2010), 23
World Cup (2014), 105
World Cup (2018), 105
World Cup (2022), 3, 26, 143, 158
World Cup (2026), 97, 158–9
World Cup (2034), 3, 133
World Expo (2030), 133
World Series Cricket, 84
World Sports Academy, 14
World Trade Organization (WTO), 28
World War I, 87
World War II, 11, 12
World Wrestling Entertainment (WWE), 77–8, 137 WTA, 150–1

X, 137
Xavi, 19
Xiaoping, Deng, 125

Yemen, 10, 32, 43, 70, 103, 121, 129, 149, 152–4
Yom Kippur War, 10
Young, Karen, 64

Zenkel, Gary, 90–1
Zico, 1, 93, 128–30
Zuckerberg, Mark, 38
Zurich, 148, 152